memos
to the
president

memos
to the
president

A Guide through
Macroeconomics for the
Busy Policymaker

Charles L. Schultze

THE BROOKINGS INSTITUTION
WASHINGTON, D.C.

Library of Congress Cataloging-in-Publication data:

Schultze, Charles L.
    Memos to the president : a guide through macroeconomics for the
busy policymaker / Charles L. Schultze.
        p.   cm.
    ISBN 0-8157-7778-7 (cloth)
    1. Macroeconomics.   2. United States—Economic policy.   I. Title.
HB172.5.S365   1992
339—dc20   92-13098
                                                            CIP

9 8 7

The paper used in this publication meets the minimum requirements of the American
National Standard for Information Sciences—Permanence of paper for Printed Library
Materials, ANSI Z39.48-1984

ⒷTHE BROOKINGS INSTITUTION

The Brookings Institution is an independent organization devoted to nonpartisan research, education, and publication in economics, government, foreign policy, and the social sciences generally. Its principal purposes are to aid in the development of sound public policies and to promote public understanding of issues of national importance.

The Institution was founded on December 8, 1927, to merge the activities of the Institute for Government Research, founded in 1916, the Institute of Economics, founded in 1922, and the Robert Brookings Graduate School of Economics and Government, founded in 1924.

The Board of Trustees is responsible for the general administration of the Institution, while the immediate direction of the policies, program, and staff is vested in the President, assisted by an advisory committee of the officers and staff. The by-laws of the Institution state: "It is the function of the Trustees to make possible the conduct of scientific research, and publication, under the most favorable conditions, and to safeguard the independence of the research staff in the pursuit of their studies and in the publication of the results of such studies. It is not a part of their function to determine, control, or influence the conduct of particular investigations or the conclusions reached."

The President bears final responsibility for the decision to publish a manuscript as a Brookings book. In reaching his judgment on the competence, accuracy, and objectivity of each study, the President is advised by the director of the appropriate research program and weighs the views of a panel of expert outside readers who report to him in confidence on the quality of the work. Publication of a work signifies that it is deemed a competent treatment worthy of public consideration but does not imply endorsement of conclusions or recommendations.

The Institution maintains its position of neutrality on issues of public policy in order to safeguard the intellectual freedom of the staff. Hence interpretations or conclusions in Brookings publications should be understood to be solely those of the authors and should not be attributed to the Institution, to its trustees, officers, or other staff members, or to the organizations that support its research.

FOREWORD

Issues of macroeconomics—inflation, unemployment, economic growth, interest rates, trade deficits, and the like—often dominate political debate. In designing economic policy, presidents, senators, and representatives have access to expert economic advice from professional staff in the executive branch and Congress. Journalists frequently consult economists, and private citizens read newspapers and watch TV talk shows. But policymakers, journalists, and the interested voter should not be at the mercy of the opinions of others. Making sensible policy, or sensibly judging those policies, requires some understanding of how the economy works and how various governmental measures affect the economy.

Despite the disagreements within the economics profession on many issues, centrist economists share a body of knowledge about the economic relationships and patterns that drive a modern economy. Often these relationships are not simple, and some of the most important ones are counterintuitive. Unfortunately, many people who make or assess policy are only vaguely acquainted with economic principles, relying on dimly remembered college courses, or rules of thumb picked up over the years, many of which are likely to be wrong. Yet few people in later life have the time or the inclination to plow through the standard college text.

In this book, Brookings economist Charles L. Schultze sets out to fill the gap. He imagines that a newly elected president commissions a newly appointed chairman of the Council of Economic Advisers (a position Schultze himself once held) to write a series of short, easy-to-read memos. These memos must briefly explain what the president ought to know about how the economy works and the effects of various macroeconomic policies. The resulting memos, twenty-nine of them, form the body of this book. They are heavily loaded with examples drawn from the economic events and policies of recent years that readers will remember. As much as possible they are free from economic jargon.

The author is a senior fellow in the Economic Studies program. He acknowledges the valuable comments received from many colleagues at Brookings and elsewhere: Henry Aaron, Alan Blinder, Barry Bosworth, Van Ooms, Peter Passell, George Perry, and Alice Rivlin. William Nordhaus and Robert Solow read an early draft of the manuscript and gave the author extensive help in shaping the later product. Finally, the author owes a special debt of gratitude to Timothy Taylor who undertook an intensive review of the manuscript and whose insightful recommendations on structure, style, and substance are reflected throughout the book. Many errors were prevented and deficiencies remedied. Those that remain are the author's alone.

Theresa Walker edited the manuscript, and Carmel Peddie and Charles Hornbrook provided research assistance. Anita Whitlock, Irene Coray, and Valerie Owens were responsible for word processing. Roshna Kapadia and Laura Kelly worked with Charles Hornbrook to check the manuscript for accuracy. Susan Woollen prepared the manuscript for typesetting, and Florence Robinson constructed the index.

Brookings gratefully acknowledges financial support from the Alfred P. Sloan Foundation as well as the Ford Foundation.

The views expressed here are those of the author and should not be ascribed to any of the persons consulted during its preparation, or to the officers, trustees, or other staff members of the Brookings Institution.

Bruce K. MacLaury
President

May 1992
Washington, D.C.

Contents

Figures

Introduction

Whenever presidents, cabinet officers, senators, and congressional representatives want economic advice, professional economists are not far away. Economic units in the administration and Congress turn out staff studies, forecasts, and simulations designed to help policymakers reach sound judgments. Journalists who write about economic policy can call on a host of experts, in and out of government, to help explain the significance of various economic developments and policy proposals. And citizens who seek to be informed about economic trends and policies now have at their beck and call a wide range of nontechnical interpretive pieces in newspapers, magazines, and television specials dealing with the economic events and policy issues of the day.

All of this is not enough. Policymakers do have to lean on experts for all sorts of technical and quantitative estimates. But in our government, experts do not make the final call, nor should they. A government is ill-served if its policymakers do not understand how the economy works. And those who report on the economic scene, and the concerned citizens who simply try to make reasoned judgments about economic affairs should not, and more to the point, will not passively accept expert opinion. In any event, experts often disagree, and without some underlying grasp about how the economy works, policymakers, journalists, and citizens are left with only half-remembered college courses and a portfolio of slogans, myths, and rules-of-thumb that are often dead wrong.

To be able to reason through most issues of economic policy one does not have to wield the mathematical tools and intricate modeling of the modern professional economist. But more than common sense and intuition is required. The economic world is, after all, a maze of mutual influences, made continually more intricate as information, goods, and capital move ever more freely among regions and nations. The causes and consequences of economic events and policies are often not what they seem. And the economic history of recent years witnessed many developments that cannot be explained without an understanding of some economic principles or relationships that are far from obvious. Common sense, in reasoning about economics as in other areas of life, is an attribute highly to be prized. But common sense alone is not enough when it comes to the ability to discern the web of relationships that make modern economies tick. An understanding of a few economic principles and some practice in applying them rigorously to specific problems are necessary.

The explanation of what determines whether a country runs a trade surplus or deficit and how big it is likely to be, for example, is highly counterintuitive. Economists are almost unanimously agreed that the size and nature (deficit or surplus) of a country's international trade balance are not principally determined by its trade policies, or those of other countries, or by the productivity of its industries, but by the relationship between how much a nation saves and how much it wants to invest at home. Yet the major political battles about trade policy in the United States in the 1980s proceeded on the opposite assumption. But it's no use asking intelligent people to accept the counterintuitive view on faith; it is necessary to explain just how the economic system produces such a result. To grasp that explanation fully requires in turn a fairly comprehensive view of how the economy operates.

The trade case is perhaps the most dramatic example of the counterintuitive results. But there are many puzzles to be explained. How did the United States, twice in the decade of the 1970s, simultaneously suffer from high unemployment and increased inflation? What happened to prevent the huge federal budget deficits of the 1980s from generating substantial new inflation? If not inflation, what are the economic consequences of sustained large budget deficits? Why, despite the long period of sustained economic growth and the sizable increase in employment that occurred from 1982 to 1990, did the real wages of American workers stagnate? When oil prices suddenly soar, it's obvious that the living standards of American consumers are harmed as they pay more to foreign producers for the gasoline and heating oil they use, but why does the economy also inevitably fall into recession, with increased unemployment and idle factories? Such oil-related recessions have happened three times in the past two decades, in 1974, 1981, and 1990. This book seeks to present and explain the essential principles and relationships necessary to understand how the macroeconomy operates by showing how they apply to these and many other issues of immediate relevance to economic policymakers.

The busy policymaker, journalist, businessman, or interested noneconomist is not likely to turn to the introductory texts used by college students as means of improving their understanding of economics. Those texts typically take the reader through the whole corpus of economic knowledge point by point and principle by principle. Policy examples are sprinkled here and there but are not central to the basic objective of communicating a comprehensive body of systematic and sometimes abstract knowledge. This approach usually means that realistic discussions of policy issues come along late in the book, since the many requisite "principles" and the complexities needed to understand any one policy issue have not yet been introduced.

However appropriate this building-block approach may be for college students, who, in theory at least, have the opportunity to devote a large part of a whole year just to absorbing the material, it is of limited help for the audience I wish to reach. And so this book is designed differently, along two major dimensions. First, it is highly selective. It concentrates principally on macroeconomic relationships and policy issues—inflation, unemployment, long-term economic growth, and the flow of international trade and capital. Sometimes, to deal with one of those issues it goes further afield, but only as necessary. Second, it teaches heavily through the discussion of actual economic events or policy debates—using, as much as possible, recent examples.

Recognizing that the audience I am trying to reach is continually involved in making judgments about complex policy issues, either as participants or deeply interested spectators, I ask the reader to plunge immediately into a discussion of such issues. In practice, this means that, to the maximum extent possible, policy issues or historical economic developments are used to illustrate, and if you will, teach, some specific line of economic reasoning. But since, in life, any important policy issue or economic development involves many economic relationships, the reader is initially asked to take some ideas and principles on faith, as others are illustrated. One by one, however, I present reasoned arguments to replace the elements of faith.

Even though I assume that most readers will have had some experience in making judgments about specific economic issues, the explanation of each topic within this book starts from scratch. It assumes no prior knowledge of the economic principles being discussed. This means, of course, that many readers will come to particular sections that tell them what they already know. Those sections can be skimmed quickly, saving time for other arguments that may be less familiar.

DO ECONOMISTS AGREE ON A CORE OF ECONOMIC PRINCIPLES?

Cynics might point out that economists disagree on numerous issues. Economists appointed by a liberal president would offer one set of economic principles while those appointed by a conservative president would offer a quite different and inconsistent set. Popular jokes and myths to the contrary, that is not true. A consensus exists on many important points. Ninety percent of the professional economists in the United States would give Boris Yeltsin similar advice about the virtues of a market system and about the principal characteristics of economic institutions needed to make such a system work. They would indeed disagree widely about exactly what priority to give each stage of economic reform and whether or not Soviet reform ought to move toward the market system gradually or try to do it cold turkey. But about the essential principles and characteristics of a free market system there would be agreement.

Even within the narrower range of issues typically confronting the chief executive of a modern industrial state, there is more consensus among professional economists than widely believed. Having served for ten years first as a staff member and then as a chairman of the Council of Economic Advisers, under presidents of both parties, and having closely observed the operations of the council in other years, I would estimate—nuances of language and emphasis apart—that the advice given presidents by Republican and Democratic CEAs is remarkably similar on about two-thirds to three-quarters of the relevant issues. The big differences come in two areas. One, in the trade-off between equity and economic efficiency, Democratic CEA chairmen and members will usually give somewhat more weight to considerations of how a proposed measure affects income distribution while Republicans will stress how the measure affects incentives to work, save, and invest. Two, historically, in considering the short-run trade-off between inflation and unemployment, Democratic chairmen have given a bit more weight to the desirability of maintaining employment, and Republicans to the benefits of avoiding inflation. But the differences, especially in the second case, are modest and do not usually reflect a wide gulf in the way the two view the cause and effect relationships in the American and the world economies.

If one thinks of the views of first-rank professional economists about issues of public policy as arrayed across a spectrum of 180 degrees, from left to right, the middle third of the spectrum would probably contain four-fifths of the economists. On such diverse matters as how changes in aggregate spending in the economy broadly affect inflation and unemployment, the factors that tend to determine the size and sign of the nation's trade balance, the way in which saving and investment influence economic growth, and the outlines, at least, of how large and sustained budget deficits influence the economy, that "centrist" four-fifths would share a large body of understanding. Although it is not the subject of this book, an even larger area of agreement exists on why, and how, economic outcomes determined by the market are (with some exceptions) preferable to solutions imposed through government price and wage controls, rationing, or subsidies to producers.

HOW IMPORTANT IS IT TO GET THE ECONOMICS RIGHT?

It is not self-evident that better economic understanding by the president, the Congress, the media, and the politically active public would have produced radically different policies. Decisions about economic matters are importantly (some would say solely) driven by the interplay of regional, class, producer group, and other forces of pure self-interest and by strong but variable currents of public opinion about economic matters that may or may not be fully rational in nature. In a truly cynical view, what the presidents, senators, and representatives believe about how the economy operates makes little difference, since their decisions are driven not by what they believe about macroeconomic reality but by what they think is necessary to be elected and reelected. But this is cynicism carried to an unreal extreme. Many elected public officials have strong views about the way the world works that cannot at all be explained by their own or their constituents' self-interest. Senators Alphonse D'Amato and Daniel Patrick Moynihan represent the same state; they vote together on a relatively modest number of New York issues but strongly disagree and vote differently on most important matters of public policy. One need only pay attention to the public debate about economic matters, especially macroeconomic matters, to realize that the advocates on each side are divided only in part by self-interest and importantly by the way they are convinced that the economic world works.

It is of no small importance that policymakers understand how the economy operates and the likely consequences of the economic policies they adopt. Historically the economic policies of the federal government—some good, some bad—have played a large role in shaping the course of economic developments. After the stock market crash of 1929, misguided monetary policies by the Federal Reserve helped turn what might have been a run-of-the-mill recession into the Great Depression. But in 1987, the economic effects of another massive stock market crash were neutralized by the skillful monetary management of the Federal Reserve. In the early 1930s the Great Depression was worsened by America's adoption of highly protectionist trade policies; enacted in the mistaken belief they could increase jobs for Americans, they triggered protectionist measures around the world and helped deepen and spread the depression. After the Second World War, America's leadership in promoting the liberalization of international trade helped bring on an era of prosperity and growth for the entire free-world economy. Judicious tax cuts early in the decade helped make the 1960s a period of prosperity, but late in the decade failure to pay for Vietnam War spending with tax increases helped launch a major round of inflation. The budgetary policies adopted in 1981—large tax cuts and increased defense spending—initially contributed to a rapid recovery from the recession of 1981–82, but the continuation of large deficits in later years helped bring about a sustained period of high interest rates, reduced national saving and investment, and massive American trade deficits.

Getting economic policies at least roughly right can make a big difference in the prosperity and growth of the nation. And in turn understanding how the economy works is a prerequisite for choosing the right economic policies.

THE FORMAT

In writing this book, I have employed a particular fantasy to help me concentrate on those elements of economic reasoning and those kinds of issues that are likely to be important for making macroeconomic policy in the decade of the 1990s. I imagined a new president promising the chairman of the Council of Economic Advisers to devote an hour or so a week to learning about the key economic relationships that a president ought to understand as a background for making macroeconomic policy judgments. My fantasy then had the president instructing the CEA chairman to prepare a series of weekly memos that would accomplish that purpose. This book was planned and written as if it were that series of memos. It was a congenial task, and one at which I have had some experience.

My fantasy includes one final element. I imagined my hypothetical president and his or her economic adviser to come from somewhere near the middle of the political spectrum. The nature of the memos would not vary much whether the two people were a little to the right or a little to the left of center, but my imaginary writer and audience are admittedly centrist in nature. Convinced supply-siders of the early Reagan administration variety or those from the left wing of the Democratic party would neither have written nor welcomed such memos.

In the end, I found it took many memos to convey the necessary information. Like the mythical president for whom these memos were planned, many readers may find that the book is best read over a period of time, one or a few memos at a sitting.

A SNEAK PREVIEW

The book consists of a set of twenty-nine memos from an imaginary CEA chairman to a newly elected president. The memos are organized into a simple three-part scheme. The four memos in part 1 lay the groundwork. The first two explain why it is important for policymakers to distinguish between those economic forces or policies that affect total demand in the economy and those that affect total supply. The third memo explains what the gross national product (GNP) is and the relationships among its major parts. By now politicians and journalists, as well as professional economists, carry on the public debate about macroeconomic policy in terms of what those policies will or will not do to the nation's GNP and its components, even though many of the participants have only the foggiest notion of what the GNP is and how its components are related to one another or to the total. The fourth memo deals with national saving, investment, and the trade balance, whose relationships with each other are critical in shaping how the economy behaves. These first four memos provide the foundations for what follows. They are a bit more like textbook chapters and are less enlivened by discussions of policy controversy that the reader will find in the remaining memos.

Part 2 of the book contains fifteen memos dealing with the problem of economic instability, that is, inflation and unemployment. The memos in part 2 explain how economic forces produce short-run changes of total demand and spending in the economy; how those changes in demand, interacting with a more stable and slowly changing supply, can generate inflation and unemployment; and how economic policies can help keep total demand and supply more nearly matched so as to avoid those consequences (or how the wrong economic policies can generate the unwanted inflation and unemployment).

Part 3 turns to the question of long-term economic growth. In a recovery from recession the nation's output can grow rapidly as previously idle workers and factories are brought back into production. But in the long run, sustained economic growth can only occur as the nation's capacity or supply potential expands. The nine memos in part 3 identify the principal forces that have determined the pace of long-term supply growth and consider possibilities, costs, and limitations of government policies to promote that growth.

The final memo, number twenty-nine, provides a summary of "principles" that ought to guide policy formulation, culled from the earlier memos. It also gives some sense of what a reader might have been told on several important issues if some other groups of economic advisers had been giving the advice—for example, moderate conservatives like Martin Feldstein, monetarists, the Democratic left, and others.

The problems of economic instability revolve principally around fluctuations in aggregate demand, while long-term economic growth can be achieved only through an expansion of supply. One way to characterize the organization of the memos, therefore, is to say part 2 deals with demand and part 3 with supply.

AN ASIDE TO MY COLLEAGUES

At almost every point in writing this book I had to struggle with decisions about the extent to which I should cover most of the qualifications and the nuances that a full treatment of any topic in this book requires. I also had to decide what important modern theories or hypotheses that run counter to received wisdom I should bring in, even if only to outline why

I think they are wrong. The Barro-Ricardo view of budget deficits, the real-business cycle explanation of economic fluctuations, and the "policy irrelevance" hypothesis are examples. As a rule I have leaned toward simplicity. Footnotes are few, and some of the newer hypotheses that the talented younger members of the profession delight in exploring receive short shrift. Conceivably, I am offering policymakers a useful summary of the economic equivalent of the Ptolemaic system just as a new Copernican system is emerging, but I doubt it. Economists dispute mightily over elaborations and implications of their theories, but the basic, common understandings of the profession emphasized in this book do not change very rapidly.

I am putting myself in the place of some future economic adviser to a president or a congressional committee. True, the hypothetical adviser may have theories that, on some matters, clash with mine. Nonetheless, if that adviser's clients master the contents of this book, they will have an easier time judging the wisdom of their adviser than if they had not.

PART 1

Background

Memorandum 1

To: The President
From: CEA Chairman
Subject: **The Supply and Demand for National Output**

You asked me and my colleagues at the CEA to give you a series of memos that would summarize, in nontechnical language, essential facts about how the U.S. economy works and how government policies affect the nation's economic performance to help you in making judgments about macroeconomic policy. This is the first of those memos.

In the interest of using your time effectively, we have made several initial decisions. First, whenever possible, we explain the logic of economic principles by applying them to economic developments and public policy issues drawn from recent history.

Second, these memos concentrate on macroeconomic relationships and policy issues—inflation, unemployment, long-term economic growth, and the flow of international trade and capital. They do not, except as necessary to explain macroeconomic issues, deal with microeconomic issues of the economy's internal structure—monopoly versus competition, minimum wages, environmental economics, agricultural subsidies, and the like.

Finally, these memos, like the economic advisers you have appointed, incorporate a centrist and mainstream approach, reflecting what we believe to be the consensus of the broad middle of the professional spectrum. Where there is a significant, even if minority view, in strong opposition to the received wisdom of mainstream economists on important issues relevant to public policy, we briefly present that view—and the reasons we believe it is wrong.

Happy—or at least profitable—reading!

13

WHY THE "MACRO" IN MACROECONOMICS?

Macroeconomics deals with the economic behavior of the economy as a whole, as distinguished from the microeconomics of the individual industry, firm, or household. Many important truths of macroeconomics are counterintuitive, especially when contrasted with what we usually believe about a firm or an individual. Differences occur not because two contradictory sets of economic principles are at work. Rather, two important principles, which don't apply at the individual level, help govern the economic behavior of the nation as a whole.

First, no one firm's or individual's actions can determine what happens to the rest of the economy. And so we can freely analyze the economics of an individual's behavior without worrying about how that behavior might change the economic environment in which the individual is operating and therefore alter the outcome. But in macroeconomics we are analyzing interactions among the principal parts of the economy—consumers as a whole, investors, government, and so on—and the most important part of the analysis is precisely how their actions, taken together, change the overall economy. Thus, changes in government affect consumer income, which strongly influences the volume of consumption spending, which affects the inventory policies of business firms, all of which will change government revenues, and so on. Second, there are not many limits on the growth of the income of a family or the output of a firm in any one year, but the growth of national income and output is limited by the overall availability of capital and labor and the state of technology. In a year one firm might conceivably double its output, or a household might get a huge windfall and triple its living standards. But national income and output cannot exceed the limits set by the nation's productive capacity. Over time that capacity can increase as the labor force grows, investment adds to the stock of new plant and equipment, and technology advances. But that process is gradual. There is, in other words, an overall constraint facing the economy that is much more binding than the constraints typically facing firms and individuals. Thus, if one sector of the economy booms, various developments will be set in motion which ensure that something gives way elsewhere in the economy. And this fact of constraints has many fundamental implications for macroeconomic behavior.

Many commonsense notions that are perfectly plausible when applied to the behavior of firms and individuals can be quite wrong when transferred to the world of macroeconomics. Let's briefly look at a few examples of apparent paradoxes, demonstrating that what is clearly true for a part of the economy is not true of the whole.

—Saving, investment, and the trade balance. Each year millions of households decide how much to save. Quite independently of their decisions, every year IBM, General Motors, and some four million other business firms and homebuilders decide how much they will invest in new plant, machinery, and houses. And finally another set of independent decisions is being made by Americans and foreigners that determines how much the nation will export and import. Yet paradoxically, for the economy as a whole, total saving is always equal to the sum of domestic investment and the trade balance (exports minus imports). How is it that all of these independent decisions end up producing that equality?

—Trade protection. Imposing a tariff or a quota on the imports of a particular good can indeed protect the market for American firms producing that product and preserve jobs in the industry in the face of foreign competition, and subsidies to particular firms can allow those firms to expand their exports. But trade protection cannot increase the total number of jobs available to American workers or, indeed, substantially alter our overall trade balance with other countries. How can something that's clearly true for one good not apply to all goods?

—Investment tax incentives. Reducing taxes on the income from certain kinds of investment—for example, an investment tax credit for business purchases of machinery—will generate more of that kind of investment. But unless the economy is in a recession, producing below its capacity, the increase in that particular kind of investment will be largely offset by decreases in other forms of investment—for example, housing or overseas investment. Why should this be so?

The memos that follow will elaborate on these and many other examples of how overall economic developments cannot be understood or predicted simply by adding up the decisions of individual households, firms, and workers.

THE SUPPLY AND DEMAND FOR NATIONAL OUTPUT

Thirty years of testifying before congressional committees and speaking before business and other groups have convinced me that the fundamental distinction between the supply and demand for goods and services, and the interaction between the two, is not well understood at all. Changes in either the overall supply or the overall demand for goods and services can lead to changes in a nation's output, income, and economic well-being. The two economic forces interact, but they operate in different ways and are subject to different economic influences. Most of the government's macroeconomic policies, with respect to taxes, spending, money, and credit, affect both the demand and supply side of the economic equation, but each does so in a different way, on different time scales, with different advantages and disadvantages, and with varying effectiveness.

How much goods and services the nation produces is determined by the interaction between the supply of and demand for those goods and services. But what do these terms "demand" and "supply" mean when we apply them not just to the output of one product or firm, but to the total output of goods and services in the nation, that is, the GNP?

> By the term "demand for GNP" I mean the total amount of domestically produced goods and services, of all types, that the four major purchasers in the economy—consumers, government, investors, and foreign buyers—are willing to buy, given current economic conditions, such as the level of consumer and business incomes, interest rates, and so on.

The total, or aggregate, demand for goods and services can be influenced by governmental policies and by economic events at home and abroad. Later memos in this series will explain how various policies and events affect the demand for GNP. But it is useful to list a few important influences on demand right now. Government budget policy can increase or decrease aggregate demand—an income tax cut will leave consumers with more after-tax income, much of which they are likely to use for buying additional consumer goods. An increase in defense spending will, of course, directly raise the government's demand for military goods. We shall later devote several memos to explaining how the Federal Reserve, the nation's central bank, can reduce aggregate demand for goods and services by restricting the growth of money and credit so as to raise interest rates, which in turn discourages the construction of new homes, lowers business investment in plant and equipment, and, through a complicated process, depresses American exports (by raising the exchange value of the dollar and making exports more costly to foreign buyers). The Federal Reserve can also work the other side of the street by expanding credit, lowering interest rates, and stimulating demand. In the 1980s the highly expansionary effects of the Reagan tax cuts and defense spending increases—which by themselves would have sharply raised aggregate demand—were countered by the Federal Reserve through the demand-depressing effects of tight money and high interest rates. The Fed's actions since 1983 prevented aggregate demand from rising so fast as to have exceeded the nation's capacity to produce goods and services and so caused a new round of inflation.

Fluctuations in the demand for GNP may stem from developments in the private sector as well as from governmental policies. Near the end of a boom, business firms may become too optimistic in their expectations of future sales growth, stocking up excessively on inventories and over-building production facilities, which may in turn lead to a later cutback in business demand for investment goods. Or, as happened in 1974 and again in 1979–80, a large rise in the price of imported oil may siphon off income from the pockets of consumers to enlarge the coffers of oil-producing countries, and since the oil producers do not immediately respend those funds in buying American exports, a net decline in the demand for goods and services will occur in the United States.

By the term "supply of GNP" I mean the potential amount of goods and services of all kinds that could be produced if the nation's labor force were fully employed and its plant capacity fully utilized. To say it another way, the supply of GNP, as the term will be used in these memos, is the amount of output that the nation's firms and workers are willing and able to pro-duce if a market can be found for that output.

Full employment does not mean zero unemployment or absolutely full use of plant capacity. In the best of circumstances some people may be temporarily out of work as they search for the new job that best suits them. And some older, high-cost production facilities are typically kept on standby. The supply of GNP is a flexible amount. Under boom conditions, capacity can be temporarily stretched as standby facilities are activated, people with marginal attachment to the labor force drawn into work, and overtime hours increased. At a later stage we can look more closely at the meaning of the terms "full employment" and "full capacity utilization." For the moment, however, think of the supply of GNP as the amount of goods and services the country could produce if it were operating with reasonably full use of its available human and capital resources, not stretched drum tight as to generate a bidding war for scarce labor or materials, but not so slack as to result in large unused capacity or idle workers. That level of GNP we can call potential GNP, and the

Potential GNP and the Economists' Aggregate Supply Curve

In these memos we want to emphasize the distinction between: (1) policies that influence aggregate demand; and (2) supply-side policies that influence the long-run growth of the nation's capacity to supply goods and services to its citizens. And so we have defined supply as potential GNP. In the economics literature, however, the term "supply" refers not to a single amount, but to a schedule or curve that specifies how the quantity produced will vary depending on the price the producer can get for it. But we can reasonably assume that in the long run, for the economy as a whole, the willingness and ability of firms and workers to produce output doesn't vary with the nominal price level. In the short run, firms and workers, depending on the state of demand, often provide more goods and labor services, or fewer, than the amount that will be provided in the long run. In the parlance of economists they are operating "off" their long-run supply curves. For our purposes, nothing is lost by defining supply simply as potential GNP.

supply of GNP can, therefore, be defined simply as potential GNP. Over time, potential GNP rises gradually as the labor force grows, as the nation saves and invests that saving in additions to its stock of productive capital, and as science and technology make the operations of workers and machines more efficient.

HOW DEMAND AND SUPPLY DETERMINE THE LEVEL AND GROWTH OF NATIONAL INCOME AND OUTPUT

There are three rough and ready but highly useful principles that will be a helpful guide through the maze when it comes to thinking about how government policy and outside events affect national output, employment, inflation, and ultimately the nation's living standards.

Principle 1: Up to the limits of the nation's potential GNP (and temporarily even beyond), business firms in the aggregate will produce to meet demand. Within those limits, therefore, the level of aggregate demand determines the level of national output and employment.

When the overall demand for goods and services declines below potential GNP—that is, when the total amount that consumers, investors, governments, and foreigners want to purchase becomes less than what the country can produce—business firms do not rush to cut prices, nor do workers promptly agree to lower wages in an effort to restore sales and employment. Rather in the face of falling sales, firms produce less output and employ fewer workers. Although the rate of wage and price inflation does begin to moderate, the principal immediate effect of a fall in demand is a reduction in actual output below potential. The economy heads into recession. Conversely, in a boom, when total spending runs ahead of potential GNP, actual output temporarily rises above potential output—workers are put on overtime to an unusual degree, unemployment falls to a very low level, and standby capacity is brought on line. In a tight labor market, wages begin to advance more rapidly as employers try to keep their labor force intact and maintain employee morale in the face of wage increases elsewhere. Firms also find it easier to pass on those and other higher costs to consumers in the form of higher prices. Inflation starts to rise but typically only in a gradual manner.

Recession and recovery, boom and bust, principally arise from fluctuations in aggregate demand around a relatively stable and slowly growing potential GNP. In recessions, unemployment and idle plant capacity rise sharply not because workers suddenly lose some of their willingness to work or business managers forget how to produce efficiently, but because firms cannot sell all they would like to produce if there were a market for it. Figure 1-1 traces the pattern of actual GNP over the past twenty-five years, as it fluctuated relative to the more stable path of potential GNP, in response to fluctuations in aggregate demand.

Principle 2: From year to year, aggregate demand and GNP can fluctuate rather sharply. But with a few exceptions most of the forces that determine supply (potential GNP) change only gradually. In the short run, therefore, most of the macroeconomic issues facing government policymakers revolve around managing aggregate demand, in particular, how to keep demand on a relatively stable path, close to potential GNP, to avoid recession and the inflation that come from excessive demand.

As noted earlier, potential GNP tends to grow each year at a rate that can change over time but usually not substantially and abruptly. The growth in the population of working age is fairly smooth, and while the percentage of women participating in the labor force has been rising steadily for many years, it is not subject to quick shifts from one year to

FIGURE 1-1. Potential and Actual GNP, 1965–90

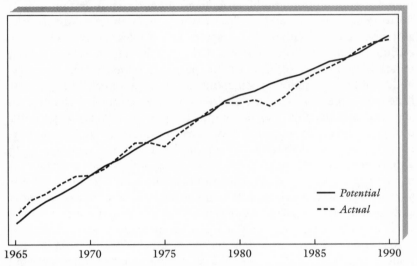

Note: GNP data are in logarithms so that equal percentage changes take up the same vertical distance in the figure.

the next. Improvements in the average skills and educational attainment of the labor force can be an important source of long-run growth in potential GNP, but such improvements occur very slowly (any one year's new crop of school or college leavers constitutes only a small fraction of the total labor force). The size of the productive capital stock cannot alter rapidly in a short time (outside of war damage); the amount added each year to the capital stock by net new investment is small relative to the size of the stock, typically only 2 to 4 percent a year. The typical fluctuations in net investment can in any one year produce only small changes in the rate at which the capital stock is growing, and even smaller changes in potential GNP. Other important factors affecting the supply of output, such as significant advances in technology, may occasionally cause quick changes in the supply capability of particular firms, but they will not occur simultaneously in many industries in a way that will produce large changes in the overall supply of GNP.[1]

In the real world, the path of potential GNP over time isn't quite as smooth as shown in figure 1-1. All sorts of disturbances occur from month to month and year to year that produce "wiggles" in the economy's capacity to produce—unusual changes in weather and crop yields, strikes, and purely random events. But these wiggles aren't large relative to the more volatile movements of aggregate demand. The short-run fluctuations in GNP and the associated social harm that comes from high unemployment and inflation stem principally from swings in aggregate demand above and below a relatively stable path of potential GNP.[2] Figure 1-1 showed how actual GNP has fluctuated around potential over the past twenty-five years. At the trough of the recession of 1981–82, the deepest of the postwar years, U.S. GNP fell some 9 percent below its potential. The social and economic damage from the recession was worse than that number suggests because its impact was not evenly spread among all citizens, but was heavily concentrated among the unemployed, whose numbers rose by some 4 million in that recession. Nevertheless, the 9 percent GNP shortfall does give some idea of the magnitude of the problem.

This description of economic fluctuations leaves out several complications. Whenever aggregate demand drops and GNP falls, the lower availability of jobs discourages some people from looking for a job; they drop out of the labor force, and the size of the labor force declines (relative to its long-run path). Similarly a drop in GNP usually will lead to a temporary decrease in the efficiency with which goods and services are produced, since production volume is below what the various enterprises were designed to produce. But these reductions in labor force and productivity do not represent a cutback in supply, or potential GNP. The discouraged workers would be glad to supply their labor if there were a market for their output; and productive efficiency would be restored to normal if only the demand were there to enable firms to dispose of the output their facilities have been designed to produce and which they are perfectly willing to supply. Again, the description of short-term economic fluctuations as movements in aggregate demand relative to potential supply is essentially accurate.

A CONTRARY VIEW

Recently a number of articles in economic journals have attempted to demonstrate statistically that the American economy does *not* tend to expand and contract in relation to the country's supply potential. Recessions should not, they argue, be viewed as the result of a fall in demand below the nation's supply potential, which can be cured by renewed expansion in demand. Rather they represent a fall in the supply potential itself, occurring presumably because of sporadic reductions in national productivity (and vice versa for booms). The policy implication is that trying to cure the recession by stimulating aggregate demand can be harmful—for example, through easier money and lower interest rates or by increasing government spending; since supply has fallen, attempts to stimulate aggregate demand so that it returns to its old path will not raise output but will create an excess of demand over supply and result in inflation.

This new view of cyclical fluctuations never explains satisfactorily why the nation's business firms have sporadically and simultaneously been hit by declines in productive potential sufficient to produce periodic recessions. To argue that unemployment in recessions comes importantly from workers voluntarily withholding their labor and quitting their jobs by the millions is out of touch with reality. The postulated downward shifts in potential GNP must, therefore, arise from the occurrence of periodic contractions in efficiency and productivity, that is, in output per worker. But as noted, recessions are not accompanied by a decline in the capital available to workers on their jobs. The only available explanation for the decline in national output must then be the occurrence of absolute reversals in the technological capabilities of business firms. But this hypothesis implies that, across the whole economy, the nation's business firms forget what they have just learned. This explanation is surely implausible, and no one has come up with convincing and specific examples.

There is also evidence that the statistical results that gave rise to this view do not really demonstrate what has been asserted. Essentially the statistical findings, which purport to show that after recessions the GNP does not bounce back to its old trend line of potential GNP, are dominated by two incidents. Apparently potential GNP shifted downward during the Great Depression. And after the big recession of 1974–75, the long-run growth of potential did slow down. That is, during the Great Depression of the 1930s and following the oil shocks of the 1970s, permanent changes occurred in the long-run path of the nation's supply capability, such that even after recovery the economy was never fully restored to the status quo ante. Once these two episodes are removed, even the particular statistical techniques on which the "new view" is based strongly reject the hypothesis that recessions and booms are caused by periodic sharp swings in aggregate supply—that is, in potential GNP.

Despite the problems with this view of economic fluctuations, it does have something to teach us. It provides us with the healthy caution that the upward path of the nation's supply capability can occasionally be altered in fundamental ways that are impossible to predict, and that are difficult to identify until quite a while after they have occurred. If the "old" path of potential GNP has been lowered, then an attempt to stimulate aggregate demand back up to that path is likely to generate excessive demand that can, as we shall discuss in a later memo, produce inflation. But with this caveat, the essential portrait of economic instability that was drawn above—movements of aggregate demand around a more stably growing aggregate supply—remains a valid description of the problem.[3]

SOME POLICY IMPLICATIONS

Keeping unemployment and inflation low requires macroeconomic policies that maintain aggregate demand roughly in balance with supply, that is, with potential GNP. If demand runs ahead of potential GNP, inflationary pressures will be set in motion. If demand falls significantly below potential, reduced output and higher unemployment will ensue. In practice, maintaining the proper balance between demand and supply means avoiding changes in taxes and government expenditures (fiscal policy) and changes in money supplies and interest rates (monetary policy) that lead to excessive or deficient aggregate demand, and, going further, using such fiscal and especially monetary policy to offset large excesses or deficiencies in demand arising from other sources, at home or abroad. With one important set of exceptions—the occurrence of a major surge in the price of oil or other large cost increases—success at that task will keep the nation from suffering serious bouts of unemployment and inflation. Serious mistakes in running macroeconomic policy can bring on inflation or recession. Mistakes of an inflationary nature can be especially costly since it may take a long period of large slack, high unemployment, and subnormal demand to wring out an inflation once well under way.

Economic stability—the absence of high unemployment and serious inflation—is not the only criterion for judging the performance of an economy or the success of its economic policies. An economy can be stable but stagnant if its potential GNP—that is, its aggregate supply—is not growing significantly over time. After a recession, GNP may briefly grow nicely as idle workers and machines are put back to work in response to improving markets and the expansion of aggregate demand. But in the

FIGURE 1-2. Potential and Actual GNP, 1870–90

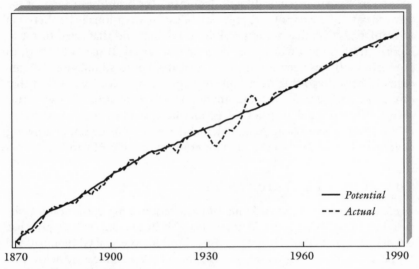

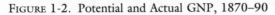

Note: GNP data are in logarithms so that equal percentage changes take up the same vertical distance in the figure.

longer run, an economy can grow no faster than its aggregate supply capabilities permit. Hence, our third principle.

> *Principle 3*: In the short run, successful economic performance depends on how well a nation avoids large fluctuations in the demand for goods and services. But in the long run—over decades and generations—economic well-being depends principally on how well a nation increases the supply of goods and services.

In the time perspective depicted in figure 1-1, the departures from the high-employment path of potential GNP can be easily observed. But when we chart the path of GNP, not over the past thirty-five years, but over the much longer time since the Civil War, as is done in figure 1-2, the cyclical fluctuations are so small against the background of the huge long-term growth in the supply of GNP, that the business cycles since the Second World War can barely be seen by the naked eye. Between 1870 and 1990 per capita GNP rose by 700 percent! The GNP in 1990 was vastly higher than it was in 1870 not because the United States in 1990 was operating closer to its economic potential than it was in 1870; any difference could have accounted for only a few percentage points of the sixfold difference in per capita GNP between the two dates. Rather, the overwhelming bulk of the advance in per capita income and output arose from the rise in potential GNP itself—that is, from the rise in supply. Even at the fullest of full employment and with a buoyant aggregate demand straining capacity at its seams, the economy of 1870 still could not have supplied anything like the per capita volume of GNP that can be supplied today.

Because we live in the present, and because the harm from recession, unemployment, and inflation is so unevenly and unfairly distributed, most of our attention and much of the substance of domestic politics focuses on problems of economic instability—avoiding the sharp swings in aggregate demand that bring on inflation and recession. But viewed in a longer time frame, the well-being of a country's citizens is chiefly determined by its success or failure in raising aggregate supply.

In the United States, the growth of aggregate supply—potential GNP—slowed very sharply after the early 1970s. GNP per worker, which had risen at an average rate of 2.1 percent a year between 1948 and 1973, rose by only 0.5 percent a year from 1973 to 1990. While the effect of the slowdown on American living standards was virtually imperceptible from year to year, the cumulative effect over the whole seventeen-year period was huge. For example, if the post-1973 fall in the long-term growth rate could have been held to half of what occurred, the income of an average American family in 1990 would have been higher by $5,000.

Even though, as I will discuss later, most supply-enhancing policies have what seem to be very small payoffs (measured in tiny fractions of a percent change in the annual growth rate), the magic of compound interest is such that even those small effects cumulate into large payoffs over long periods. Suppose, for example, the growth in output per worker could be speeded up from its current sluggish 0.5 percent a year to 0.8 percent a year, which would still be well below its performance in the 1950s and 1960s. If that could be done, then twenty-five years from now, average income for the next generation of families in today's purchasing power would be $3,000 a year, or almost 8 percent higher than will be the case under current trends.

NOTES

1. However, see the following section under "A Contrary View."

2. A drop in aggregate demand may be set in motion by a sharp rise in the price of an important raw material, like crude oil, whose supply has been dis-

rupted—as was true in the deep recessions of 1974–75 and 1981–82. (We will discuss these kinds of disruptions in memo 12.) But even here, the fall in GNP was because of the drop in aggregate demand triggered by the surge in oil prices, not because of the physical shortage of oil itself.

3. For a powerful demonstration of the statistical point made in this paragraph, see Pierre Perron, "The Great Crash, the Oil Price Shock, and the Unit Root Hypothesis," *Econometrica*, vol. 57 (November 1989), pp. 1361–1402.

MEMORANDUM **2**

To: The President

From: CEA Chairman

Subject: **Supply, Demand, and the Importance of Knowing the Difference**

Probably no one point about economic policy is more important to understand than the fundamental difference between those policies that affect aggregate demand and those that affect aggregate supply. Confusion of the two can lead to serious mistakes in policy. Thus, for example, in the early 1960s, the Kennedy-Johnson tax cuts raised output and reduced unemployment because they were principally demand-side measures that raised the depressed level of aggregate demand back up toward potential. But many of the supply-siders of the early 1980s became convinced that aggregate supply could be just as quickly and powerfully stimulated by large tax cuts. A decade of huge budget deficits resulted, which harmed the U.S. economy in many ways, especially by eroding the forces that promote long-term economic growth.

The memos that follow will explain in some detail how demand- and supply-side policies affect the economy. But even before we begin, a basic explanation of how important it is not to confuse the two types of policies is useful.

Aggregate demand policies are powerful. Tax cuts, government spending increases, or a big expansion of money and credit are effective ways to stimulate spending. A $10 billion personal income tax cut, for example, puts an extra $10 billion of spendable income into the hands of taxpayers, and they will spend a large part of the extra income on consumer goods. A similar tax cut for business firms will, with high probability, induce an increase in business purchases of plant and equipment. Government purchases of military hardware increase demand for those kind of goods, and a rise in social security benefits or other entitlements quickly translates into increased spending by the recipients. And, under most circumstances, an aggressive policy by the Federal Reserve to provide more money to the economy so as to lower interest rates will also induce more spending for housing construction and business investment as credit terms are eased.

If the economy is operating below potential—if aggregate demand falls short of aggregate supply—GNP will rise in response to the increase in aggregate demand. However, if aggregate demand already equals potential GNP, the principal effect of a further increase in demand, which creates an excess of demand over supply, will be to produce a rise in inflation. For good or for ill, depending on the circumstances, the tools of aggregate demand policy can usually be effective in substantially raising (or lowering) aggregate demand.

Raising aggregate supply is a different matter. The federal government can seek to raise potential GNP in several broad ways. It can spend more money directly for investment in education, roads, research and development (R&D), and related projects that enhance the nation's ability to produce. It can, through reductions in taxes or through subsidies, seek to improve the monetary incentives of entrepreneurs, workers, and investors to take actions that raise supply, for example, a reduction in tax rates to induce individuals to work more or to be more willing to take risks, or special tax incentives for business investment. Either one of these types of policy will raise spending somewhere in the economy; the increase in government investment spending will obviously do so, and general tax reductions or special tax incentives will also raise the consumption or investment spending of those who receive the lower taxes. But once the economy is already operating near potential, any increase in total spending—that is, in aggregate demand—is unwelcome; as we said, it will simply lead to inflation. And so government policies to increase supply, since they will almost always raise spending somewhere in the economy, must also provide for an offsetting decrease in spending elsewhere. Thus, growth-oriented increases in government investment-type spending, or supply-side tax incentives, need to be accompanied by a restrictive monetary policy and high interest rates in order to reduce private spending, or by cuts in other forms of government spending, or by offsetting tax increases somewhere else in the system.

In short, aggregate demand policy aims at changing the level of GNP. Most frequently, aggregate supply policy has to achieve its objectives by changing the composition of GNP—more investment and less consumption or lower tax rates accompanied by a reduction in government spending. Numerous qualifications aside, aggregate demand policy can be very potent in changing demand. But it cannot, on any sustained basis, raise GNP above the level of its potential; overstimulation of demand will lead to inflation. Successful aggregate supply policies, however, can increase potential GNP on a sustained basis. But achieving that result will usually require a painful and difficult reallocation of GNP away from the consumption of public or private goods. Moreover, some supply-side policies seek to promote additional saving and investment through tax incentives for savers and investors. But since these groups are typically upper income, such policies mean a redistribution of income in the direction of greater inequality.

Supply-side policies are often difficult to sell politically because the resulting increase in aggregate supply is likely to seem modest. For example, a shift of $10 billion from consumption to investment may add only $1 billion to $2 billion a year to the annual flow of national income.

Several lessons, or better, cautions, for economic policymaking emerge from this important distinction. In the first place, confusing demand effects with supply effects is dangerous. Second, unless the economy is operating below potential, most macroeconomic supply-side measures—for example, tax incentives to promote additional investment or additional spending on government infrastructure—must be accompanied by other measures (usually highly unpopular) to reduce spending elsewhere; otherwise the policies will lead to excess aggregate demand and inflation or be frustrated as the Federal Reserve raises interest rates to quash the excess demand.

THE DEMAND-SUPPLY BALANCE AND THE IDEOLOGICAL BATTLE

Although government can have large effects on aggregate demand, through tax and spending policies and through the monetary actions of the Federal Reserve, we are still uncertain, despite decades of empirical research, about the magnitude and timing of many of these effects. And so managing the economy to achieve economic stability is no easy task. Making a mistake in one direction can bring on a recession; mistakes of the opposite nature will generate a new round of inflation that will be difficult and painful to remedy. Even with the best will in the world, reasonable people have much room to disagree.

Government policies of many kinds, including taxes and spending and monetary policies, can affect the growth of aggregate supply. Usually, however, unlike the case of demand, large policy actions are needed to have noticeable effects on supply, and even aside from extremists, experts disagree over the size of those effects. Moreover, some supply-oriented policies will provide increased monetary rewards for those who are already doing well in the marketplace, at the expense, initially at least, of those who are less well-off.[1] Finally, when the policies do work, they do so gradually and almost imperceptibly. Asking the voters to approve such policies is a politician's nightmare. As we have already seen, however, when cumulated over many years, they can have large effects on living standards.

Liberals and traditional conservatives tend to have their own blind spots in regard to one aspect of the demand-supply balance at the expense of the other. The two groups disagree along several dimensions. One can usually separate a liberal from a conservative on macroeconomic issues by asking the person to fill in the blanks in the sentence, "Take care of the _____ run and the _____ run will take care of itself." Liberals will enter "short" and "long" in that order; traditional conservatives will reverse the order.

Generally, liberals have historically tended to emphasize keeping demand high to minimize unemployment and avoid recession. It is not always clear, for example, when the policy dials should be turned down to keep the economy from overheating. Usually a noticeable lag occurs between the time of taking action to influence aggregate demand and the time those actions take effect. And the precise point when the rising pressure of demand on supply begins to yield dangerous inflationary consequences is never so obvious as to preclude reasonable people from disagreeing about whether that point has been reached. When in doubt, liberals often err in the direction of budgetary and monetary ease. They are more willing to take chances on letting demand rise too far relative to potential supply, with inflationary consequences, rather than prematurely applying restrictive monetary or budget policy that might keep unemployment above the full-employment level. Even though the improvement in employment may only be temporary, liberals tend, when considering the inflation-unemployment trade-off, to prefer an immediate and relatively certain gain in employment to the longer-term and more speculative

---

The Psychology of the Liberal-Conservative Argument

It is a fascinating commentary on human nature that in the public debates about these matters, the two sides articulate their disagreements not so much in terms of their different values but in the context of different assessments of the facts. Thus, a debate about the merits of a proposed tax incentive to stimulate saving seldom concentrates on whether the resulting increase in economic growth is "worth" the accompanying redistribution of income in favor of the rich. The issue is virtually never posed this way. Rather, the conservatives argue that the incentive will have large growth effects, while the accompanying redistribution of income is likely to be small. The liberals will pooh-pooh the efficacy of tax incentives in spurring growth and argue that the income redistributions will be large.

---

gains from the avoidance of future inflationary trouble and subsequent employment correction. And until recently, the liberals were more willing to tolerate some government deficits in order to get some stimulation of demand and employment. (Most sitting presidents, whatever their original ideological tendencies, tend to acquire more liberal leanings about expanding aggregate demand as election day nears.)

Old-fashioned conservatives usually give high priority to making sure that restrictive actions are taken early enough to prevent inflation even at the cost of forgoing some further improvement in the unemployment situation. These conservatives were loathe for years to accept any of the Keynesian doctrine about the benefits of demand stimulation during recessions, and they were the quickest to decry federal budget deficits under almost any circumstances.

The two camps disagree over the priority of a more equal distribution of income versus the provision of incentives for the sake of increasing the supply of GNP. Thus, in the interests of promoting a more equal distribution of income and providing a social safety net, liberals are inclined to play down potential negative effects of higher taxes, social benefits, and more extensive government social regulations on the supply of GNP. When tax measures are discussed, liberals devote much of their attention to the question of fairness, and less consideration to the consequences of the measures for economic efficiency and growth.

Among conservatives, measures to improve the supply side of the economy take precedence over managing demand and income distribu-

TABLE 2-1. Promises and Performance[a]
(1986 as promised in 1981)

Item	Promised	Actual
GNP (1982, billions of dollars)	3,952	3,718
Business investment (percent of GNP)	15.0	10.3
Personal saving (percent of disposable income)	7.9	4.1

a. "Promised" performance from Department of the Treasury, press releases, R-53 (Washington, February 26, 1981), and R-81, "News" (Washington, March 20, 1981). These forecasts had already been toned down from what were apparently even more optimistic original estimates. Promised GNP was calculated by applying to the actual 1980 GNP the forecasted percent changes between then and 1986 set forth in the February release as likely to occur if the administration's proposed tax and budget program were enacted.

tion—the concept of trickle-down is a crude but useful caricature of such attitudes. And in public debate about whether to increase taxes and social benefits, and to extend government regulations, conservatives give great weight to their potential negative influence on the supply of GNP and far less emphasis to their effects on demand or income distribution.

THE SUPPLY-SIDERS: A NEW BREED

In the 1980s a new breed suddenly emerged, the supply-siders. They managed to combine and exaggerate the blind spots of both liberals and conservatives, while often confusing the distinction between demand and supply. Nevertheless, they did achieve a virtual political revolution in 1981, setting in motion the basic policies that dominated the scene in the 1980s and producing a decade of huge budget and trade deficits and unprecedentedly high interest rates.

First, in 1981, the supply-siders vastly overstated the ability of lower federal tax rates to expand the supply of GNP. They took the traditional conservative emphasis on the supply-creating effects of tax cuts and multiplied their promised payoff by something like a factor of ten. Some sense of the overstatement can be gleaned from table 2-1, which compares the promises made in early 1981, as administration witnesses testified in favor of the tax cut, with actual outcomes five years later.

Second, some supply-siders promised to make it easier for conservatives to support popular spending programs. The supply response would be so large, they claimed, that the old-fashioned political dilemma of choosing between low tax rates and high social spending could be put aside, once and for all. As one of the proponents of the new doctrine, Senator Orrin Hatch, said at the time, "What the supply-siders have done is to point out that the war between the proponents of incentives and the federal government's spending constituencies is not necessary. It is possible to attack at another point: to get tax rates down and stimulate growth sufficiently to pay for the current rate of social services, hence bypassing the question of whether social spending is too high."[2]

Third, because of their faith in the efficacy of tax cuts to raise aggregate supply sharply, many supply-siders severely criticized the efforts of the Federal Reserve during most of the 1980s to restrain the growth of aggregate demand to prevent it from overrunning potential GNP. The failure of GNP to grow as originally promised when the supply-side policies of the 1980s were adopted is blamed by the remaining band of supply-siders (many have fallen by the wayside in recent years) on excessively restrictive policies of the Federal Reserve. Here they have assumed, again in exaggerated form, the traditional liberal tendency to avoid putting on the brakes as the economy enters into the danger zone of potential inflation.

IMPLICATIONS

The supply-siders' exaggeration of what could be gained from attempts to improve the growth of aggregate supply should not be allowed to divert attention from the importance of supply-side considerations in the design of macroeconomic policy. Memos 20 through 28 will discuss aggregate supply and what government policies can and cannot do to raise its level and speed its growth.

NOTES

1. Once the economy is at full employment, the revenue loss from tax incentives to stimulate saving and investment must be offset by tax increases elsewhere or by government spending cuts. The tax incentives will tend to favor

the well-to-do while, if history is any guide, the offsetting tax increases or spending cuts are most likely to affect those with middle and lower incomes.

2. Orrin G. Hatch, "The Politics of Supply-Side Economics," in Lawrence H. Meyer, ed., *The Supply-Side Effects of Economic Policy* (Boston: Kluwer-Nijhoff Publishing, 1981), pp. 255–62.

To: The President

FROM: CEA Chairman

SUBJECT: **The Nation's Income and Output: The Basic Structure**

In 1990 the U.S. gross national product (GNP) amounted to $5.5 trillion dollars, almost $22,000 dollars for each person in the country. After eliminating the effect of rising prices on the market value of goods and services, we can calculate that the amount of GNP produced in 1990 was more than three and one-half times higher than in 1950. But the annual rate of growth of GNP has slowed sharply in the past several decades, from 3.6 percent a year in the two decades before 1973 to 2.5 percent a year since then. Nevertheless the United States still has the highest per capita GNP in the world, above Germany and Japan and vastly greater than in the developing countries of the world.

By now references to GNP have become commonplace not only in the business section but on the front pages of newspapers, and the term has entered the vocabulary of television news anchors. Most of those who read about and listen to the term probably have a pretty good even if rough idea of what the GNP is—the total value of all the goods and services produced by the economy in a given year. But far fewer people are aware of several highly important relationships among the various elements of GNP—relationships central to understanding how a modern economy works.

For example, did you know that: for every dollar of GNP produced, there is a dollar of wage, profit, or some other kind of income created—output is income and income is output. The total amount that a country can invest at home and abroad can never exceed the amount that it saves. A country's international balance-of-payments deficit will always be equal

Gross National Product vs. Gross Domestic Product

At the end of 1991, the government published a revised set of national income and product statistics and began to emphasize the gross domestic product (GDP) rather than the gross national product (GNP). The difference between the two is very small—in 1990 GDP was two-tenths of 1 percent smaller than GNP. The GDP excludes, while the GNP includes, the interest, dividends, and reinvested profits earned by U.S. residents and corporations from their investments abroad (minus the earnings of foreign residents on their earnings in the United States). These net earnings are assumed to measure the net contribution of U.S.-owned investments abroad to production in other countries. Thus the GDP is the value of goods and services produced within the United States while the GNP is the value of goods and services produced by residents of the United States. This change brings the U.S. system of national income and product accounts into line with those of other industrial countries. These memos continue to use the GNP measure of national production, since the change was introduced just as they were going to press. A substitution of GDP for GNP would change nothing of any significance in any of the memos.

to the excess of its domestic investment over its saving, while a balance-of-payments surplus will mean that it has an excess of saving over domestic investment. Thus the United States has been saving little relative to what it wants to invest domestically and so has been running a trade deficit. Japan saves a lot, even relative to its large domestic investment, and so it has been running a trade surplus. It's time to take a close look at the GNP, the elements that make it up, and some of the important relationships among those elements.

THE GNP: WHAT'S IN AND WHAT'S OUT

For some fifty years the Department of Commerce has put together the national income and product accounts (NIPA), which is the accounting framework within which the gross national product is calculated. By convention the GNP is expressed as an annual amount; and so, for example, the estimates of GNP in a calendar quarter are always multiplied by four to express them at an annual rate. The statisticians who compile the NIPA statistics accept the decisions of the marketplace in deciding how to value the myriad goods and services that are produced. In the world of aesthetics a book of poetry may be worth its weight in precious metals. But in the GNP it takes one thousand $12 books of poetry to count as much as one $12,000 automobile.

With a few exceptions that we need not worry about here, only those goods and services bought and sold in the marketplace are included in the GNP. Thus the homemaking services of the housewife are not included, but the services of a paid housekeeper are, leading one well-known economist to note that by marrying his housekeeper he would lower GNP. The value of the weekend labor put in by the homeowner fixing up his house is not part of GNP, but the materials he buys at the hardware store are, as are the amounts he pays the plumbing or roofing contractor he might employ.

The GNP is not an index of human happiness or human welfare. It does not include, for example, any allowance for the condition of the environment or the status of worker safety. But it is a reasonable measure of how the nation is faring in the production and distribution of those goods and services that can be valued in the marketplace. And the GNP also provides important data for the analysis of the forces that increase or decrease the nation's output of goods and services.

GNP AND INFLATION

Prices have risen in almost every year of the past fifty. As a consequence the increase each year in the market value of goods and services produced, that is, in GNP, partly reflects an increase in the physical volume of production—more automobiles, dresses, and haircuts—and partly represents the effects of price inflation. And so the NIPA statisticians construct a second measure of the GNP, which eliminates the effect of inflation. In every year they assign to each unit of goods and services the price at which that unit sold in a base year; in the United States that base year is 1987.[1] And so the price at which each unit of goods and services is valued does not alter; any change over time in this second measure of GNP represents a change only in the volume of physical production, "clean" of any effect of inflation. Thus we have two measures of GNP: GNP in current dollars, whose changes from one period to the next reflect alterations in the volume of output and in prices; and GNP in constant (1987) dollars, whose changes reflect alterations in output only. GNP in current dollars is often called nominal GNP, while GNP in constant dollars is labeled real GNP. In 1990, for example, current dollar GNP, the market value of all the goods and services produced, rose by about 5 percent. But some 4 percent of that rise in market value was because of inflation. Constant dollar GNP, the volume of output produced, rose by only 1 percent.

SERVICES ARE AN IMPORTANT PART OF GNP

Notice the phrase "goods and services" in the definition of GNP. Services are an integral part of GNP. The wages and salaries of schoolteachers, nurses, and civil servants are entered in the GNP as reflecting their production of educational, health, and governmental services. Concert tickets, hotel charges, haircuts, and health spa fees are part of GNP. In 1990 goods production amounted to only 40 percent of GNP; the production of services accounted for 50 percent and construction for the remaining 10 percent. And of the 40 percent of GNP that were goods, only a little over half represented the contribution of the manufacturing industry; most of the other half was contributed by the services of transportation and distribution firms. Manufacturing output represents only a little over one-fifth of GNP. One of the peculiarities of the economic accounting of the former Soviet Union and the Eastern bloc countries—reflecting a peculiarity of Karl Marx's reasoning—was that they tended to include only goods production, or closely connected activities, in their GNP accounts.

OUTPUT EQUALS INCOME

The single most important relationship in macroeconomics is embedded in the NIPA accounting framework:

☆ **National income is identically equal to national output**

Every dollar of output produced creates an equal dollar of income. Take, for example, an American-made automobile sold to a consumer for $12,000. The transaction is entered as part of GNP; it represents $12,000 worth of production. But the $12,000 that the consumer handed over to the dealer for the car is in turn paid out as income to the firms and workers who helped produce, transport, and distribute that automobile: the salesman's commission, the dealer's profits, the wages and profits of the firm that trucked the car from factory to dealer; the wages, fringe benefits, and profits of the auto manufacturing firm, and similar incomes for the many firms and their workers who produced the materials, components, and parts that went into the vehicle.

If one thinks about some possible changes in the hypothetical income flows used in this example, one can see how the identity continues to hold. Suppose, for example, that the dealer, to sell the car, has to offer an extra $500 rebate. The value of the retail purchase is now $11,500, and that value would be entered into GNP. But, simultaneously, there would now be only $11,500 of income to be distributed. In this instance, the profits of the dealer would be lower if it was his discount, or the manufacturer would be poorer by $500 if it was a manufacturer's rebate.

Suppose by the end of the accounting period the car had not been sold. It would, however, have been added to the dealer's inventory at invoice cost, say $11,000. The GNP would show an $11,000 entry—under the category "change in business inventories"—and $11,000 would have been distributed as income further back in the distribution and manufacturing chain. In this instance, however, the dealer and the salesman would not yet have earned their profits and commissions.

Gross national product is thus matched by an equivalent total, "gross national income," which consists of all the incomes earned in the production and distribution of GNP. Its main components are the compensation of employees (wages and fringe benefits), which constitute two-thirds of the total, and various forms of income from invested capital (interest, rent, profits, and depreciation allowances). The duality of output and income is more than an accounting convention, however. As we saw in the automobile example, it reflects economic reality.

THE MAJOR CATEGORIES OF GNP

In the GNP data, the hundreds of thousands of different kinds of goods and services produced each year in a modern industrial economy are grouped into four major categories: consumer goods; investment goods (new homes, factories, office buildings, machinery and equipment, and additions to business inventories); goods destined for government use; and exports. These categories were chosen to correspond closely to the four major groups of decisionmakers in the economy: consumers, investors, governments, and foreigners.

Several aspects of the various categories of GNP require special mention. In the first place, the terms "investment" and "investors" have a more limited meaning than they do in common parlance. Investment refers to the purchase of tangible capital goods and investors to those who directly make such purchases—GM buying a new machine tool or a family buying a newly constructed home. The term does not include the purchase of the stocks, bonds, or mortgages that may be providing the financing for those investments. Second, government purchases refers to the purchase by government of currently produced goods and services—weapons, computers, dams, roads, space vehicles, the services of government employees, and so forth. The government also spends large sums in making transfer payments to individuals as part of social security, welfare, unemployment compensation, veterans' pension, and other programs. But these payments do not represent the purchase by government of a good or service, and so they are excluded from the government purchases line of GNP. (The recipients of these transfer payments do of course use the money they receive principally to buy consumption goods, and those purchases do show up in the consumption category.)

As a first approximation, one might think of GNP as simply the sum of purchases of goods and services by American consumers, investors, and governments, and by foreign buyers. But GNP is a measure of the total *production* of *U.S.* goods and services, and the above definition doesn't quite match that concept. In the first place, some purchases by consumers, investors, and governments are imported goods and do not represent production of U.S.-made goods. To measure GNP, purchases of imported goods have to be subtracted out of total purchases to arrive at an estimate of goods and services produced at home.

For various reasons, the NIPA statisticians don't subtract out imports from each category of purchases. Rather they define each of the categories as total purchases (including imports), but then make a global adjustment by subtracting total imports from the export figure and entering into GNP a number representing net exports—that is, total exports minus total imports. And so, as reformulated, GNP is the sum of consumer purchases, investment, government purchases, and net exports (exports minus imports). Table 3-1 shows the comparison of GNP among those major compositions and how it has changed over the past thirty years.

A second important modification to the initial definition of GNP involves goods that have been produced but not sold—that is, business inventories. Simply adding up purchases won't catch those goods, and GNP so estimated would understate the volume of production when inventories were rising and overstate production when inventories were

TABLE 3-1. Shares of GNP
Percent

Item	1960	1970	1980	1990	Dollar value (billions) 1990
Consumption	64.2	63.0	63.4	66.9	3,657
Gross investment	15.2	14.7	16.0	13.6	741
Government purchases	19.5	21.5	19.4	20.1	1,098
Net exports	1.1	0.8	1.1	−0.6	−31
(Exports)	(5.8)	(6.8)	(12.8)	(12.3)	(673)
(Imports)	−(4.7)	−(6.0)	−(11.7)	−(12.9)	−(704)
Total GNP	100.0	100.0	100.0	100.0	5,465
Addendum: Consumption plus government pur- chases	83.7	84.5	82.8	87.0	4,755

falling. And so the NIPA statisticians, as we noted earlier, include under the category of investment an item labeled change in business inventories (or, informally, inventory investment), which is positive when inventories are being accumulated and negative when they are being run down.

Besides providing a bird's eye glimpse of the underlying structure of aggregate demand and GNP in the American economy, table 3-1 highlights three developments that will be discussed in later memos. One, the international sector of the economy grew markedly over the past thirty years as exports and imports greatly expanded their share of aggregate demand. Two, in the 1980s, the export share temporarily stopped rising while the growth of imports sharply accelerated, leading to the creation of a major trade deficit; imports exceeded exports. In 1989, total spending by the three domestic purchasers of output—that is, the sum of consumption, gross investment, and government purchases—exceeded GNP by 0.6 percent, precisely the size of the trade deficit. Americans spent more than the country produced, and the only way that could be accomplished was by importing more than we exported. Three, during the 1980s, the share of GNP devoted to government and consumer purchases combined rose well above its postwar average (to 87 percent in 1990 from 83 percent in earlier decades). That rise in the joint consumer-government share was achieved partly by reducing investment and partly by running a large trade deficit, with imports exceeding exports.

THE DUAL ROLE OF INVESTMENT

Investment purchases play two important roles in the operations of the economy. In one way, purchases of investment goods are like all other purchases of goods and services—they add to the aggregate demand for output. When business firms add to their purchases of new factories, machinery, and equipment, the firms who produce those goods increase their demand for labor and raw materials to fill the additional orders they have received. If the economy is operating below potential, GNP rises. If, however, the economy is already at full employment, the added demand for labor and raw materials is likely to lead to higher inflation. (We haven't yet discussed what causes inflation, but at this point we can take for granted that when demand for goods and labor exceeds the available supply, the existing pace of wage and price increases is likely to speed up). So far, there is nothing special about this event. The same thing could be said of a change in demand in any other sector of the economy. Unlike other goods, however, investment goods also add to the future productive capacity of the economy. They not only increase demand, they increase supply. But, as mentioned earlier, a dollar's increase in investment adds a dollar to total spending and demand, but only a modest fraction of a dollar to the annual supply of goods and services. Thus, in an economy already producing at or near potential, an increase in investment spending, by raising demand more than supply, will lead to inflationary problems.

The upshot is that a policy to stimulate long-term growth by providing additional investment incentives in the tax code must simultaneously make provision for reducing aggregate demand elsewhere in the economy if inflation is to be avoided. For example, any tax incentives introduced to promote more investment must be accompanied by cuts in government spending or by tax increases on consumers.

AN EXPORT SURPLUS IS AN OVERSEAS INVESTMENT

A country with a positive net export balance is investing abroad. When a country exports more than it imports, it is sending some of its goods and services abroad for which it is not immediately receiving payment (in the form of imports). When Japan, for example, runs a large trade surplus with the United States, Japan necessarily ends up increasing its ownership of dollars. That is, U.S. receipts of yen from exports to Japan are not enough to pay the Japanese for their exports to the United States, so the Japanese must accept dollars in payment for their exports. But except for fairly small amounts, no one holds such foreign currency earnings in noninterest-bearing cash. Thus, the Japanese invest their dollar holdings in U.S. Treasury securities, American stocks and bonds, and U.S. real estate and business ventures, all of which yield a stream of earnings to the Japanese. A country with a net export surplus is, thus, making an investment just as real as additions to domestic plant and equipment. Both types of investment increase the stream of national income and output in the future—the domestic investment by raising national productivity, and the foreign investment by securing the right to a stream of interest, dividend, and profit payments from abroad. The converse of course is that a country's trade deficit is matched dollar for dollar by its borrowing from abroad—the incurring of obligations to pay a future income stream to foreigners—and is equivalent to disinvestment. Because of its investment nature, net exports can also be designated net foreign investment.[2] This component of GNP can of course be positive or negative, depending on whether the country is exporting more than it imports or vice versa.

GROSS VERSUS NET NATIONAL PRODUCT AND INCOME

Every year some part of the nation's stock of tangible capital—machinery, factories, and other structures—wears out or becomes obsolete and is no longer available to contribute to the production of output. And to avoid future declines in output and income, some fraction of the nation's annual production of investment goods must be devoted to replacing what has been worn out or depreciated. As a consequence, that part of GNP—replacement investment—does not represent goods freely available to use as we wish for consumption or as an addition to the nation's wealth.

The GNP represents the nation's total output of goods and services, including the goods that must be used simply for replacing the depreciated capital. Net national product (NNP) excludes those replacement items. For purposes of analyzing short-term fluctuations in national production and employment, we normally use the GNP data. Net national income, which is the term for the income counterpart of net national product, includes all the items of income except depreciation charges. For simplicity, in all of the succeeding memos I will call this income total *national income.* (This nomenclature is slightly different from that of the official Department of Commerce statistics, which define national income to exclude not only depreciation but also the value of sales and property taxes.)

In an exactly matching way, gross national income includes all of the income generated in the production of GNP, including not only wages, profits, interest, and other such income, but also the allowances for depreciation included in the prices charged by business firms to cover the cost of the wearing out and obsolescence of their plant and equipment. Net national income, normally abbreviated to national income, includes all the other items of income but excludes depreciation charges.

NOTES

1. In the recently revised GNP/GDP data the base year was changed from 1982 to 1987. (For various technical reasons it is not desirable to have a base year that is very many years in the past.)

2. Actually, net foreign investment is defined a little differently than net exports, but for our purposes the two terms are equivalent.

MEMORANDUM 4

To: The President

From: CEA Chairman

Subject: **National Saving and Investment:**
         Why Are They Important?

In the 1980s, national saving in the United States virtually collapsed, as shown in figure 4-1. In the three decades prior to the 1980s, net national saving averaged a little more than 8 percent of national income; publicly and privately the nation consumed a bit under 92 percent of its national income. The 8 percent national saving rate that existed in the 1950s, 1960s, and 1970s was not unusually high or low for the United States— outside of war and recession, national saving had fluctuated around that level for most of the preceding century. During the 1980s, however, the national saving rate fell dramatically, to 3 percent at the end of the decade. Measured on a comparable basis, the national saving rate for the late 1980s was 17 percent of national income in Japan, 13 percent in Germany, and averaged about 12 percent for the advanced industrial countries outside the United States.

NATIONAL SAVING AND ITS MAJOR COMPONENTS

Why should we care what happens to national saving, and how does it affect national well-being?

Total national saving is made up of several components, each undertaken by a different sector of the national economy. On average, households save—that is, do not consume—a modest fraction of their income after taxes. Business firms, after paying dividends, interest, and taxes, are left with their retained earnings, which is business saving. The sum of household and business saving equals the nation's private saving.

FIGURE 4-1. The Collapse of Net National Saving, 1959–90

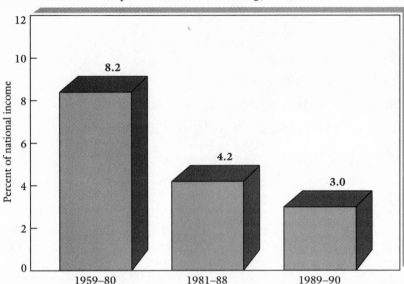

A Definition of National Saving

National saving is that part of a nation's income not used for private or public consumption.[1] But since national income and output are the same, that part of a nation's income that is not consumed constitutes output available for purposes other than consumption, that is, for investment, either domestic or abroad.

If, in the aggregate, governments (federal, state, and local) run a deficit and spend more than their income, they *dis*save; their borrowing to finance the deficit soaks up some of private saving and reduces the amount available for business to borrow and invest. If, less typically, governments spend below their revenues and run a surplus, they redeem outstanding government debt and in that way supplement the funds available from private saving to finance investment. Thus national saving is equal to *private saving* less the government *budget deficit* (or plus the government

FIGURE 4-2. The Components of the Collapse in National Saving, 1959–90

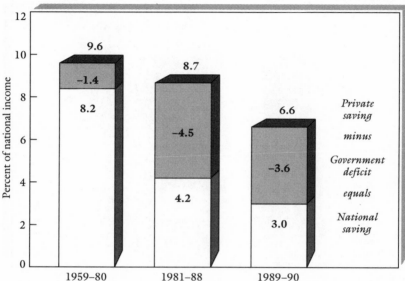

surplus). It is the amount of national income that has not been consumed publicly or privately and is, therefore, available for investment. The components of national saving are shown in figure 4-2.

The decline in national saving during the 1980s just discussed occurred because of a fall in the private saving rate and a large increase in the federal budget deficit, as shown in figure 4-2. In the three decades before 1980, the private saving rate (the sum of personal and business saving) averaged 9.6 percent of national income. On average government budget deficits absorbed 1.4 percent of the private saving, leaving the United States a national saving rate of 8.2 percent. By 1989–90 the private saving rate had fallen to 6.6 percent, and of that shrunken amount, the budget deficit absorbed 3.6 percent, leaving an overall national saving rate of only 3.0 percent.

We can also examine the decline in national saving by looking at the opposite side of the coin—the rise in public and private consumption; during the 1980s, public and private consumption, which had earlier averaged 92 percent of national income, rose to 97 percent. The tax cuts of 1981 and the increase in government transfer payments, which contributed to the rising budget deficits, raised household incomes and

FIGURE 4-3. The Relationship of National Saving and Investment

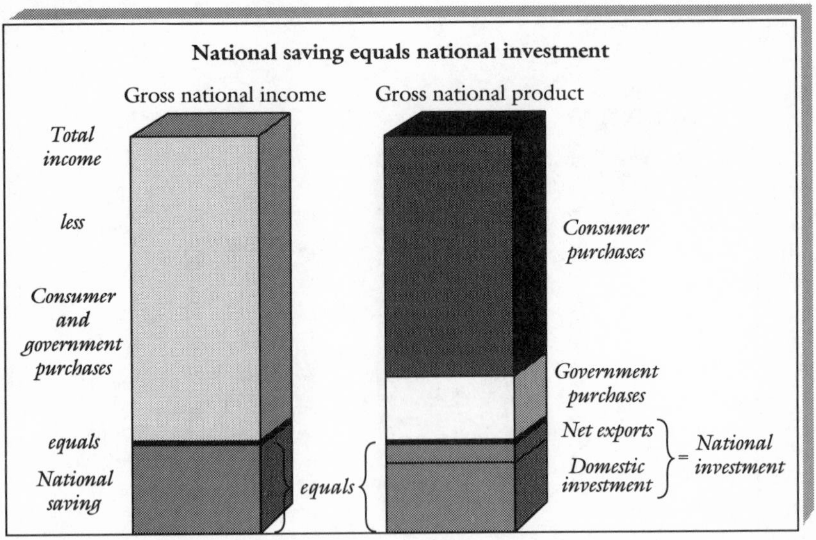

so consumers spent more. And the rise in defense purchases increased government consumption. Not only did households, through deficit-financed tax cuts and transfer payments, receive an enlarged share of national income, but they in turn consumed a larger share of the income they did receive. By these routes the country sharply raised the percentage of national income going to public and private consumption and correspondingly lowered the share going to national saving.

SAVING, INVESTMENT, AND THE TRADE DEFICIT

A nation can invest only what it saves. Broadly defined, there are really two destinations for the goods a nation produces: consumption (public and private), and investment (domestic and foreign, that is, an excess of exports over imports). The only way we can make part of our national output available for investment is to refrain from consuming, that is, to save. The relationship between national saving and national investment is shown in figure 4-3.

We can measure either gross national saving or net national saving. Gross national saving includes, while net national saving excludes, the depreciation allowances that are part of business firms' gross retained earnings.[2] Correspondingly, we can distinguish gross investment, which includes the purchase of investment goods for replacement purposes, from net investment, which does not. Net investment thus represents only net new additions to the nation's stock of productive capital. Both concepts are useful. But on balance the volume of net saving and net investment is probably the better indicator of what the nation is doing to provide for its future.[3] Figures 4-1 and 4-2, depicting the recent decline in national saving, are based on the net saving concept. Since depreciation allowances have risen as a share of national income, the decline in the gross saving rate has been smaller than the decline in the net rate.

SAVING, INVESTMENT, AND THE TRADE BALANCE

In figure 4-3, net exports (which are also net foreign investment) are shown as positive. But, as pointed out in memo 3, that net foreign investment can be negative. In that case, total spending for domestic purposes—consumer purchases plus government purchases plus domestic investment—is larger than GNP; domestic spending is greater than production. We accomplish that feat by importing more than we export—net exports are negative. And, by the same amount, national saving is less than domestic investment; to finance our excess of spending over production, we borrow saving from abroad. Thus, a country can spend more on consumption and domestic investment than it produces, by importing more than it exports and financing the difference on the world capital market. It can, in other words, provide resources for domestic investment despite an increased use of resources for consumption purposes, through borrowing from abroad and importing more than it exports. It thereby supplements the resources that its own saving makes available for domestic investment through the device of borrowing the saving of other countries. The experience of the United States in the 1980s nicely illustrates these facts.

ADJUSTING TO LOWER NATIONAL SAVING IN THE 1980S

As implied by the preceding discussion, a nation can adjust to a drop in its national saving rate in only two ways: it can reduce the fraction of output going to domestic investment, or it can supplement its shrunken saving by borrowing the saving of other countries, that is, it can meet the

FIGURE 4-4. Adjusting to a Lower Saving Rate, 1959–80, 1989–90

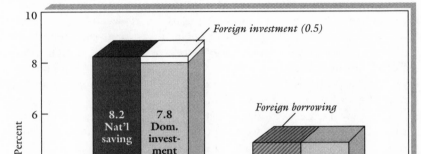

rise in consumption and government purchases by spending more than it produces, thereby running a trade deficit, necessarily financed by overseas borrowing.

As figure 4-4 depicts, the United States did some of both. In the decades prior to 1980, when we saved 8.2 percent of our national income, we used 7.8 percentage points for domestic investment and invested 0.5 percent abroad, that is, we ran a small trade surplus matched by our loans abroad. When, during the 1980s, the national saving rate fell to 3 percent, we cut domestic investment but not by as much as saving fell; domestic investment dropped from 7.8 percent to 4.9 percent of national income. We maintained domestic investment at that level, despite the fall of saving to 3 percent, by converting the trade surplus to a trade deficit and shifting from being net lender to the rest of the world to net borrower.[4] We supplemented our shrunken national saving by borrowing saving from abroad. By 1990, more than half of our reduced net investment total was directly or indirectly supported by the importation of foreign saving.

This discussion begins to explain some apparently paradoxical propositions about countries' trade balances to which virtually all economists subscribe but which most people neither understand nor believe. As we just saw, if a nation begins to consume a very large fraction of its national income, or what is the same thing, saves very little, then the sum of its domestic and net foreign investment *must* also be small. If, for whatever reason, domestic investment stays relatively high, then net foreign investment (net exports) must be negative—the country will run a trade deficit and borrow saving from abroad as a means of simultaneously consuming and investing at a high rate. That has been true of the United States for more than a decade. However, a country whose domestic saving is high relative to its domestic investment needs will have some saving left over; it will run a trade surplus and lend some of its savings to foreigners— Japan in the 1980s. In short, it is not a country's trade policies or those of its competitors that principally determine whether it has a trade deficit, but the relationship between its national saving and the investment demands of its homeowners and business firms. Trade policies do importantly influence national well-being but not through their ability to produce trade surpluses or deficits.

SAVING, INVESTMENT, AND THE FLOW OF FINANCIAL FUNDS

The flow of saving that households, business firms, or governments undertake each year becomes available to finance investment. But how new saving each year is channeled into investment may be indirect and complex. For business saving, the process is indeed fairly direct. Business firms retain part of their after-tax profits rather than paying them all out as dividends, and they use most of the resulting funds to finance their investments. But a very large share of the funds that households save is channeled into investment not directly through purchases by those households of stocks, bonds, or residential mortgages, but indirectly through the actions of banks, savings and loan institutions, money market funds, and other financial intermediaries—that is, institutions who collect funds from savers and use them to finance home purchases and business investment.

Households deposit much of the money they save into these financial intermediaries who in turn finance business and residential investment by making loans to business firms and mortgages to homebuyers or by buying stocks and bonds newly issued by business firms. (There is of course a huge volume of purchases and sales each year of existing stocks and bonds, but for the economy as a whole, this action simply reshuffles existing ownership of securities among holders and doesn't represent a transfer of new saving into new investment.) Households also save and buy securities indirectly through the operations of the pension funds that most business firms set up for their employees. Part of the employee compensation comes in income that is not paid out to them but deposited in pension funds, which in turn use the proceeds to buy stocks, bonds, and mortgages.

Subject to an important qualification that we will come to in a later memo, households will, for convenience, keep a certain balance in their regular checking accounts, but once their average deposit is large enough to meet convenience needs, they will use the rest of their savings in ways that earn higher returns–thrift deposits, purchases of mutual fund securities, direct purchases of stocks and bonds, and so on.

When a government runs a deficit, it sells securities to the private marketplace absorbing some of the funds that would have otherwise been available to finance private investment. Thus government deficits reduce national saving. When governments run a surplus, however, they use it to retire some of their outstanding debt—that is, they buy back debt from existing holders. But those holders in turn place the cash they have received into various other financial instruments, and thus the government saving is channeled into private investment. At the present time, for example, the federal government's social security trust fund is running a large annual surplus. By law, it must use those surpluses to buy Treasury securities. If the rest of the government's budget were in balance, however, the Treasury would not be issuing any net new securities for the social security fund to buy. The only way it could buy the government securities it needed would be to purchase them from existing private holders. But, as we said, those holders would use the proceeds to buy private securities. In other words, if the budget outside the social security funds were in balance, the social security surpluses would add to the funds available for private investment, even though the surpluses were used to purchase Treasury securities. To channel the social security surplus into private investment, it is not necessary to have the social security fund buy private securities.

In sum, the flow of real resources made available for investment purposes, as society refrains from consuming all of its income, is matched by a flow of financial resources from savers to investors.

What's to Come

We have seen that because of the nature and definitions of income, output, saving, and investment, a nation's total investment (domestic and foreign) must rise and fall in exact parallel with national saving. Yet the people who do much of the saving are not the same people who make the decisions about investment. The managements of a few hundred large business firms make the decisions that account for most of the nation's investment in plant and equipment, and millions of small businesses make the remainder of those decisions. In any one year, housing construction depends on the actual and projected homebuying decisions of several million homebuyers. And the magnitude of net foreign investment is determined by a different set of decisionmakers, involving exports and imports by thousands of business firms and flows of financial capital by individuals and firms all over the world. Scores of millions of households save, to some extent directly and to some extent through their company's pension plans. The decisions of the savers and the decisions of the investors have little direct connection with each other. Yet, when it is summed up, national saving equals national investment. How this occurs and how it eventually generates movements in aggregate demand and thus in employment, output, prices, and interest rates is the subject of the following memos on aggregate demand and economic instability.

NOTES

1. This statement, and what follows, implicitly assumes that all of government purchases represent goods for public consumption and that none are for investment purposes. That is obviously not correct; governments do invest in productive assets—roads, schools, and so forth. But it is a temporarily useful fiction, which we can later abandon. That's not as far from the real world as one might first think. In 1990 gross government investment in (nonmilitary) tangible assets was 2.5 percent of GNP, and after depreciation, net investment was only 1 percent of NNP.

2. After paying the out-of-pocket costs it incurs, as well as taxes, dividends, and interest, firms are left with their gross retained earnings. These can be allocated into two components: depreciation allowances, representing, as noted in memo 3, the cost of the wearing out and obsolescence of the capital stock, and net profits. The former are included in gross and excluded from net saving.

3. The choice is not an easy one. While net investment is a measure of how much the nation is increasing its stock of capital—which is highly relevant to how fast the economy can grow—a speedup in the rate at which existing capital goods are replaced by newer capital can hasten the introduction of new technology into the workplace.

4. Remember that the lending and borrowing referred to include all sorts of methods by which one country provides capital to another: loans, purchases of stock, and direct investment in business and real estate enterprises.

PART 2

Managing Demand

To: The President

FROM: CEA Chairman

SUBJECT: **What Causes Recessions and Booms:**
          An Overview

Earlier, in memo 1, recessions and inflationary booms were explained as the result of total spending in the economy falling below or racing well ahead of the economy's supply capabilities, as measured by its potential GNP. And that memo also noted that these imbalances between demand and supply arise mainly from fluctuations in aggregate demand; aggregate supply changes more gradually and smoothly over time.

But what causes the movements in aggregate demand that produce supply-demand imbalances and economic instability? Essentially two different kinds of problems give rise to instability. The first one arises from a characteristic of our economy that we can label "the inertia of inflation" and from government efforts to tame inflation. The term "inflation" simply means rising prices; if prices are rising at 4 percent a year, we say the inflation rate is 4 percent. The term "wage inflation" is similarly used to denote rising wages. In the United States, and to a greater or lesser degree, in all other modern market-based economies, inflation is marked by a high degree of inertia. That is, workers and firms modify their wage- and price-setting decisions only gradually and grudgingly to meet changing demand-supply conditions. In particular, it normally takes rather substantial unemployment and idle capacity to get workers and firms to lower the rate of wage and price increases. And so, once a new round of inflation gets under way, and becomes part of the wage and price-making process, it takes a sustained period of depressed aggregate demand, economic slack, and higher unemployment to wring the inflation out of the system.

In a related vein, whenever some large economywide cost-raising shock hits the economic system—such as a fall in productivity growth or a big rise in oil prices—wage and salary workers have to accept a cut in their real incomes; costs are higher and so prices have to rise relative to wages. But, typically, if the economy is at high employment with little economic slack when the cost-raising shock occurs, wage and salary workers will try to avoid any cut in their real income—they will demand higher wage and salary incomes sufficient to offset at least a good part of the higher cost of living that came about because of the cost increase. Prices will then begin increasing even faster, and a new cost-based inflation will begin. Again, the only way to head off this response is by pursuing monetary and fiscal policies austere enough to reduce aggregate demand, thereby creating some economic slack and unemployment, thus making it less likely that wage and salary workers will demand, and their bosses will grant, the troublesome wage and salary increases.

Many of the recessions of the postwar years arose from these inflation-related causes, and the recessions of 1974–75 and 1981–82 were especially noteworthy: oil shocks and productivity slowdowns were converted to wage-price spirals, which in turn could be conquered only by periods of exceedingly tight money and high unemployment. Sometimes inertial wage and price behavior causes the government to bring on a shortfall in aggregate demand as the only way of preventing cost-induced inflation or reversing an inflation that has started from whatever cause.

In memos 11–13, we will look more closely at this first source of economic instability, arising from the inertial character of wages and prices in modern economies. But aggregate demand can and does fluctuate relative to supply, and economic instability can and does occur for reasons other than government policies designed to suppress or prevent inflation. This second set of reasons for fluctuations hinges on the fact that there is instability in aggregate demand itself. In the remainder of this memo, and in memos 6 through 10, we examine the features of the economy that produce that instability, and others that limit it.

THE STABILITY OF AGGREGATE DEMAND

Let's look at the behavior of aggregate demand in the context of the economy's saving-investment balance. Imagine an economy with a nice equality between aggregate demand and long-run supply, with GNP equaling but not exceeding its potential. Consumers, investors, governments, and foreign buyers together are purchasing goods and services sufficient to provide a market for the potential high-employment output of the economy. To the extent that the citizens of the economy, privately and collectively, are not consuming all of national output, that is, to the extent they are saving, the remainder of national output is being sold to investors in the form of new structures and equipment or is being invested overseas in the form of a surplus of exports over imports.

But now suppose that, for whatever reason, some component of aggregate demand falls off. A fall in aggregate demand will show up as a tendency for national saving to exceed national investment. Thus, if consumer spending declines, saving will increase. If government consumption, say for defense purchases, declines (and is unaccompanied by a tax cut), national saving will also increase. Alternatively, the fall in aggregate demand and the associated tendency for saving to run ahead of investment could come about not by a rise in saving but by a fall in the demand for investment goods by business investors or for exports by foreigners. In either case, some part of potential GNP that was being sold for consumption or for investment purposes can no longer find a market; aggregate supply becomes larger than aggregate demand, and by exactly the same amount, saving threatens to exceed the sum of domestic and foreign investment. The lack of a market for some of the output of business firms causes them to cut back their production, GNP falls, and workers are laid off or put on short workweeks.

Remember, national income equals national output. When GNP (output) declines, so does GNI (gross national income). Wages, salaries, profits, and government revenues fall. Consumers will have less income and their saving falls. Profits decline and so does business saving. Government takes in less revenue and its deficit rises (that is, the government *dis*saves). National saving and investment will continue to be equal to each other, but now at a lower level. The drop in aggregate demand, which showed up as an initial tendency for an imbalance between saving and investment, reduces national output and income, which then lowers national saving, bringing saving and investment into equality but at a lower level. And the same story could be told in reverse when aggregate demand increases relative to supply. That creates a tendency for investment to run ahead of saving, which leads to an increase in aggregate demand, raises GNP and GNI, and brings saving back into equality with investment but now at a higher level.

In sum, a decline in aggregate demand relative to potential GNP sets up a situation in which the savers in the economy are seeking to save a larger amount than investors are willing to use for investment purposes. The result is a fall in national output, that is, in GNP, and an equally large fall in GNI.

At some point the decline in GNI lowers national saving to the point at which it is equal to what the economy wants to invest. GNP then stops falling and (at least temporarily) rests at a level below the economy's potential.

Remember that aggregate supply—potential GNP—increases gradually as the labor force grows and productivity slowly rises. To provide jobs for the new entrants to the labor force and for workers whose jobs are displaced by growing productivity, aggregate demand, which determines how much GNP is actually produced, also has to increase. A constant level of aggregate demand, maintained year after year in the face of growing potential GNP, would mean an increasing shortfall of demand relative to supply and a growing level of unemployment. For example, aggregate demand and GNP (in constant dollars) rose by 1.3 percent from 1960 to 1961. But this rise was less than growth of potential GNP, which at that time was growing at about 4 percent a year. And so unemployment rose, from an average of 5.5 percent in 1960 to 6.7 in 1961.

WHY DOES AGGREGATE DEMAND FLUCTUATE?

At first glance, the puzzle is not why aggregate demand fluctuates, but why—except for the Great Depression of the 1930s—it has not fluctuated more. Figure 5-1 provides a measure of the volatility of the major components of GNP during the past forty-odd years. Each bar shows the average quarterly percent change (whether positive or negative) of each component relative to its long-term trend. The average change in the volume of residential construction, for example, was 4 percent, which is a very large change for one quarter. Except for the (very sizable) consumer nondurables and services component and state and local government purchases, the other major components of aggregate demand are also characterized by a tendency to fluctuate substantially.

The most volatile component of GNP, inventory investment (the change in business inventories), isn't shown in figure 5-1. Since it often swings from a positive to a negative amount and back again, a calculation of percentage changes is meaningless. But we can express the average quarterly change in inventory investment as a percentage of GNP; this is

FIGURE 5-1. The Average Volatility of GNP and Its Components
Quarterly percent change, relative to trend

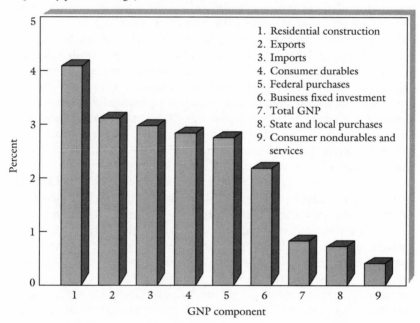

a measure of the immediate impact of changes in inventories on total aggregate demand. The average quarterly change in business inventories over the postwar period was enough to swing total GNP by an annual rate of 2.7 percent, which is no small amount.

SOME DESTABILIZING FORCES THAT MAGNIFY THE EFFECT OF INITIAL CHANGES

The relatively volatile sectors of aggregate demand (consumer durables, investment of all types, net exports and federal purchases) make up less than half of the total, while the more stable elements of demand, consumer nondurables and services, and state and local purchases account for more than half. Nevertheless, the instability among the volatile elements is large, and there are forces that magnify the effect on aggregate demand of a change originating in one sector of the economy.

The first of these is the so-called *multiplier* effect. When demand in one sector of the economy declines—let's say purchases of automobiles—production of those goods will also fall, workers will be laid off or will have to go on reduced workweeks, and their incomes will drop. They reduce their purchases of consumption goods, which leads to a second round of reduced demand and layoffs in other consumer goods industries, producing still a third round, and so on. The ultimate decline in aggregate demand from this process is a multiple of the initial decline. And of course the chain effect described works in reverse, potentially turning initial increases in demand in one component of GNP into a larger increase in aggregate demand. The concept of the multiplier and its use in analyzing economic fluctuations are closely connected with the work of the famous English economist John Maynard Keynes.

Another economic process that magnifies the effect of initial changes in demand into larger changes in GNP results from what is known as the *investment accelerator*. A major reason for businesses to purchase new plant and equipment is to expand capacity to meet expectations of a growing market. The faster the growth in the demand and sales that business firms expect, the larger the investment they will undertake. Imagine, for example, that aggregate demand and actual GNP are growing steadily, in line with the growth of potential GNP, that business firms have come to expect this rate of growth to continue, and are investing accordingly. But then suppose that developments in some sector of the economy cause the growth of aggregate demand to slow down—total demand doesn't actually fall, it simply grows more slowly. To the extent that business firms now expect their future sales to grow more slowly, they will need a smaller growth in production capacity and so will reduce the investment they are making in new plant and equipment.

In other words, a mere slowdown in the rate of growth of aggregate demand may, if it forces a reevaluation of business expectations about the future, cause an absolute drop in business purchases of plant and equipment, and by the same logic, a drop in production devoted to building up inventories to meet future growth in sales.

In this way an initial decline in one sector of the economy, even if it isn't large enough to lead to an absolute decline in aggregate demand, may through the multiplier process slow or halt the growth of demand and GNP and call into play the investment accelerator that induces a decline in business investment purchases. That will lead to further weakness in aggregate demand, to further multiplier and accelerator effects, and so on into recession. And the scenario can be replayed the opposite way to produce overheated booms and inflation.

So far it seems like a witches' brew—a number of very volatile sectors of aggregate demand and several highly destabilizing chain effects that multiply and accelerate initial fluctuations in certain sectors into much larger and widespread fluctuations in overall demand, production, and employment. And indeed in the first ten to twenty years after the Second World War, bolstered by the memories of the Great Depression and in the flush of excitement generated by the newly emerged Keynesian analysis, what was called knife-edge economics gained prominence. According to this view, the economy was prone to bounce regularly from deep recession to overheated boom and back again. The then-recent memory of the Great Depression reinforced this concept of a highly unstable economy.

Gradually it became apparent, however, that the postwar economy wasn't behaving that way, and that even in the prewar era, the Great Depression was the exception rather than the rule.[1] Glance back at figure 5-1 and notice that despite the large volatility of several components of aggregate demand and the existence of the multiplier and accelerator processes, the typical fluctuations in GNP relative to its long-term trend, while hardly trivial, were not nearly as large as would have been the case had the knife-edge view been correct. Nine recessions have occurred in the postwar era. But in none of them did GNP fall by more than 2.5 percent from one year to the next. There must, therefore, be some stabilizing elements in the economic system that tend to counteract, even if only partially, the knife-edge characteristics outlined. Some of these stabilizing elements are built into the private economic system, others reflect the operations of government monetary and fiscal policies (although it's also true that badly timed or otherwise mistaken monetary and fiscal policies have on some occasions contributed to, rather than moderated, economic instability).

The above discussion suggests two questions. One, what are the stabilizing features in the economy that normally moderate the processes that would otherwise produce large and frequent cyclical swings? And two, why aren't those stabilizing features effective enough to prevent the recessions and inflationary booms from which we still on occasion suffer? The next three memos sketch the answers to these questions.

NOTE

1. But as we have mentioned, the GNP, quite apart from the depression of the 1930s, fluctuated more sharply in the years between the Civil War and the Second World War than it has done since.

To: The President

From: CEA Chairman

Subject: **The Behavior of Consumption Spending**

The operations of the private economy moderate the potential for economic instability in several ways. First, certain characteristics of the behavior of households and business firms with respect to their purchases of consumer and investment goods attenuate the operation of the multiplier and accelerator processes. And, second, when aggregate demand falls below potential GNP and saving correspondingly threatens to run ahead of domestic and foreign investment, changes in interest rates, credit conditions, and exchange rates are set in motion that induce increases in aggregate demand that partially offset the initial decrease.

In this and the next memo, we examine the forces that drive consumer and investment spending and consider how consumer and investment behavior damp down, even though they do not eliminate, the strength of the multiplier and accelerator processes. As a bonus, an understanding of the important influences on consumption, saving, and investment will be a useful background for some of the discussion in the supply-side memos that follow.

CONSUMPTION SPENDING

In economic policymaking, two main aspects of consumer spending are important to understand, both of which figure 6-1 illustrates: one, in the short run, what major factors cause consumption to fluctuate from year to year, and in particular, to what extent do period-to-period changes in consumer spending mimic changes in household income?

FIGURE 6-1. The Behavior of Consumer Spending and Saving, 1950–90

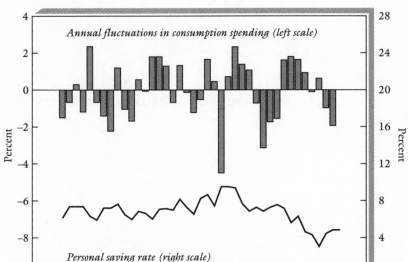

Note: Fluctuations in consumption are measured relative to trend.

Two, over the longer run, what determines the fraction of income that consumers save, and why has that fraction fallen so sharply over the past fifteen years?

A glance back at figure 5-1 reveals that spending on consumer durables is highly volatile and contrasts sharply with the behavior of spending on consumer nondurables and services, whose fluctuations are much smaller. The cyclical behavior of spending on consumer durables is more nearly comparable to that of business investment, and indeed the two are driven by many of the same forces. Purchases of consumer durables are an investment by households in relatively long-lasting consumer capital goods, which produce a stream of services for the consumers lasting many years. Autos provide transportation services, washing machines produce laundry services, and so forth. And like other purchases of investment goods they are heavily influenced by the accelerator phenomenon outlined in memo 5. We will postpone a discussion of consumer durables purchases until memo 7, and concentrate now on the behavior of consumer demand for nondurables and services.

Consider two kinds of fluctuations in consumer purchases (of nondurables and services). First, changes in consumption spending can occur because household income changes. This is what drives the multiplier process just discussed. When, for example, an initial decline in demand and output occurs somewhere in the economy, workers are laid off or go on short time; their incomes fall, and their consumption spending consequently declines. In this case, the changes in consumer spending are not what initiates the fall in GNP, but the response of consumption spending to the initial change of demand elsewhere in the economy spreads and deepens the overall decline. Second, consumption can change independently of any alterations in income, responding to various developments, such as large swings in the stock market or fears of future economic disturbances. But the evidence suggests that these factors are much less important, on average, than changes in income as an explanation for fluctuations in consumption.

How Consumption and Income Are Related

In the aggregate, consumers spend about 80 percent of their income on the purchases of nondurable goods and services. At first glance, this sum would seem to make for a very large "multiplier" and imply that an initial loss in income caused by a fall in demand and output anywhere in the economy would induce very large secondary effects. If each $100 loss of income by a group of laid-off workers caused them to reduce their consumption spending by $80, resulting in a second group of laid-off workers who in turn cut spending by four-fifths of their loss of income, the resulting chain effect would be strong indeed, making for a very volatile overall economy.

In fact, however, even though households on the average spend a very large share of their income on consumer goods, they do not typically react to every change in income with proportionately large changes in spending. One can think of any change in income experienced by consumers as composed of two parts: that part of the change they believe permanent and that part they believe transitory. Overwhelming empirical evidence shows that the consumption response to permanent changes in income is much greater than its response to what are believed transitory changes in income. When income falls, then, unless households have reason to believe the fall will be permanent, they dip into past savings, they borrow, in the event of layoffs younger ones may move in with parents, and so forth. The smoothing of consumption isn't complete of course and families in different circumstances do more or less of it in bad times.

The same smoothing occurs when income rises sharply; families save (sometimes by repaying debt) a large part of any surge in income they believe to be a temporary windfalls—an unusual amount of overtime work, a particularly good crop on a farm, or a sharp jump in profits in a small business.

Consumers of course often don't know precisely what part of any large income change is permanent and what part is transitory. However, common sense and the evidence of studies of consumer behavior suggest that initially households only consider a part of any sizable change in income as likely to be permanent. But the longer the change persists, the more they come to see it as permanent and adjust their consumption fully to it.

Milton Friedman, the father of the permanent income theory of consumer behavior, proposed it in a strong form: consumers will spend no part of any income change considered transitory; consumption will respond only to what are perceived as permanent changes in income. But that idea is surely an exaggeration. Even if consumers were very foresighted long-term planners, and wanted, for the purpose of smoothing their consumption patterns, to ignore temporary changes in their fortunes, many of them couldn't do it fully. To maintain their consumption spending during temporary periods of low income, consumers would have had to save up substantial emergency funds in earlier periods or have access to borrowing precisely when their income was low or nil. Especially for low- to moderate-income households, saving up an emergency kitty for bad times is extremely difficult. And in any event, since households usually have no idea how long the bad times might last, they are still likely to use any emergency funds sparingly. And although the typical consumer these days does have considerable access to credit, that access is not unlimited; among lower-income consumers, credit is quite restricted. For these reasons many consumers are what economists call liquidity constrained. And so for many households, consumption rises and falls more closely with year-to-year changes in income than is consistent with the pure form of the permanent income theory.

Studies of consumer behavior support a modified version of the permanent income explanation for consumer behavior. The evidence is strong that cyclical or transitory fluctuations in household income bring forth some change in consumption but a good bit less than proportionally. The multiplier is not eliminated, but it is much smaller than would be true if consumers fully adjusted their consumption to every fluctuation in income. The proposition that for purposes of making decisions about consumption, households treat temporary changes in income differently from changes they consider permanent implies that changes in taxes that are announced as temporary should have a smaller effect in increasing or decreasing consumption than permanent changes in taxes. To the extent this conclusion is true, it has important implications for policies aimed at smoothing out economic fluctuations (for example, what is the efficacy of temporary tax cuts in stimulating consumer spending during a recession?). We will return to this point, and what the empirical evidence tells us, in the memo on government fiscal policy (memo 19).

THE LIFE CYCLE THEORY OF CONSUMER SPENDING AND SAVING

We want to understand consumer behavior not only to discern how it changes over the business cycle but also to explain other aspects of the economy—for example, how demographic changes affect national saving and investment, and how consumption and saving respond to changes in the stock market, to savings-oriented tax incentives, or to changes in interest rates. Nobel Prizewinner Franco Modigliani many years ago put forth a fundamental proposition about consumer behavior, consistent with the idea of consumption smoothing, but going well beyond that notion. He argued that consumers take a lifetime view of their income prospects and plan their consumption patterns accordingly.[1] In its simplest version, workers recognize that their incomes will probably increase gradually over the early to middle portion of their working lives, perhaps drop slightly before retirement, and then fall sharply after retirement. But they would prefer a more even pattern of lifetime consumption. And so they save and build up assets over their working lifetime—with the saving and the asset building largest in the middle years when their incomes are highest—and then run down their assets to provide for consumption in retirement years. Moreover, in Modigliani's version of this approach, households over their lifetime consume most or all of their lifetime income, typically leaving only small bequests to their children.

Though it can be stated fairly simply, this theory of consumption has some important implications for understanding what causes changes in consumer spending. In the first place, as we said earlier, it is consistent with the view that consumers smooth their consumption in the face of what they believe are temporary fluctuations in their income. Second, Modigliani's theory predicts that a small fraction of any unexpected rise in household wealth will be spent on consumer goods each year. Suppose, for example, households experience a significant increase in wealth because of a rise in the price of the common stocks they own, a rise they think will be permanent. They won't spend this windfall all at once. Rather the lifetime stream of income available to them has risen, and they will spend a small fraction of that increased wealth every year—older people with a shorter period to live will each year spend a larger fraction of the extra wealth than younger people who have to spread the increased consumption over a longer period into the future.

There are other aspects of the theory that need not concern us here— for example, a country's saving rate will depend importantly on the age of its population, since young and middle-aged people are saving for retirement while old people are *dis*saving, drawing on their earlier saving to support their consumption patterns.

How well does the life-cycle theory explain the observed behavior of consumption spending? We have already seen that although consumers smooth their consumption relative to their income, they do not seem to behave as if they were operating on a lifetime consumption budget, completely ignoring temporary ups and downs in their income. This behavior may reflect, as mentioned earlier, liquidity constraints—they cannot borrow against the likelihood of better income in the future—but it may also mean that human beings on average don't behave like the farsighted rational optimizers beloved of economists. Human nature may simply be such that most people find it very hard to put away today for the far-distant future. That is one reason we have social security programs and employer pension plans that force people to save.

Partly because accurate data on consumer saving, dissaving, and wealth data, cross-classified by age, income, and other characteristics, are very hard to come by, there has for years been a cottage industry of research studies trying to confirm or reject other aspects of the theory.[2] The evidence strongly shows that households respond to a change in their wealth along the lines predicted by the theory—when household wealth increases, a small fraction of the additional wealth is added, or subtracted as the case may be, from the annual value of household consumption.

The only changes in wealth sharp enough to have a significant effect on cyclical fluctuations in the economy are changes in stock prices. Even though the population holding the great bulk of stock ownership is small,

---

FIGURE 6-2. Consumption and the 1987 Stock Market Crash

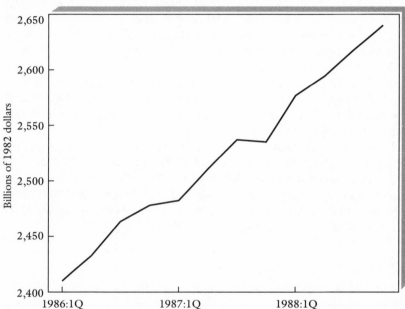

its consumption is a large enough share of total consumption that large swings in the stock market can have observable effects on consumption spending. Figure 6-2 shows the small dip in consumption that occurred after the October 1987 stock market crash, and its subsequent disappearance as the market recovered. One cannot be sure the stock market crash caused the dip in consumption, but such a result would have been consistent with the evidence from earlier empirical studies demonstrating a positive relationship between consumer wealth and the volume of consumer spending. However, several studies have concluded that the post-1982 boom in the stock market, though it may have had some effect in reducing saving, can at best explain only a modest part of the fall in personal saving that has occurred in the past decade.

CONCLUSION

Cyclical changes in household income will lead to changes in the same direction in consumer purchase of nondurable goods and services, but the consumption response will be less than proportional to the change in income. Correspondingly, when demand and output change somewhere in the economy, the multiplier effect will enlarge and spread that initial change throughout the economy, but the size of the multiplier is far less than would be the case if consumption spending responded proportionately to cyclical changes in income.

Large increases or decreases in stock market values can also lead to modest increases or decreases in consumer spending. But the boom in the stock market can explain only a modest part of the recent fall in the personal saving rate.

I will wait until memo 24, which focuses on long-term changes in saving and investment, for a discussion of the extent to which changes in the after-tax return that households earn on their saving balances can induce them to change their saving and spending rates. This issue is obviously of great importance in judging the merits of various proposed tax incentives aimed at raising the household saving rate.

NOTES

1. Robert E. Hall, "Stochastic Implications of the Life Cycle—Permanent Income Hypothesis: Theory and Evidence," *Journal of Political Economy*, vol. 86 (December 1978), pp. 971–87.

2. For most households, saving is only a small fraction of income. It is very difficult to extract, through questionnaires and interviews, a complete accounting of consumption in a year, comprehensive and accurate enough to provide a good measure of saving. And that difficulty is compounded manyfold when one realizes that, ideally, what is needed to test various theories about consumption behavior are data covering a number of years so that household responses to various economic changes can be examined. The alternative, trying to deduce saving data from information about changes in the value of household financial and other assets, is fraught with different but also formidable difficulties. And finally, the need to get the information by demographic groups—for example, households in the third income quintile, with children, headed by a 35–44 year-old black male, with a working spouse—obviously compounds the problem by requiring very large sample sizes for the surveys.

MEMORANDUM 7

To: The President

From: CEA Chairman

Subject: **The Behavior of Investment**

As in the case of consumption, two aspects of investment are of principal concern: what are the forces that generate year-to-year fluctuations in investment, and what determines, over longer periods, how much a country invests? While consumption fluctuates less than income does, investment fluctuates vastly more. And this generalization holds for investment by business firms and for investment-type purchases by households—residential housing and consumer durable goods. A glance back at figure 5-1 shows how volatile the various components of investment have been during the past three decades.

THE KINDS OF INVESTMENT AND WHY THEY ARE UNDERTAKEN

Both households and business firms purchase investment goods, that is, long-lived goods whose purpose is to produce other goods and services. Business firms purchase factories, stores, machinery, and equipment. They also have to carry an inventory of raw materials, a pipeline of work-in-progress, and usually a stock of finished goods. Households invest in durable consumer goods, such as autos and appliances, which produce transportation and other kinds of household services; they buy homes, which produce shelter. Theoretically we might even classify the purchase of clothing and shoes as an investment—they yield up their services gradually over time. But by convention, household purchases of all kinds of nondurable goods and services are treated as consumption, reserving the term "investment" for household purchases of the longer-lasting durable goods and housing.

Four main types of investment purchases can be distinguished: business investment in plant and equipment; changes in business inventories (a form of investment that can be either positive or negative); consumer purchases of durable goods; and residential construction. They share certain similarities, but they also behave in some ways differently from one another.

Broadly speaking, business firms invest in capital goods for several different reasons: for the replacement each year of the capital goods that have become worn out or obsolete; to expand capacity to serve an expected growth in sales and markets; and to adopt new cost-saving methods of production or to introduce new and improved products. Because there are different reasons to invest, purchases of investment goods can respond to different kinds of economic developments and different types of government policy.

THE VOLATILITY OF INVESTMENT—THE ACCELERATOR

Figure 7-1 shows how much larger the fluctuations in investment are (the total of all four types) compared with the much smoother path of GNP. That part of investment—in plant and equipment, in consumer durables, and so on—devoted to replacement of the capital goods that wear out or become obsolete each year is relatively steady, rising slowly over time as the stock of assets grows and replacement needs become correspondingly larger. But the part of investment spending that represents new additions to the capital stock—that is, net investment—tends to be very volatile. I have already mentioned (memo 5) one of the major reasons for the volatility of investment purchases, the accelerator phenomenon. When business firms expect their future sales to be constant, they do not have to invest in additions to capacity. Investment for this purpose will be zero. In a similar vein, if business sales are expected to remain unchanged, business firms have no reason to add to inventories of goods on hand; inventory investment will also be zero. The faster the growth in consumer income or business sales, however, the higher the level of purchases of investment goods. The level of investment depends on the rate of change in sales and income. Thus, a mere slowing of the pace at which income and sales are advancing can lead to an absolute decline in investment. Given this characteristic, the high volatility in investment purchases is hardly surprising.[1] And it also means that any economic development that

FIGURE 7-1. The Volatility of Investment

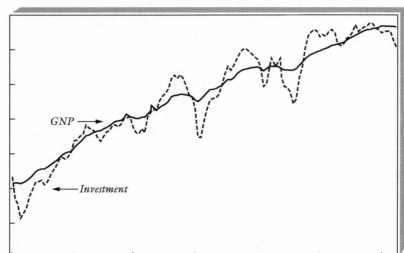

Note: Indexes = 1.00 for both GNP and investment in first quarter 1977. Data have been converted to logarithms so that equal percentage changes take up the same vertical distance in the figure.

significantly speeds up or slows down the growth of GNP is reinforced by an induced, accelerator-type response in business and investment.

The same phenomenon holds for consumer purchases of durable goods; if income is constant, consumers as a rule will not be expanding their demands for the services that the ownership of durable goods like automobiles and appliances can provide. While their purchases for replacement purposes will continue, their net purchases of new durable goods will tend toward zero. Thus, when the growth of consumer income slows down substantially, the absolute level of consumer durable goods purchases is likely to fall.

OTHER REASONS FOR THE VOLATILITY OF INVESTMENT

Business firms will not normally expand their capacity and their sales simply for the sake of growth—they have to believe they can sell the additional output at a profit. Adding large new capacity whose output can be sold only at cut-rate prices, yielding little or no profit, is hardly an appealing prospect. Decisions about adding to capacity require some estimate of the profits obtainable from the added capacity. Similarly, a decision to invest for the purpose of cutting costs or producing a new kind of product is based on some estimate of the additional profits that will be earned by the investment. And what is relevant to all of these types of investment decisions is an estimate of future profits, not the level of today's profits. But like everyone else, business managers have to peer into the future through a thick fog of uncertainty.

As John Maynard Keynes eloquently pointed out more than fifty years ago, the factual basis for estimating the future yield from a long-lived investment decision "amounts to little, and sometimes to nothing." With such a flimsy connection to today's realities, longer-term business investment decisions are likely to be influenced by contagious moods of optimism or pessimism—by "animal spirits," to use Keynes's term.

Except by appeal to animal spirits, it is hard to explain, for example, the behavior of developers, investors, and banks during the boom in office and commercial construction during the 1980s. The vacancy rate in office buildings by the mid-1980s had already reached record highs. Through 1986, tax shelters and other provisions in the building code strongly favored commercial real estate development. But those provisions were eliminated in the 1986 tax reform act, yet for several more years the commercial real estate boom continued. Supposedly conservative banks were making loans to developers with nothing down, in amounts generous enough to cover interest payments during the construction period, and with only speculatively priced land as the collateral. It was not until 1989 and 1990 that the boom finally burst.

The postponability of most investment purchases can also contribute to large declines of investment purchases in recessions. The automobile can usually be used for another year, the decision to buy a new house put off for a while, and the addition to capacity postponed. A long-planned investment project does not have to be completely scrapped when doubts about the economic environment begin to appear. The project can be often be put on hold until more favorable developments override the doubts. This feature of investment purchases also contributes to investment instability.

SOME STABILIZING FACTORS

So far we have concentrated on the features of investment decisions that make for volatility. But the picture is far from as bleak as this discussion

FIGURE 7-2. Actual versus "Permanent" Sales

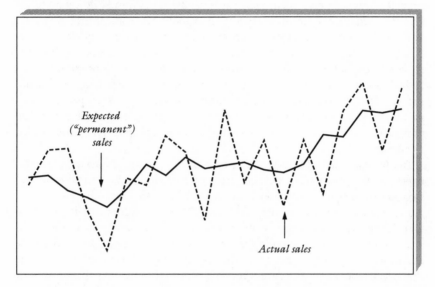

alone seems to indicate. Some forces are at work to moderate the swings in investment.

Business firms invest in capacity addition to meet expected long-term increases in sales. But simple experience teaches that not every upward blip in sales means a permanent increase in the size of the market. Just as we saw for consumers' income expectations, what is relevant for business decisions are increases in sales that are believed permanent. And so, when some economic development occurs that boosts the growth of GNP, sales, and income, business firms do not immediately rush off to add to capacity. Actual sales increases or decreases only gradually get reflected in changes in permanent sales expectations. Estimates of the prospect for markets over the long-term future—which, in parallel with the earlier discussion of household income expectations we might call permanent sales—are what counts in investment decisions. Those decisions tend to respond in a smoothed fashion to current sales experience. Figure 7-2 illustrates the concept. The volatility otherwise imparted by the accelerator is substantially damped down, because the relevant "permanent" changes in sales from period to period are a good bit smaller than the actual changes in sales.

To be able to meet temporary surges in sales without having to expand capacity immediately, business firms typically keep some idle capacity on standby. Since that standby capacity is usually older and more costly to operate, the decision about whether or not to add capacity often turns out to be a trade-off between the possibility of lowering costs through replacing the standby capacity with new capacity, and the possibility that today's increased sales may not be a permanent addition to the firm's market. In any event, provision of standby capacity gives firms the ability to wait and see if current sales increases are going to be temporary or permanent. And this capability tends further to damp down the volatility of the accelerator.

An increase in sales that has persisted long enough to change the expectations about future sales does not immediately and in one fell swoop translate into additional purchases of plant and equipment. There are several lags in the process. A decision about a significant investment takes time; there are plans to be drawn, cost estimates to assemble, and various levels of managerial approval to obtain. Once the order for new machinery and equipment, or for new plant construction has been placed, the economic activity related to the production or construction and installation of the new capital goods stretches over time—in the case of a major project, perhaps over years. Again, the impact of the accelerator is smoothed. When economic expansions are under way, the additional investment activity set in motion is spread out over time. And if the expansion turns into recession, there is a backlog of uncompleted work on investment projects to be carried out that softens the effect of the recession on employment and income.

In sum, because fluctuations in current sales only gradually translate into expectations of permanent changes in sales, and because large investment projects are carried out over long periods of time, the inherent volatility of investment is greatly attenuated. But as figure 7-1 clearly shows, the smoothing is not so great as to eliminate all of the volatility of the investment process.

INVENTORY INVESTMENT

Business inventory investment has several characteristics that make it more volatile than other forms of investment. Inventories can be quickly built up and drawn down; mistaken judgments about inventory building can be reversed with far less cost than mistakes made about adding new plant capacity. Suppose, for example, that after balancing the cost of carrying inventories with the desirability of having goods in stock for its customers, a particular business firm carries inventories equal to two months' sales—which is a little higher ratio than the average for American business as a whole. If the firm makes a mistake in its sales forecast and orders too much, so that inventories turn out to be, say, one-fifth higher than the ideal level, the firm by keeping new orders for merchandise 20 percent below sales can get its inventories back into line within two months. A firm might be stuck for several years, however, with an investment decision that added an excessive 20 percent to its plant capacity. Thus, business firms can afford to adapt inventories more closely to current changes in sales than is the case with longer-lived investments in plant and equipment. Moreover, lags in ordering and acquiring additional inventories are typically short. For all of these reasons, inventory investment behaves more closely in accordance with the predictions of the raw accelerator model than do other forms of investment. Correspondingly, even though the average level of inventory investment is small—something like 1 percent of GNP goes into building inventories during normal times—changes in inventory investment over the postwar period have contributed more than twice as much to fluctuations in GNP as any other single component.[2]

HOUSING INVESTMENT

Next to inventory investment, residential construction—the building of new single-family homes and apartment units—is the most volatile form of investment. On average, it accounts for 25 to 30 percent of the total domestic investment in the economy. The demand for new housing responds to several economic developments. An increase in the number of families obviously increases the demand for housing. And as income rises, families want to use some of the gain to improve the quality of their housing. The price of the stock of existing houses rises as more customers bid on houses that are up for sale. It becomes profitable for real estate developers and construction firms to increase the volume of new home construction to satisfy the rising demand and take advantage of the higher prices. When income growth slows, or there is a drop in the number of new families formed each year, the demand for new housing falls and residential construction declines.

The most important fact about the demand for new housing, in regard to fluctuations in GNP, is that it is very sensitive to interest rates and other credit conditions. Most houses are purchased with mortgages that cover a very large fraction—80 to 90 percent—of the value of the house and are expected to be paid off over a long period. As a consequence, mortgage interest payments in turn account for a large share of the monthly payments that homeowners and landlords pay out for the housing they own. For example, on a $200,000 home financed with a thirty-year mortgage at an 8 percent interest rate, the interest payments over the life of the mortgage will be more than one and one-half times the initial value of the house. A rise in the mortgage rate from 8 to 10 percent would increase the monthly payments by 20 percent and raise the homebuyer's annual payments from $17,610 to $21,060. Thus, changes in interest rates face prospective homebuyers with large changes in the effective price of new homes, which in turn affects the demand for new housing.[3]

BUSINESS INVESTMENT AND THE COST OF CAPITAL

As we have seen, business firms invest not only to expand capacity to match expected growth in sales but also as a means of reducing costs. At any time, a business firm has a range of alternative techniques of production in which it could invest, each one using different combinations of labor, raw materials, energy, and capital. At the cost of acquiring more capital, the firm can economize on labor or other costs. It can use a less or more automated production line; it can rely more or less heavily on computers versus clerks for handling and processing information; it can choose among a whole range of more or less sophisticated and labor-saving material-handling equipment, with correspondingly more or fewer workers devoted to such tasks; it can centralize production facilities and lower costs but at the expense of using highly capital-intensive transportation facilities to distribute products nationwide.

When a business firm is considering an investment in more capital-intensive means of production, it must weigh the cost of the additional capital against the reduction in other costs that the investment can make possible. Given economic conditions and the available state of technology, the lower the cost of capital, the higher the volume of cost-saving investment is likely to be. Thus, investment tends to be determined not only by the expected growth in sales (the accelerator) but also by the cost of capital.

There are two main elements to the cost of capital: the price of the capital good (relative to prices of the goods that it produces) and the cost of borrowing or otherwise acquiring the funds to pay for it.

The Relative Price of Capital Goods

Some recent research by Harvard economists J. Bradford Delong and Lawrence Summers has documented that in advanced industrial countries, the prices of machinery and equipment are much lower relative to the prices of other goods and services than is true in less developed, poorer countries.[4] Thus, in the United States, the average prices paid for machinery and equipment are about 30 percent lower than in countries with half the average U.S. income and almost 50 percent below the equipment prices that prevail in those developing countries with one-quarter of U.S. income (although much variation occurs among individual countries).

In the United States, one of the more important economic developments of recent years has been the dramatic fall in the cost and reliability of computation and information processing. The capital cost per unit of computation or memory storage and retrieval has fallen steadily for a decade. Adjusted to reflect increases in their speed, reliability, and other performance characteristics, the average price of computers in 1989 was only one-third its level as recently as 1982! Because the cost of this kind of capital has fallen so sharply, its use has exploded. Together with communications equipment, purchases of information processing and related equipment now account for about one in every four dollars spent for machinery and equipment by business firms in the United States.

The prices of machinery and equipment in an advanced country, relative to prices of other goods, depend heavily on the state of technology and the country's underlying economic structure. It is not something that economic policy can easily manipulate. But at least one important economic mistake should be avoided—the temptation to yield to special interest groups and provide price-propping protection for industries producing capital goods or their components. But that mistake is exactly what the United States committed in 1986, when at the urging of U.S. semiconductor firms, America used its economic leverage to force the Japanese to establish a worldwide cartel, setting a high floor under semiconductor prices. That agreement significantly raised the costs and prices of American-made computers.

The Cost of Funds

Securing the funds with which to purchase capital goods does not come free. To be a worthwhile decision for the stockholders, an investment must yield a return at least high enough (over and above its annual depreciation charge) to cover the cost of acquiring the funds used to buy the capital goods. As a first approximation, one can think of the cost of funds as the interest rate the firm must pay to borrow the money. Even if a firm uses its retained earnings to buy a capital good, it cannot consider those funds costless. Instead of purchasing the capital good, it could have bought a government or corporate bond and earned interest on those funds. Hence, to determine the true cost of buying the capital good, the firm must calculate as a cost the interest earnings forgone. Similarly, the firm could have retired some of its debt, raising future profits by the amount of the interest payments it no longer would have to make. Alternatively, the firm could have used the retained earnings to buy back some of its stock, decreasing the number of shares among which future earnings have to be split up and thereby raising the earnings per share for shareholders. And if instead of borrowing or using retained earnings, the firm had issued new stock to secure the funds, there would have also been a cost to the firm's shareholders. The additional stock dilutes future earnings for existing shareholders; those future earnings must now be spread over a larger number of shares, lowering the amount of earnings per share. However one considers it, a firm must pay, directly or indirectly, a cost for the funds it uses to make an investment in capital goods. Indeed the cost of funds for investing in capital goods can best be defined as the return those capital goods must be expected to earn in order for it to be worthwhile for the firm to devote the necessary funds to their purchase.

Taxes and the Cost of Funds

Taxes levied on the earnings of a firm—corporate taxes, for example— tend to raise the effective cost of funds. As just noted, the cost of funds is the amount the firm has to earn on an investment simply to cover what it cost to raise the funds. Clearly, if out of its earnings it must pay some fraction to the government, the amount the investment will have to yield before taxes is now higher than it would be in the absence of taxes. Effectively, therefore, the cost of funds is higher. As a general proposition, an increase in taxes on the earnings of capital will raise, and a reduction in taxes will reduce, the cost of capital.

The effect of taxes is complicated, however, by several provisions in the tax code. Business firms can deduct their interest payments from the income subject to tax. They cannot, however, deduct their dividend payments. Thus, the tax system penalizes equity financing relative to debt financing. Inflation has several complicated effects on the taxes firms pay and on the cost of capital. While the overall effect of higher inflation and the cost of capital is small, there are wide variations among different types of assets and industries.[5]

Per dollar of revenue loss to the government, some reductions in business taxes are likely to have a greater stimulative effect on business investment than others. In particular, a tax reduction that applies only to a new investment will provide a "bigger bang for a buck" than a general reduction in tax rates on all business income, since business firms would get the benefits of the latter whether they invested or not. An investment tax credit, which provides a tax reduction proportionate to the value of a new investment, is an example of the former.

HOW IMPORTANT ARE CHANGES IN THE COST OF CAPITAL?

Recent studies have suggested that changes in GNP and business sales play the dominant role in explaining changes in investment from year to year. Changes in the cost of capital seem to have had a much smaller effect on investment. But pinning down the effect of changes in the cost of capital is notoriously difficult, and the study results cannot be taken with great certainty.

If we knew how much, on the average, a given increase in the capital intensity of production reduced other production costs, then it would be possible to calculate approximately what additional volume of capital goods would be installed when the cost of capital dropped from, say, 15 to 14 percent. And some economists, by making a relatively optimistic assumption about that relationship, have produced studies showing that modest declines in the cost of capital have rather large effects in stimulating investment. In fact, however, the conclusions follow from the initial assumptions. If we don't want to start by assuming the answer, it is necessary to employ statistical techniques to try to dig the answer out of the data on the behavior of investment, sales, and the cost of capital over the past four decades. But history is against us in this effort. Fluctuations in real interest rates and the cost of capital were moderate during the first thirty years of the postwar period. The past fifteen years did witness much larger changes in the cost of capital—through changes in interest rates and changes in taxes. But many other aspects of the economy were also changing rapidly, and fifteen years may not have been long enough to differentiate accurately the effects of changes in the cost of capital from other economic developments affecting the volume of business investment.

One survey of the evidence concludes that changes in the cost of capital do indeed have effects on business investment in plant and equipment but that these effects are modest and occur gradually over a long period.[6] Applying these results to tax policy, a good middle-of-the-road estimate would be that one dollar's worth of annual tax reduction devoted to lowering the cost of capital has a decent chance of gradually bringing about one dollar's worth of additional business investment. This estimate assumes that the tax reduction applies only to new investment—for example, through an investment tax credit or accelerated depreciation. But we have to be careful about the policy implications of this "fact." If the economy is already at full employment, it is impossible to increase business investment or any other kind of spending on a sustained basis without reducing spending somewhere else in the economy by an equivalent amount. And so if the government introduces an investment tax incentive costing, say, $25 billion in lost revenues, it must raise other taxes, reduce government outlays, or institute a policy of tight money and high interest rates in order to generate an offsetting reduction in aggregate demand and spending elsewhere.

NOTES

1. Investment in new homes is affected not only by income growth but importantly by demographic trends. When the number of new families is growing rapidly, a large amount of residential construction will take place, even if income is growing relatively slowly.

2. The measure used for comparison was the mean (1948–89) of the absolute quarterly change in the variable as a ratio to the prior quarter's GNP, all variables in 1982 prices.

3. This is an example of a more general principle. The higher the value of a capital good relative to the annual flow of services its ownership provides—in this case the cost of the new home is large relative to the annual flow of rental services it provides its owner—the greater will be the effect of a change in interest rates on the profitability of owning the asset. For this reason, changes in interest rates have a greater effect on the profitability of long-lived assets than they do on short-lived assets. The construction of long-lived buildings will be more greatly affected by a change in interest rates than will the purchase of, say, short-lived computers.

4. J. Bradford De Long and Lawrence H. Summers, "Equipment Investment and Economic Growth," *Quarterly Journal of Economics*, vol. 106 (May 1991), pp. 445–502.

5. Barry P. Bosworth, *Tax Incentives and Economic Growth* (Brookings, 1984), p. 197.

6. Bosworth, *Tax Incentives*, pp.109–10. Much of the analysis in the last several pages is adapted from chapter 4 of the Bosworth book.

MEMORANDUM **8**

To: The President

From: CEA Chairman

Subject: **Interest Rates as a Stabilizing Force—
and Why They Are Not Always Sufficient**

The following two sentences summarize the information in the preceding three memos about the problem of economic instability.[1]

Fluctuations in demand originating in one sector of the economy are transmitted to other sectors and magnified as consumer spending responds to changes in household income (the multiplier) and investment spending rises or falls in response to changes in the pace of economic growth (the accelerator).

Several characteristics of consumer and investor behavior, however, moderate—but do not eliminate—the transmission of instability from one sector to another through the multiplier and accelerator mechanisms.

Another important set of forces also tends to reduce potential economic instability, namely, the rise and fall in interest rates during economic expansions and recessions. Like the moderating factors discussed earlier, the behavior of interest rates cuts down the size of recessions and overheated expansions but, as history shows, does not automatically keep the economy on an even keel.

REAL AND NOMINAL INTEREST RATES

Before discussing the importance of interest rates, one must recognize the difference between real and nominal rates. Imagine a person or business firm borrowing $1,000 for a year at, say, 6 percent interest while inflation in that year was also 6 percent. At the end of the year, the borrower would owe the lender $1,060—the $1,000 loan plus the interest of $60. But because of inflation the real purchasing power of the $1,060 would be no higher than the initial loan of $1,000. The lender would have earned no real interest over the period. In a similar vein, because of the inflation, the borrower could have bought a (nondepreciating) asset worth $1,000 at the beginning of the year, sold it for $1,060 at the end of the year, and with the proceeds paid off the loan plus interest. He would have had use of the asset for the year at no real interest cost. In other words, what is important to both borrower and lender, when making their decisions about whether to lend and borrow, is the difference between the nominal interest rate they pay or receive and the rate of inflation they expect to occur over the year. That difference—the nominal interest rate *minus* the expected inflation rate—is the *real* interest rate, which is the rate most relevant to economic decisionmaking.

The real interest rate is easy to define but hard to measure, since the rate of inflation *expected* by lenders and borrowers is what counts. At any time, we do not observe the inflation rate that people expect, we can only estimate it indirectly and imperfectly from surveys of expectations or from other economic data. In short-term—say three-month—interest rates, it is conventional to calculate the real rate by assuming that people expect the recent pace of inflation to persist at least for a little while, and to subtract that from the nominal rate to get the real rate. But when inflation is jumping around a good bit from quarter to quarter, that simple technique may not give the proper results. And for long-term interest rates, the relevant expectation is the inflation expected over the life of the loan, and estimates of that number are likely to be highly imperfect. In the discussion that follows, the term "interest rate" means the real rate, recognizing that actually measuring its magnitude is a highly uncertain business.

INTEREST RATES AND THE BALANCE BETWEEN SAVING AND INVESTMENT

When aggregate demand falls relative to aggregate supply, there is a surplus of what some people want to save over what other people want to invest. Stated simply, the supply of funds available for lending begins to exceed the demand for such funds, and several consequences follow.

FIGURE 8-1. Change in Real Short-Term Interest Rates before and after Business
Cycle Peaks

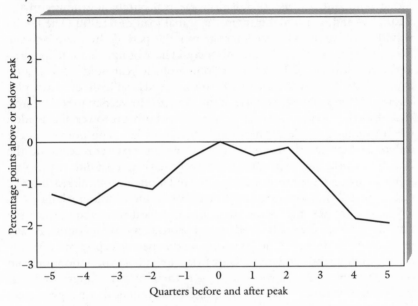

First, interest rates fall. Rates on short-term loans will fall by more than
the fixed interest rates on long-term loans. When lending money for a
period of, say, ten years, one has to consider what the economic conditions
are likely to be over the whole ten years. And today's recessionary tendencies in the economy will probably not last for most of that period. So
as long-term interest rates begin to fall, lenders will put more of their
funds into short-term loans, so that they will have them available again
to lend in the near future when interest rates are likely to have rebounded.
As the supply of loans for long-term lending shrinks, the decline in
long-term interest rates is moderated. Nevertheless, both long and
short rates will tend to fall. In strong economic expansions the opposite
occurs.

Figure 8-1 shows how short-term interest rates have tended, on average, to rise and then decline before and after the peaks of business cycles
during the postwar years.[2] But the average conceals wide variations. The
interest rate peak sometimes preceded the business cycle peak, and the
period before the 1973–75 recession was an exception to the average

tendency, since nominal interest rates did not keep up with rapidly rising inflation. In the 1990–91 recession, economic growth was quite weak in the year and a half before the recession began; interest rates started down long before the business cycle peak occurred. (Of course, as we shall see in memo 19, the historical pattern of interest rates was also strongly affected by the policies of the Federal Reserve.)

There is a second way in which credit markets will reflect the drop in aggregate demand and the excess of loanable funds supplied. During periods of prosperity, when investors' demand for funds to borrow is high, institutional lenders, such as banks and insurance companies, will restrict the supply of loans they make within the bounds of the funds they have available. Lenders will not only keep interest rates high enough to limit the demand for their funds but will also become more selective among borrowers and more stringent in the terms and conditions they impose. They will favor long-term steady customers over new ones; they will require larger down payments and, for business firms, place some restrictions on their future borrowing as a condition of making the loans. But when the supply of loanable funds begins to be excessive relative to the demand, the various rationing devices will be loosened—lower down payments, fewer restrictive conditions, a more favorable reception to newer borrowers.

Lower interest rates and easier credit terms reduce the cost of capital and stimulate domestic investment. And the better loan terms may induce additional purchases of durable goods by consumers. In memo 9, I explain how lower interest rates in the United States also reduce the overseas value of the dollar and thereby stimulate the expansion of U.S. exports and the decline of imports. In these ways, the reduction of interest rates and the easing of terms for loans offset some of the decline in aggregate demand.

LOWER INTEREST RATES AND THE STABILITY OF AGGREGATE DEMAND

Despite the stabilizing forces described here and in memo 7, the United States and other industrial countries experience periodic recessions, not to mention episodes like the depression of the 1930s. Why aren't the stabilizing forces of lower interest rates enough? When savers are offering more funds to investors than the investors want to borrow, why don't interest rates keep plummeting until enough investment and exports are created to wipe out the potential excess of saving over investment and restore the equality of aggregate demand and potential GNP?

There is a real puzzle to be solved. Remember that every dollar of output is matched by a dollar of income; GNP equals gross national income (GNI). And so when the economy produces at a level of high employment—that is, at its aggregate supply capability, potential GNP—it generates income exactly equal to the value of the GNP produced. When that income is spent, either directly for consumption (public and private) or lent to business firms and consumers to buy plant, equipment, and housing, the resulting purchases should be precisely enough to take off the market everything that was produced. Why then should aggregate demand ever fall below aggregate supply?

Many economists, in the century preceding John Maynard Keynes, pointed out that people produce and earn income only to use it; to the extent they refrain from consuming all of their income, they don't typically hoard the cash; they put it to work by lending it, directly or through banks and other financial institutions, to finance investment of one kind or another. So shouldn't there always be enough aggregate demand to match aggregate supply? If demand starts to fall, why doesn't the pressure to lend out the idle funds push interest rates low enough and investment high enough to restore aggregate demand to equal aggregate supply? Why should there ever be recession—and by similar reasoning—why should we occasionally suffer from excess demand and economic overheating?

Initially, the sheer size and complexity of the economy might seem an obvious candidate for playing the villain. Suppose, for example, that forces were always at work to push the economy to full employment—weaknesses of demand in one sector of the economy were always balanced by growing demand in other sectors. Even so, the labor and capital freed by declines in demand in one sector of the economy may not be of exactly the right kind or in the right locations to meet the new demands. Making the transition can take time. Suppose, for example, that the markets for durable consumer goods become temporarily saturated, so that sales, production, and employment fall. Even if the rise in consumer saving (consumers are now buying fewer autos and television sets) does lead to a fall in interest rates, inducing more housing construction and greater exports, it takes time for the shift in the pattern of production to occur. The unemployed workers aren't where the new jobs are, the idle automobile and appliance factories can't produce housing or the export goods wanted by foreigners, and the firms that do produce the goods whose sales are now increasing may not be able to expand immediately. In the transition period, excess unemployment and idle capacity occur.

But this is not the reason we have recessions. If it were, some parts of the economy would be in recession while others were booming, with large unfilled orders, bottlenecks owing to shortages, and job vacancies. What we observe in recessions, however, is an overall problem of slack demand. To be sure, recession conditions aren't equally distributed throughout regions and industries in the country, but they are widespread and not matched by boomlike conditions elsewhere.

A similar possible explanation for recessions and for booms is that the stabilizing changes in interest rates are indeed enough to keep aggregate demand in balance with supply, but that changes in interest rates take time to affect the actions of homebuyers, business investors, and foreign customers. Significant lags do occur between changes in interest rates and the consequent change in economic activity. And these lags are important in making fluctuations in aggregate demand worse than would otherwise be the case. Moreover, the lags greatly complicate the job of the Federal Reserve in managing the nation's monetary and credit conditions. But they are not the principal reason for recessions.

If lags between changes in interest rates and changes in investment spending were the main problem, we would then observe that just as economic activity was sagging into recession, signs of future recovery would be sprouting up all over the place. Business firms would be revising upward their investment plans; new orders for plant and equipment would be starting to rise; and business confidence would be reversing itself, even though actual production and employment were still falling. Typically, however, the decline of the economy into recession is characterized by downward revisions of investment plans and sagging indicators of business ebullience. The shortfall of aggregate demand in recessions reflects more than a temporary pause taking place while the medicine of low interest rates is accomplishing its cure. Something else must be at work to keep interest rates and credit terms from improving enough to prevent recessions.

John Maynard Keynes was the first (in 1936) to find an answer to this puzzle. He pointed out that households and business firms get benefits of convenience and liquidity from holding some assets in the form of cash, or money. Liquidity is that characteristic of an asset that allows it to be converted into another asset with minimal transactions costs and risk of loss because of an unfavorable price at the time of liquidation.

Different assets vary greatly in their liquidity. Money is the most liquid asset. In modern economies most money is in the form of checking accounts. In Keynes's day, and until recently, banks paid no interest on checking accounts. Even now, checking deposits of business firms are paid no interest and individuals receive only a low rate, compared with the rate available for bonds or stocks or other assets. Thus the convenience and liquidity benefits of holding money are not costless. Firms and individuals give up interest income to hold money.

The higher the rate of interest available on bonds and other financial assets, the more costly it is to hold money. When interest rates fall, it becomes less costly for individuals and business firms to secure the convenience and liquidity of holding a larger share of their assets in the form of cash. *And so the desire to hold money declines as interest rates rise and increases when interest rates fall.* In the 1970s as interest rates soared to what were then unprecedented heights, corporate treasurers began to devote more and more effort to minimizing their company's cash holdings, since the income forgone from holding cash became larger and larger.[3]

Because the demand for money rises when interest rates fall, interest rates are kept from falling enough to prevent recessions. When the onset of a decline in aggregate demand starts to drive down interest rates, business firms and individuals begin to revise their financial plans to increase the proportion of their assets held in cash. If we assume that the Federal Reserve does not increase the overall supply of money or cash in the economy, then in order to try to get more cash into their portfolios, households and business firms reduce their demand for bonds, securities, and other financial assets that provide financing for residential and business investment. As the supply of funds available to buy bonds and similar securities shrinks, the decline in interest rates is checked.

The same phenomenon can be looked at in another way. The downward pressure on interest rates that occurs when saving starts to run ahead of investment is partially dissipated by a diversion of some of the "excess" saving into a demand for additional cash balances and away from a recession-correcting demand for bonds and other securities. The fall in interest rates is partially thwarted, and it cannot proceed far enough to generate new investment or other forms of spending sufficient to offset the shortfall in demand occurring elsewhere in the economy. In the aggregate, demand falls below supply, and recession occurs. The rising demand for cash has, so to speak, shortcircuited the self-correcting feature of the economy that runs from demand decreases to lower interest rates to offsetting demand increases.

The same logic explains how excessive aggregate demand can occur. Imagine an economy, already at full employment, in which a surge in spending occurs, either because saving has declined or investment increased. The flow of funds to investors, made available out of national saving, now threatens to fall below the amount of funds sought to finance investment. If nothing intervened, this potential deficiency of saving and available lending below the needs of investors would keep driving interest rates up until investment demand and saving, aggregate demand and aggregate supply, were brought back into line again. Unfortunately, as interest rates begin to rise, business firms and individuals want to switch their portfolios away from cash to take advantage of the higher interest rates and to avoid losing that extra income through holding large cash balances. The potential deficiency of saving below investment, which would have driven up interest rates enough to squelch the excessive spending in the economy, is weakened. The demand for bonds and other securities is supplemented by an additional demand as individuals and business firms seek to switch some of their unwanted cash into securities of various kinds. The rise in interest rates is muted, and the boom takes place.

In all of this discussion, I am trying to show how the private economy operates in the absence of any countercyclical policies by the government. Clearly, if the major problem in recessions is that the demand for money rises, dissipating some of the stabilizing potential from falling interest rates, the Federal Reserve could alleviate the problem by creating an increased supply of money to meet the higher demand for it, allowing interest rates to fall enough to stabilize the economy. And the opposite policy should clearly be pursued when aggregate demand threatens to become positive. This, indeed, is the rationale for an activist countercyclical monetary policy. But there's many a slip 'twixt the cup and the lip, and there are many reasons why it is not a simple and easy matter for the Federal Reserve to achieve virtually complete economic stability. One reason has already been alluded to: the lags between the time interest rates fall and the effect on the economy is felt. To offset this quarter's drop in aggregate demand, the Federal Reserve would have had to act six months to a year earlier—that is, to stabilize the economy, it must forecast, and forecasts are often wrong. There are other reasons why choosing appropriate stabilizing monetary policy, while highly desired, is neither easy nor obvious, as we will explore in memo 17, which deals with monetary policy.

SUMMARY

We have examined two features of the modern economy. One, when aggregate demand starts to depart from aggregate supply, interest rates begin to change and help to moderate the change in aggregate demand, diluting the forces leading to recession or boom. Two, typically, if government policy is passive, the change in interest rates will not be enough to do the full stabilization job. Recession and booms can and do occur.

AN IMPORTANT LESSON FOR A CURRENT POLICY ISSUE

Often in recent years, when the debate about the federal budget deficit was under way, the question was asked whether or not a reduction in the deficit would have to be accompanied by an active policy of monetary ease by the Federal Reserve. That is, would the initial decreases in aggregate demand resulting from tax increases (consumer after-tax income and spending would fall) or government expenditure cuts automatically generate a decline in interest rates sufficient to produce offsetting increases in aggregate demand and keep the economy operating at high employment? Or would the Federal Reserve have to weigh in with an active policy of monetary ease?

The preceding discussion tells us that the Fed would have to act. The initial declines in aggregate demand induced by the deficit reduction would indeed lead to some stabilizing reduction in interest rates, but consumers and business firms would then want to hold greater cash balances, and that would attenuate the drop in interest rates. In the end, interest rates would not fall enough to keep GNP and employment from falling. To avoid recession or a serious slowdown, the Federal Reserve would have to intervene with a policy of monetary ease, pushing interest rates further down than they would "naturally" fall following the cut in the budget deficit.

NOTES

1. Remember that in memos 6 through 10 we are ignoring the problems of economic stability created by the stubbornness and inertia of inflation and examining the other reasons why aggregate demand can be unstable. We will turn to the problems arising from inflation inertia in memos 11 and 12.

2. Figure 8-1 is based on the ninety-day Treasury bill rate, with inflation measured as a two-quarter moving average of the GNP deflator. Interest rates were averaged for the recessions of 1953–54, 1957–58, 1960–61, 1969–70, 1973–75, 1981–82, and 1990–91. The 1980 recession was excluded because it was so short (although interest rates in the trough of recovery from the 1980 recession are included in the period prior to the 1981–82 recession).

3. The 1970s saw the invention of "overnight repo's," through which corporations at the close of the day's business loaned to a bank their cash balances for repayment the next day. The banks often need such brief access to cash to match fluctuations in the inflow and outflow of funds through their accounts. Modern computers have aided business firms in planning and managing their flows of revenues, costs, and financial investments to reduce the cash that business firms need to hold relative to their activities.

M E M O R A N D U M **9**

To: The President

From: CEA Chairman

Subject: **Exports, Imports, and International Investment**

During the past forty years, international trade in goods and services has become the most rapidly expanding sector in all the advanced economies. Exports and imports have grown twice as fast as GNP, and their share in GNP has doubled. Three major developments paved the way for this growth. First, improved technology and greater efficiency in transportation sharply lowered the cost of shipping goods, internally and across borders and oceans, thereby encouraging specialization and trade. Increasingly, producers with low costs and high quality could look to the world for their markets, and consumers around the world saw their living standards markedly improve.

Second, for more than four decades, the United States led the world in cajoling, bargaining, arm-twisting, and otherwise persuading other nations to operate under a system of free international trade. That system as it now exists is far from perfect; there are many sinners and the United States is among them. Nevertheless, after more than four decades, trade barriers have steadily fallen in round after round of multilateral trade negotiations—almost always initiated by and kept alive by pressure from the United States. In 1947 the average level of tariffs in the major industrial countries was 40 percent; by the late 1980s the average level had declined to something in the neighborhood of 5 percent. U.S. leadership in this area constitutes a record of which the nation can well be proud.

The third principal source of the expansion of world trade was the trend toward the production of specialized, high-quality, and technologically

FIGURE 9-1. U.S. Exports, Imports, and Trade Balance as a Percent of GNP, 1948–90

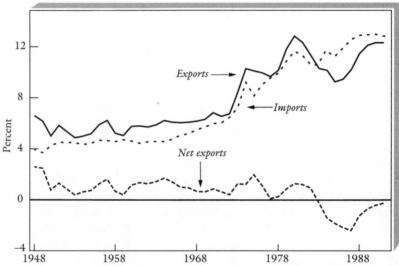

sophisticated goods throughout the world. No longer do countries' trade advantages depend chiefly on their natural resources—soil, climate, or raw materials—and to a lessening degree on the availability of capital, but on the ability of individual firms and entrepreneurs to find a niche in making a specialized set of attractive, high-quality products. In most industrial countries, almost every advanced manufacturing industry is characterized by having large exports and large imports. Thus, the United States in 1989 exported $23 billion in office machines and computers and imported $26 billion in the same category of goods. In the same year, while Germany was exporting $43 billion worth of chemicals, it was importing them to the tune of $25 billion.

THE GROWTH OF U.S. INTERNATIONAL TRADE AND ITS MAJOR COMPONENTS

Figure 9-1 traces the rapid growth of U.S. exports and imports of goods and services, and the balance between them, over the last forty years. Trade grew much faster between 1960 and 1990 than did the rest of the

TABLE 9-1. Components of the U.S. Balance of Payments,
Current Account Balance, 1979, 1990
Billions of dollars

Component	1979	1990
Goods	− 28	− 108
Services	3	26
Investment income	30	12
Other	6	− 22
Current account balance	− 1	− 92

economy, and the value of exports and imports as a share of GNP more than doubled. One can easily see from figure 9-1 the effects of the large devaluation of the dollar that occurred after 1971 (exports soared), and of the huge dollar rise and subsequent fall in the 1980s (exports plummeted and then began recovering), and the fact that after three decades of modest surpluses of exports over imports, the United States in the 1980s began to import more than it exported, that is, its net export balance turned negative. One can also see the effects of the two oil price shocks, in 1974 and again in 1979-81, when soaring oil prices sharply boosted the value of U.S. imports.

THE COMPONENTS OF THE U.S. BALANCE
OF INTERNATIONAL PAYMENTS

The United States receives payments from abroad for three kinds of exports. Correspondingly, America pays foreigners for three kinds of imports. The balance of receipts and payments on each of these three kinds of transactions are shown in the first three lines of table 9-1. One, the United States exports and imports *goods*. In 1990 we exported and received from foreigners $390 billion for goods exported and paid $498 billion abroad for imports leaving a deficit of $108 billion—often referred to as the merchandise trade balance. America is a major net exporter of capital goods, industrial materials and supplies (excluding petroleum), and farm products, with a combined positive trade balance in these items of $89 billion in 1990. We are a major net importer of consumer goods (including autos) and petroleum products, with a negative 1990 trade balance of $172 billion in these categories.

Two, the United States exports and imports *services* of all kinds: shipping charges and airline fares, insurance fees, payments for telephone calls and computer leases, and similar items are part of the category of services. Expenditures of American tourists abroad represent U.S. imports of services, and spending by foreign tourists in this country is an American export. In 1990 we exported $133 billion of such services and imported $107 billion for a favorable balance of $26 billion.

Three, business firms, governments, and individuals also export and import the services of capital across international borders—Americans lend and otherwise invest capital abroad, and conversely foreigners lend and invest capital in the United States. The receipts of *investment income* from the capital invested abroad are a U.S. export, and the payments of interest dividends and other forms of capital income paid to foreigners for the capital they have invested here are an import.[1] In 1990 we received $130 billion from foreigners as income on U.S. investments abroad and paid out $118 billion, for a surplus of $12 billion. Ten years ago the United States had a much larger net surplus of investment income from abroad, but since then, Americans—business, government, and consumers—have borrowed and otherwise imported capital in such large amounts that our net investment income has fallen sharply. In fact, the United States is a net debtor abroad, and were it not that the United States, for various reasons, earns on average a higher rate of return on investments abroad than foreigners do in the United States, the U.S. investment balance would be negative.

We obtain foreign capital not only when foreigners buy our private and government debt instruments, but also as they make equity investments—buy U.S. stocks and real estate or directly invest funds in foreign-owned business firms in this country. To say that the United States is a net debtor country is a shorthand way of stating that the total amount of foreign assets we own is less than the amount of U.S. assets owned by foreigners.

In summing up total U.S. overseas payments and receipts, we have to add to the balance on exports and imports various overseas transfer payments—remittances of immigrants to their home countries, U.S. social security checks paid to beneficiaries who have retired abroad, and government grants to other countries. The net balance on these transactions (with a few technical statistical adjustments) came to a net negative balance of $22 billion in 1990.

The total balance of these receipts and payments, called the *current account balance*, amounted to a deficit of $92 billion in 1990 (down from a peak of $160 billion in 1987). In the years before 1982, the United States had seldom run significant current account deficits. But in the eight years from 1983 through 1990, the cumulative total of the deficits amounted to almost $900 billion.

FINANCING THE CURRENT ACCOUNT DEFICIT— THE CAPITAL ACCOUNT

When the U.S. economy imports more than it exports or otherwise pays more abroad than it receives in payments from foreigners, then one way or the other it must obtain the necessary financing to do so. There are only two ways: we can sell some of the overseas assets we own to get the foreign currency we need, or we can borrow (or otherwise obtain capital) from abroad. One way or the other, there must be a net inflow of capital to match the deficit in the U.S. current account balance.

Note the use of the word *net*. During the 1980s, when the United States was running a current account deficit and needed to import capital to finance it, many U.S. firms and individuals were still investing abroad. And so the total gross inflow of foreign capital had to be larger than the amount needed to finance the current account deficit—it had to cover both the current account deficit and the overseas investments of Americans.

To repeat, a country's current account deficit must be matched with a net inflow of foreign capital. Thus, from 1983 to 1990, the string of large U.S. current account deficits had to be financed by a corresponding net inflow of foreign capital. By 1990 the net overseas assets of the United States (U.S. assets abroad minus foreign assets in the United States) had declined by $620 billion. At the end of 1982, the United States was a net creditor abroad in the amount of $260 billion; by the end of 1990 America was a net debtor to the tune of $360 billion. While conceptually the nation's current account deficit ought to be exactly matched by the inflow of foreign capital and a corresponding decrease in America's net asset position, the statistical measures of these flows of transactions are far from perfect. Thus, as measured statistically, there is a discrepancy each year between the reported current account deficit and the net flow of foreign capital into the United States, as estimated from the net change in our assets and liabilities to foreigners. Sometimes this statistical discrepancy is small, but once in a while it is embarrassingly large.

INFLUENCES ON EXPORTS AND IMPORTS

The major forces that produce changes in a country's exports and imports are changes in domestic and foreign *output and income* and changes in the *price* or *quality* of exports and imports. For simplicity we can talk about changes in quality-adjusted prices (defining a 1 percent increase in quality to be that change which increases exports by the same amount as a 1 percent fall in price).[2]

—Income. Everything else being equal, the faster the growth in national income and output among U.S. trading partners abroad, the faster the rise in U.S. exports. And correspondingly, the faster the growth in U.S. national income and output, the greater the demand for goods of all kinds, including those imported from abroad. Moreover, there is a tendency for exports and imports to respond somewhat more than proportionately to a growth in income here and abroad. According to one recent study, a 1 percent rise in income among other countries in the Organization for Economic Cooperation and Development (OECD) will typically generate a rise of something like 1.5 percent in American exports. And, according to the same study, a 1 percent rise in American income will lead to a rise of perhaps 2.5 percent in imports into this country.[3]

When Europe has a recession not shared by the United States, its income will fall, imports from the United States will decline, and the U.S. trade deficit will grow. Europe had a much slower recovery than did the United States from the recession of 1982; American exports to Europe experienced feeble growth, while U.S. imports rose sharply as recovery proceeded rapidly here. This difference in cyclical recovery patterns explains a little of the widening U.S. trade deficit of the period.

—Prices. A reduction in the quality-adjusted price of American-made "tradable" goods relative to prices charged by other producers around the world will stimulate U.S. exports and discourage imports into this country. Lower American prices will directly increase the competitiveness of American goods in the home markets of other industrial countries and improve the ability of American exporters to win out in the competition for markets in third world countries. At the same time, a fall in the relative price of American-made goods will make it harder for importers to compete in the U.S. market. And of course a rise in the price of American goods relative to foreign prices will work in the opposite direction.

The prices of U.S. tradable goods can change relative to the price of foreign goods in two ways: first, and obviously, if the U.S. inflation rate is lower or higher than the average inflation rate of trading partners; and second, if there is a change in the value at which the U.S. dollar exchanges for other currencies.

—Inflation. More often than not, manufacturers of U.S. exports set their prices by applying a relatively fixed markup to their wage and raw materials costs. If inflation in the United States is proceeding more rapidly than elsewhere, those costs will be advancing faster here than abroad and the prices of American exports will begin rising above the prices of comparable products manufactured abroad, and American export sales will drop, typically more than proportionately to the rise in prices. In some cases, American goods are sold in highly competitive markets where there is one world price. When costs rise in the United States faster than abroad, prices can't be raised to compensate, profit margins are squeezed, and those firms become less interested in making export sales. In that case exports will drop. And by the same reasoning, imports will rise because the inflation in their costs of production is less than for the domestic American manufacturers with whom they compete. All of this works in the opposite direction when inflation in the United States is lower than it is abroad.

—Changes in the overseas value of the dollar. Whenever the value of the U.S. dollar rises (appreciates) relative to another currency, it takes more of that currency to purchase a given amount of dollars; it becomes more expensive for importers in the foreign country to buy goods made in America. For example, if a particular brand of American personal computer sells for $2,000 and it takes Fr 5 to buy $1 on foreign currency markets, a French wholesaler of computers has to pay Fr 5,000 to get enough dollars to buy that computer for sale in France. If the value of the dollar goes up, so that it now costs Fr 6 to buy $1, the French wholesaler will have to pay Fr 6,000 to purchase the same computer. Japanese or locally made French computers will now look more attractive. Sales of American computers to France will fall. The American computer manufacturer, faced with falling sales, may cut prices, but there is a limit on how much it can cut and still remain profitable.[4] And even if the price cuts do limit the fall in sales, export business is now less profitable and firms will put less effort into exports. One way or another, the rise in the value of the dollar will depress the sales of American exports. A fall in the value of the dollar (a depreciation of the dollar) will work in the opposite direction to reduce the price of American goods to foreign buyers and boost U.S. export sales.

Imports into the United States will also be affected by a change in the overseas value of the dollar. When the dollar rises, so that Fr 6 buys a dollar instead of Fr 5, an American importer has to pay fewer dollars to buy French goods. The importer can now sell the French merchandise more cheaply in the United States, boosting the sale of French imports. And a dollar devaluation will work the other way, making French goods more expensive in the United States and depressing sales.

In any period, the change in the relative price of U.S. tradable goods in world markets is equal to the change in the exchange rate plus the differential inflation rate in the United States relative to the rest of the world. Thus, if in a particular year, the dollar appreciates by 10 percent and the U.S. inflation rate is 5 percent greater than the average in our trading partners, the relative price of U.S. goods will have risen by 15 percent. If, however, a 10 percent appreciation of the dollar is accompanied by a 10 percent lower inflation rate than elsewhere, it is a stand-off—there is no rise in U.S. relative prices, and no pressure on U.S. imports or exports in either direction. This measure—the change in the U.S. nominal exchange rate plus the differential U.S. inflation rate—is called the change in the *real exchange rate*. It combines the two main factors producing changes in the competitiveness of American goods around the world, our relative inflation rate and movements in our exchange rate.

During most of the past three decades, our inflation rate didn't vary much from the average inflation rate of our trading partners (it ran a little higher than in Germany and Japan, and lower than in England, France, and Italy). The real and nominal exchange value of the dollar moved rather closely together. And so from now on, we will concentrate on changes in nominal exchange rates as the major influence on the competitiveness of U.S. goods around the world.[5]

EXCHANGE RATES AFFECT EXPORTS AND IMPORTS WITH LONG TIME LAGS

Although changes in the prices of one country's goods relative to those in other countries do affect the volume of its imports and exports, they do so only gradually. Prices for expensive capital goods may have been set at the time the good was ordered, which often precedes the actual export of the finished good by a long time. Rather than lose markets, importers faced with a rise in the price of foreign goods may, at least for a while, absorb some of the increase so that the price to the customer doesn't change as much as might have been expected. If the value of a currency has risen and remained high for some time, and that country's exporters have suffered a loss in sales over several years, they may have dismantled part or all of their distribution channels abroad. Since getting back into markets is often expensive, once lost, a fall in the country's currency to its old level may not induce a reentry of those exporters into foreign markets for some time—until they have become convinced the new exchange rate is more than a temporary fluke.

The study of American manufactured exports and imports referred to above estimated that a year after a change in import prices, only half of the effect on import volume would have been felt. The lag estimated for the export response was even longer—only about a third of the response would be felt by the end of the first year; even by the end of eighteen months, less than half of the eventual volume change would have occurred. Thus the exchange rate of the dollar peaked in early 1985, but the volume of U.S. net exports began a substantial recovery only in 1987.[6]

THE J-CURVE

As we have just seen, when the dollar's exchange rate rises or falls, the resulting changes in exports and imports take time to develop. But the effect on the dollar value of imports is immediate. Suppose the value of the dollar falls. The effect of that devaluation in depressing the volume of imports is delayed. But the prices that importers have to pay for most imported goods are fixed in foreign currencies—Fr 500, let's say, for a case of French wine. As soon as the value of the dollar falls, say from Fr 6 to the dollar to Fr 5, the importer has to pay more dollars for foreign goods; the dollar price of the case of wine goes from $83 dollars (500 ÷ 6) to $100 (500 ÷ 5). Thus, the immediate effect of a dollar depreciation is to raise the dollar value of imports and push the current account balance in a negative direction. But eventually the higher dollar price of imports reduces the volume of imports, and the current account balance recovers from its earlier fall and moves in a positive direction. And so, when the value of the dollar falls, the American current account balance traces the shape of a J. The opposite reaction occurs when the dollar rises; the current account first moves in a positive direction and then gradually turns toward the negative, forming an inverted **J**.

Earlier, estimates were cited showing that an equal rise in national income in the United States and abroad seems to produce a growth of American imports faster than the growth of American exports. If these estimates are even roughly correct, they would support a controversial hypothesis that has been debated for some time, namely, that to keep the United States from running an increasingly large trade deficit U.S. trading partners must grow faster than America, or, lacking such differential growth rates, a small but continuing depreciation of the dollar must take place to keep American firms competitive in world markets.[7] In the years before 1980, the long-term growth of the Japanese and most European economies was a good bit larger than that of the United States, helping to keep the United States from running sustained deficits in international payments. But as noted, foreign growth slowed relative to U.S. growth during much of the 1980s, helping to produce the trade deficits of the period.

NOTES

1. Foreign holdings of U.S. government bonds are much larger than American holdings of foreign government bonds. There is a substantial net outflow of government bond interest from the United States to foreign owners of Treasury securities ($38 billion in 1990). Until recently, the national income account statisticians did not consider the interest payments on government bonds as a service and excluded them from investment income payments and receipts in calculating exports and imports. However, a comprehensive picture of the American balance of international payments, as shown in table 9-1, has to include this net outflow. For this reason and several other less important ones, the net export figure in the national income accounts (shown in figure 9-1) is more positive (less negative) than the more comprehensive balance shown in the table.

2. A common way to measure the change in quality is to ask how much more consumers would be willing to pay for the extra quality. If the producer introduces a quality improvement for which the consumer is willing to pay an extra 10 percent, but charges the same price as before, that is equivalent to a 10 percent price cut.

3. These estimates exclude petroleum products and computers, which have several special features not shared by the broad run of other goods and services. Robert Z. Lawrence, "U.S. Current Account Adjustment: An Appraisal," *Brookings Papers on Economic Activity* 2: 1990, pp. 343–82.

4. The problem is compounded for the exporter because most countries have antidumping laws that prohibit a foreign firm from selling in the foreign country at prices below what it charges at home. So the exporter has to cut prices on its sales everywhere.

5. Admittedly, for most goods, the available measures of inflation are not corrected for quality changes, and such changes may have played a role in influencing the pattern of exports and imports. But even if that is true, changes in the quality of U.S. goods relative to those of other countries are likely to be a slow and gradual matter, and unlikely to have produced the dramatic swings in the U.S. competitive position that we will be discussing. See Lawrence, "U.S. Current Account Adjustment."

6. Of course, if the dollar exchange rate had remained at its fantastic peak of early 1985, the U.S. trade deficit would have reached a much higher level than it eventually did. So the effect of the decline in the exchange rate on the improvement of the trade balance, in comparison with what it otherwise would have been, came about more quickly than it appears from the dates cited in the text.

7. This proposition is known as the Houthakker-Magee hypothesis, named for the two economists who first proposed it in 1969.

To: The President

FROM: CEA Chairman

SUBJECT: **Exchange Rates, the Trade Balance, and the U.S. Economy**

Throughout the 1980s many senators, congressional representatives, and business and labor leaders argued, and they still do, that America's trade deficits were importantly the result of the "unfair" trade practices of other countries, especially Japan. Trade barriers of various kinds were proposed to deal with the trade deficit, and as devices to increase jobs for American workers. But my main message in this memo is that such approaches will not achieve these objectives. Trade policies and practices, here and abroad, are important. They can affect the composition of national output and employment, but not its level. They can affect the volume of exports and imports, but not the balance between them. They can affect living standards, but not by providing more aggregate employment. Aggregate demand, national output, and employment and the size of a nation's trade balance are determined by macroeconomic conditions, especially by the relationship between national saving and domestic investment opportunities.

WHAT DETERMINES EXCHANGE RATES?

Until 1973 the major trading countries operated under an agreement that fixed the exchange rates of their currencies relative to one another. Rates were indeed changed. But the changes were major events that usually required international agreement and came at infrequent intervals. Given the rapid postwar recovery and increasing competitiveness of Japan and Europe, the exchange rate of the dollar was getting more and more out of line; it was too high, and U.S. trade was beginning to suffer. In 1971 President Richard M. Nixon more or less unilaterally devalued the dollar by 10 percent. And in 1973 exchange rates were set free to float, that is, to be determined by market forces (although, as we shall see, with some occasional nudging by the governments of the major countries).

What determines the rate at which dollars are exchanged for marks or yen or sterling on the market? We can say demand and supply, but that answer just pushes the question further back—what determines the demand and supply of various currencies?

To make it simple, let's start with a situation in which a country, say the United States, each year has a balance in its current accounts—total payments to foreigners for importing goods and services and for interest on overseas debts are equal to total receipts from foreigners (when all the various transactions are valued in dollars at the current exchange rates). The total amount of dollars in the hands of foreigners who have sold goods to the United States and who want to convert it back to their home currencies is exactly matched by foreign currencies in the hands of U.S. exporting firms from their sales abroad, who are now looking for dollars to bring home. The demand and supply of dollars and foreign currencies seeking to be exchanged for each other are equal.

But now suppose that the United States begins to experience a wage and price inflation higher than in other countries. As we saw in memo 9, this event causes a fall in U.S. exports more than proportional to the rise in the relative prices of U.S. export goods. The dollar value of exports declines.[1] The United States begins to run a current account deficit; receipts of foreign currencies from abroad fall short of the amount of dollars in the hands of foreign importers. There is a relative surplus of dollars and a shortage of foreign currencies. The price of the dollar—that is, the dollar exchange rate—falls; the dollar is said to depreciate. The cheaper dollar, however, now means that foreign buyers have to offer less of their own currency to buy American exports. Exports start to recover. When the value of the dollar has fallen enough to bring the prices of American goods in world markets back into line again, the U.S. deficit in its international balance of payments will be wiped out.

This line of reasoning led many people for a long time to accept the view of exchange rates called purchasing power parity. According to this view, the rate at which the dollar was exchanged against any other currency would essentially settle down at a point determined by U.S. prices relative to foreign prices; if, on average, it took two deutsche marks (DM) to buy in international markets what could be bought for one dollar, the exchange rate of DM to dollar would be 2 to 1. If, because of relatively high inflation, American prices doubled relative to German prices, so that a dollar would now buy only what one DM would buy, the dollar exchange rate with the DM would fall to 1-to-1. Thus, under the purchasing power parity interpretation of exchange rates, differences among inflation rates among countries—because they lead to divergences in price levels— would be dominant in explaining exchange rates. Exchange rates would move until they offset the effects of divergences in domestic price levels and restored the parity among currencies in terms of what they could buy on international markets. This theory has one serious flaw—it doesn't fit the facts.

EXCHANGE RATES AND INTERNATIONAL CAPITAL FLOWS

As noted in memo 9, the real exchange rate is a measure that corrects the nominal exchange rate for differences in inflation rates between the United States and its major trading partners. If most of the movement in exchange rates simply reflected differences in price movements among countries, as the purchasing power parity doctrine predicts, the real exchange rate would be flat—it would move very little. In fact, the real exchange rate has moved up and down sharply over the years. Although differences in inflation rates among countries can and do lead to changes in the exchange rates of their currencies, most of the major recent movements in the dollar exchange rate have not been associated with differential inflation rates. And that shows exchange rates can and do move substantially apart from the level needed to preserve the parity of purchasing power among countries.

The key reason why exchange rates often move sharply in ways that cannot be explained by the concept of purchasing power parity is that individuals and business firms often want to obtain a foreign currency not to buy imports of goods and services but to invest in the financial or other assets of the foreign country. The net demand for a currency, therefore, is determined not only by the flows of payments and receipts for the export and import of goods and services—as implied by the purchasing power parity concept—but also by the demand for that currency from investors who want to use it to buy assets denominated in that foreign currency. A German investor seeking to buy a U.S. Treasury bond or a

FIGURE 10-1. Interest Rate Differentials and the Exchange Rate for the Dollar

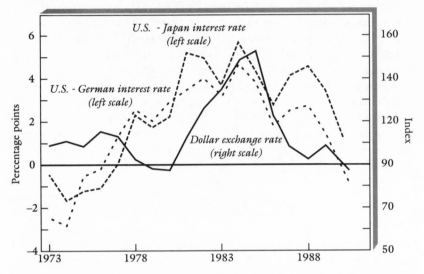

corporate stock has to sell his DM for dollars in order to make the purchase—he cannot buy those securities directly with marks.[2] Even if a country's current account is in balance, the demand for that currency may greatly exceed or fall short of the supply available, depending on whether investors are trying to increase or decrease their holdings of that country's assets.

A chief reason why the citizens of one country, say Germany, would want to invest in dollar assets is because they believe they can earn a higher return on their money by so doing. The investment demand for dollars will be high when interest rates or other returns to investment in the United States are higher than they are in Germany, and vice versa. Thus, differential interest rates, as well as differential inflation rates, move exchange rates. (From now on we will, for the sake of simplicity, use the term "interest rates" as shorthand to mean the yield on assets of various kinds; but remember that while most foreign investment is in interest-bearing assets, foreign firms and individuals also put their money in stocks, real estate, and direct investment.) Figure 10-1 shows how movements in the exchange for the dollar during the 1980s were linked with movements in U.S. interest rates relative to those in Germany and Japan. The massive rise in the dollar's exchange rate in the first half of the 1980s occurred in response to the large upsurge in U.S. interest rates relative to those available abroad. (Before 1971, the dollar exchange rate had been fixed for many years and had become far too high to be consistent with the U.S. competitive position in the world. During the period immediately after exchange rates were cut loose to float in 1973, the dollar was gradually adjusting to the new situation and for a while its movements didn't parallel the movement of interest rate differentials as they did later).

THE GROWING MOBILITY OF INTERNATIONAL CAPITAL AND ITS CONSEQUENCES

In the past fifteen years or so, world financial markets have evolved significantly—financial capital has become highly mobile. Because computers can keep track of massive, complicated transactions, institutional and private investors are now able to shift huge sums inexpensively from financial investments denominated in one currency to those denominated in another, as actual and expected interest rates and other financial returns change among countries. As recently as 1980, the combined total of foreign bonds bought and sold by U.S. citizens and U.S. bonds bought and sold by foreigners was in the neighborhood of $40 billion. In 1989 that total substantially exceeded $1 trillion dollars! And in the New York financial markets on a typical day some $130 billion in foreign currencies changes hands. Increasingly, fluctuations in exchange rates have occurred because of changes in the investment demand for currencies connected with differences in interest rates among countries.

The total return that can be earned from investing in assets denominated in a foreign currency depends on the foreign interest rate *plus or minus any gain or loss experienced because of movements in the exchange rate* during the time the foreign assets are being held. For example, if interest rates on a five-year bond are 5 percent in Japan and 8 percent in the United States, a Japanese pension fund will earn an extra 15 percent over the five years on any funds it places in a U.S. five-year bond. But if the exchange rate for the dollar in yen falls by 15 percent over this period, all of the extra earnings will be wiped out when the pension fund converts the dollars back into yen. And of course if the dollar should fall by more than 15 percent, the pension fund will have done worse by investing in dollar rather than yen securities. And so *the demand by international investors for a foreign currency will depend on the height of its interest rates relative to those in other major financial centers minus any expected decline in the exchange value of that currency.*

When a country's interest rates go up relative to those abroad, investors around the world increase their demand for that country's currency. But there is, at that moment, no increase in the supply of that currency available to satisfy the new demand. That currency's exchange rate begins to rise; people have to pay more units of foreign currency per unit of the favored currency. Thus in 1980 it took DM 1.8 to buy $1 of U.S. currency. But by 1985, after a period of very high U.S. interest rates, it took 2.9 DM to purchase $1. The currency of a high-interest-rate country will keep rising until it gets high enough that investors begin to worry it will fall again by enough to wipe out any extra earnings they might have made from the higher interest rates. At that point the value of the currency stops rising; the extra interest yield is now matched by the expected future loss from currency depreciation.

The rise in a country's exchange rate produced by an increase in its interest rates relative to those abroad will gradually lead to a fall in its exports, a rise in imports, and a worsening of its international payments balance.

This view of what drives the exchange rate mechanism—and it is the standard explanation widely accepted by economists and financial experts—highlights expectations about the future value of a currency. Expectations can be volatile, and speculation can at times play a major role. Those who deal professionally in foreign currency markets, like those who deal in stocks, can make money if they can anticipate what others are going to believe about the future value of an exchange rate, regardless of whether those beliefs are consistent with the underlying economic forces that will ultimately determine the movement of the exchange rate. Moreover, the preceding analysis of the exchange rate mechanism is a good surface description of what drives exchange rates but not a deep one—it doesn't tell us what determines at any moment whether an exchange rate is above or below its likely long-term value. Economists have not yet produced a fully satisfactory analysis of the determination of exchange rates. Nevertheless, a good bit about how interest rate differentials can drive exchange rates is understood.

INTERACTIONS WITH THE DOMESTIC ECONOMY

When an economy is operating with a great deal of slack, when unemployment is high and plenty of productive capacity is idle, any development that raises exports or causes a substitution of domestic goods for imports will expand U.S. aggregate demand and lead to an expansion of output and employment. An increased growth of GNP and income abroad or a fall in the exchange value of the dollar will move the economy in that direction. And, conversely, U.S. aggregate demand, GNP, and employment will fall when economic growth among U.S. trading partners sags or the dollar appreciates in value. Changes in the economic fortunes of other countries and developments affecting the exchange value of the dollar, like changes in domestic consumption and investment spending, also can alter aggregate demand relative to potential GNP and thereby produce fluctuations in GNP, employment, and income for the American economy.

But even when high employment has been achieved and maintained, changes in the world economy or in the value of the dollar can affect other aspects of the American economy. To be more precise, let's assume that the Federal Reserve successfully manages monetary policy to keep aggregate demand approximately equal to potential GNP—raising interest rates to damp down demand when aggregate demand is excessive and lowering rates to stimulate additional spending when demand is weak. In that case, an expansion of demand and spending in one sector of the economy requires a contraction somewhere else. How does a change in net exports then affect the national economy, and conversely how do changes in aggregate demand elsewhere in the economy affect net exports?

In memo 4, we examined this situation by looking at the relationship between national saving on the one hand and the sum of domestic and foreign investment (= net exports) on the other. Suppose, for example, that the sum of consumer and government spending increases relative to national income—in other words, national saving declines. Since we cannot as a nation invest at home and abroad more than we save, we know what the end result must be; either domestic investment spending must decline, or net exports must fall, or some combination of the two must occur. We can now use what we learned in the previous memos to understand the process that forces this outcome to occur.

Because the supply of saving has fallen below the demand for saving by investors, interest rates will naturally rise. But this rise in rates will not normally be enough to insure that aggregate demand remains within the bounds of potential GNP. The Federal Reserve will have to act to push rates up enough to produce the requisite fall in investment. We saw in memo 7 on domestic investment that higher interest rates will reduce various components of domestic investment. And memo 9 explains that higher interest rates in the United States will also reduce net exports. The higher rates make investment in U.S. securities attractive to foreigners, the overseas value of the dollar rises, American exports become more expensive abroad and foreign imports cheaper here, exports fall while imports rise, and so the net export balance moves in a negative direction. In a similar vein, an expansion of investment relative to saving will produce the same result—a rise in interest rates that will choke off some of the surging investment demand and reduce net exports. And of course one can see these developments in reverse: a fall in consumer and government spending or a decline in domestic investment demand will produce a fall in interest rates, a depreciation of the dollar, and an expansion of American net exports with some reversal of any initial decline in investment.

When saving declines relative to investment and interest rates rise, how much of the adjustment takes the form of a fall in domestic investment and how much shows up as lower net exports? The mix of the two effects is different now than what it was fifteen or twenty years ago. Since exchange rates were fixed by international agreement in the 1950s, 1960s, and early 1970s, differences in interest rates between the United States and other countries did not lead to major appreciation or depreciation of the dollar and had little effect on American net exports. Hence when the saving rate changed up or down, the accompanying changes in interest rates had their major effect on domestic investment—changes in saving were pretty closely matched by changes in domestic investment. More recently, however, with exchange rates free to fluctuate more or less as market forces dictate, a substantial fraction of any change in national saving, perhaps a third to a half, is likely to show up as a change in net exports, and the remainder as a change in domestic investment.[3] Thus, when the U.S. national saving rate fell from roughly 8.2 percent of national income in the period prior to 1980 to 3 percent in 1989–90, 3 percentage points of the fall were reflected in a decline in domestic investment and 2.5 percentage points in a decline in net exports as a share of national income. (Net exports shifted from a small surplus to a big deficit; correspondingly, a positive U.S. net investment abroad was converted into substantial net borrowing from abroad.) Figure 4-4, in memo 4, summarizes these developments.

There is another way to view this phenomenon. When a country greatly expands public and private consumption relative to income, and aggregate demand is kept within the bounds of potential GNP, the society can adjust in two possible ways: first, spending for domestic investment purposes can be cut to make room for the extra consumption spending; or second, the economy can maintain its domestic investment spending, import more than it exports, run a trade deficit, and thereby spend in the aggregate more than it produces. (The excess of imports over exports is equal to the excess of domestic spending over domestic production.) In the 1980s, as already mentioned, the United States did some of both—boosted public and private consumption partly at the expense of domestic investment and partly by spending more than it produced, through the expedient of importing more than it exported.

Because we can cut national saving and still maintain domestic investment spending does not mean that we have found the secret to attaining Nirvana. As we have seen, a deficit in our balance of payments has to be financed by issuing debt or other obligations to foreign investors. Running large net export deficits year after year, as a means of supporting a high level of consumption, produces a rapidly mounting overseas debt on which we will have to pay debt service out of our future national income. Thus a large reduction in national saving will inevitably penalize future living standards in one of two ways: to the extent we adjust by cutting domestic investment in productive assets, the growth of national income will slow down. To the extent we maintain domestic investment and spend more than we produce by running a large trade deficit, we will have to devote an increasing share of future national income to debt service payments abroad.

During much of the nineteenth century the United States spent more than it produced and ran substantial balance-of-payments deficits. However, the extra spending and the overseas borrowing was devoted to greater domestic investment in railroads, steel mills, and the like, not in increased consumption. The additional national income made possible by the extra investment could be used to pay the debt service, and since the return to the domestic investment was higher than the interest rates we had to pay, we came out ahead on the operation.

GOVERNMENT POLICIES TOWARD EXCHANGE RATES

Since, as we have seen, changes in interest rates can greatly influence exchange rates, government policies that affect interest rates can also affect exchange rates. But governments sometimes try to alter exchange rates, in the absence of policy actions that change interest rates, by making large sales or purchases of a currency. Thus, in September of 1985, Secretary of the Treasury James Baker secured the agreement of other major financial powers to cooperate in a program of driving down the very high exchange value of the dollar through a program of concerted sales of dollars (for other currencies) by other governments, most importantly Japan and Germany. This move was the famous Plaza accord (named for the New York hotel where the meeting took place). Whether such "exchange intervention" can significantly alter currency values is a disputed question. The amount of U.S. dollar-denominated financial assets held privately by foreigners exceeds $1 trillion, and the daily volume of currency transactions runs into the hundreds of billions. If all governments do is buy and sell a few billion or even tens of billions of dollars for other currencies—while no change has occurred in monetary policies or other fundamentals affecting exchange rates—it is unlikely that in most situations intervention alone can have any long-lasting effects on currency values. The dollar's value did indeed decline after the Plaza accord. But it had begun declining some months earlier and some economists believe that the fundamental economic forces at work would in any event have pushed the dollar down.

To the extent that intervention in the exchange market is accompanied by changes in monetary policy that alters interest rates, currency values can be altered. And the intervention may be a signal to financial markets that speeds up the response of currencies to the interest rate action. Moreover, from time to time a heavy speculative element may be at work in foreign exchange markets, pulling currency values a good bit away from a level warranted by underlying economic forces. Conceivably, a coordinated and publicized decision by governments to intervene in the market with the announced aim of altering a currency's value may be able to take some of the speculative element out of the market and so alter currency values. But of course no one really knows the extent to which a currency's value at any one moment is or is not in line with longer-term fundamentals, and there is no basis in history for markets to assume that governments are any better than private currency holders in judging that question. Agreement on this subject is hard to come by. Nevertheless it would be wise to discount the possibility of exchange intervention alone to bring about large and lasting changes in a currency's value, although intervention may prove useful when employed with other, more basic, policy changes, and in the presence of heavy speculative activity, intervention may conceivably be useful on its own.

THE SAVING-INVESTMENT BALANCE, NOT TRADE POLICY, DETERMINES A COUNTRY'S TRADE BALANCE

As noted in memo 4, the balance between a nation's saving and its domestic investment demand, not its trade policies, is the principal determinant of a nation's balance-of-payments deficit or surplus. This memo has explained the mechanism that produces this result. Suppose, for example, that the United States began to levy a heavy tariff on Japanese imports. Initially, to be sure, Japanese exports to the United States would fall, and Japan's trade surplus with the United States would start to shrink. As long, however, as the underlying saving-investment balance in the two countries and their relative interest rates remained unchanged, Japanese investors would remain as interested as they ever were in buying U.S. securities. If U.S. imports from Japan were to fall significantly, there would be fewer dollars available for Japanese investors to buy; the dollar would become scarcer and its value would rise, making American exports more expensive and Japanese imports cheaper, offsetting some of the effects of the import surcharge. Dollar and yen exchange rates with third countries would also change, in a way that penalized American competitiveness with those countries. In the end, there might be some reduction in the Japanese trade surplus with the United States, but the overall trade balances of Japan and the United States with the rest of the world would tend to move back toward their original levels. There would be fewer Japanese imports into the United States but also fewer American exports into Japan and probably elsewhere. The overall volume of American trade with the rest of the world, both exports and imports, might well decline but not the balance between them.

Changes in trade laws, policies, and practices can change the composition of trade flows and influence the level of exports and imports for good or for ill but cannot produce important alterations in countries' overall trade balance. It is alleged, and some fairly strong evidence supports the allegation, that various Japanese business practices make it difficult for other countries to export manufactured goods to Japan. Changes in those practices would undoubtedly expand the volume of foreign imports into Japan. The value of the Japanese yen would fall. Both imports into Japan and exports from Japan would rise. Living standards in Japan and elsewhere would expand; Japanese consumers would benefit from consuming many foreign goods now discouraged from entry, and consumers throughout the world would enjoy more high-quality Japanese goods. But as long as the Japanese save far more than they can profitably invest at home, and without any major changes in the saving-investment balances in Japan's trading partners, the overall Japanese trade balance is not likely to shrink significantly.

FLOWS OF REAL AND FINANCIAL CAPITAL

When, as in the 1980s, U.S. national saving fell relative to its domestic investment demands and U.S. interest rates rose relative to those abroad, the market mechanism started to work to transfer foreign saving into this country. Foreign investors increased their demand for American securities. But as a savings-short country, we needed the resources. We were trying to spend, on consumption and domestic investment together, more than we were able to produce. We could not literally use DM or yen or British pounds or the other pieces of paper, which the foreign investors had to offer. What happened, as we have seen, is that the increased demand for dollars by foreign investors raised the value of the dollar and gradually reduced U.S. exports while increasing imports. The United States began running trade deficits, thereby importing more goods and services than it exported. The initial financial flows were thus translated into a flow of real resources into the United States, allowing the nation to spend on consumer and investment goods together more than it produced of those goods. Other countries with an excess of saving relative to domestic investment—for example, Japan—used their own real resources to "invest" in the United States; they received our IOU's and in the future will be receiving debt service payments for the excess of U.S. imports over U.S. exports that they provided us.

What such a course of events portends for the future depends on whether we were using the resources furnished from abroad to augment our consumption spending (public and private) or were using those resources to add to domestic investment that would increase our income in the future. The U.S. trade deficits of the 1980s were an example of the former. The trade deficits that we frequently ran in the nineteenth century were an example of the latter.

A FINAL REMINDER

In thinking about the relationships between domestic spending, trade balances, and international capital flows, one must realize that all of the following magnitudes are the same:

☆ **Excess of domestic spending over domestic production**

equals: **Excess of domestic investment over national saving (equivalently: shortfall of national saving below domestic investment)**
equals: **Net export deficit**
equals: **Inflow of international capital**

NOTES

1. When the U.S. inflation rate is higher than average, the prices of imported goods fall relative to those of domestically produced goods. The volume of imports expands. Empirical studies suggest that the rise in volume will approximately offset the fall in prices. The dollar volume of imports will remain approximately unchanged. The changes in the current account balance thus come mainly on the export side.

2. This sentence is not quite correct. Some firms, and some governments, issue bonds denominated in the currency of a foreign government. A Swedish municipality might issue yen bonds in Tokyo, receiving yen proceeds when the bonds are sold and obligating itself to pay interest and principal in yen rather than Swedish kronor. Technically speaking, we should talk about the demand not for foreign assets but for "assets denominated in a foreign currency." But this technical nicety would only make the text more clumsy and so we will talk simply about the demand and supply of foreign assets.

3. See, for example, Andrew Dean and others, "Saving Trends and Behaviour in OECD Countries," *OECD Economic Studies*, vol. 14 (Spring 1990), p. 18, table 2.

MEMORANDUM **11**

To: The President

From: CEA Chairman

Subject: **Inflation: History, Measurement,
         and Economic and Political Costs**

So far we have concentrated on the problems of economic instability that can arise from fluctuations in aggregate demand. But periods of recession or stagnation can also occur because of events related to inflation.

This and the next two memos discuss inflation: its causes, consequences, and the policy problems it poses. Memo 13 focuses on the features of our wage- and price-setting institutions that make inflation so stubborn and so costly to get rid of.

Though the market-based economic systems of modern industrial nations have generally worked marvelously well over long stretches of time to generate high and rising living standards, they have difficulty dealing with inflation. Unfortunately, the only way they seem able to reduce an inflation once it is under way or to prevent a major cost increase—such as a big jump in oil prices—from turning into a new wage-price spiral, is through a heavy dose of unemployment and economic slack. The major recessions of 1975 and 1982 were importantly, although not solely, brought on by the restrictive monetary policies enacted to deal with severe inflation. Figure 11-1 shows the relationship between the rate of inflation and the change in unemployment one year later, portraying the rise in unemployment that followed the increases in inflation in the late 1960s, 1973–74, and 1979–81.

POSTWAR INFLATIONS

Figure 11-2 shows the history of inflation since the Second World War. Six distinct inflationary episodes have occurred. The first four were the

120

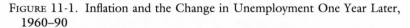

FIGURE 11-1. Inflation and the Change in Unemployment One Year Later, 1960–90

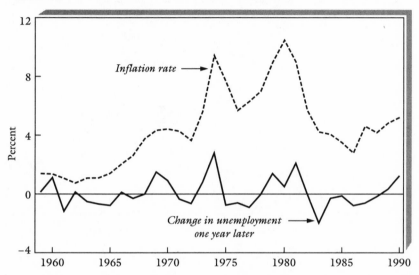

product of an overheated economy with aggregate demand in excess of aggregate supply, classic cases of too much demand chasing too few goods. Those episodes were the immediate postwar inflation, connected with the release of huge pent-up demand, amply financed by liquid assets piled up by consumers during the wartime shortages; the brief Korean War inflation, sparked by consumer and business panic buying on fears (which turned out to be groundless) of a return to wartime shortages; the modest inflation of 1955–57, in which aggregate demand wasn't excessive, but excess demand in a few key sectors of the economy raised inflation in those sectors while sluggish demand in other sectors failed to produce offsetting declines in inflation there; and the Vietnam War inflation, when the large extra defense expenditures were not covered by taxes, and interest rates were not raised sufficiently to neutralize the resulting excess of demand over supply. The last two inflations, starting in 1974 and 1979, were of a kind not experienced before. Though some excessive demand was present, especially in 1973, these inflations were chiefly caused by extremely large increases in the cost of energy, based on dramatic increases in the world price of crude oil, associated with politically caused disruptions of oil supplies from the Middle East. The

FIGURE 11-2. Consumer Price Inflation, 1946–90

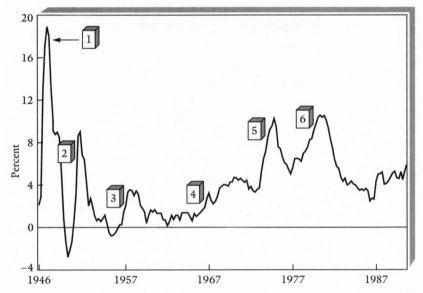

latest disruption in Middle East oil supplies, during the Iraqi invasion of Kuwait, didn't last long enough to tick off a severe inflation, although it did for a short time set off fears of future inflation.

Five of the six inflationary episodes were followed by a recession, stemming at least partially from the restrictive monetary policy (and in several cases the restrictive fiscal policy) put in place to reverse the inflation. The exception was the Korean War inflation, which was mostly a brief speculative bubble; the initial price increases never found their way into wages and no wage-price spiral was set off, so that the inflation quickly collapsed without having to be wrung out with a recession.

One final set of distinctions: the first three inflations were almost completely reversed, and eventually inflation returned close to zero. But the recessions following the Vietnam War and the 1974 oil shocks didn't eliminate much of the underlying inflation.[1] The subsequent rounds of inflation took off from successively higher levels. After the 1982 recession, the underlying rate of inflation was brought down significantly but stayed in the neighborhood of 4 percent.

MEASURING INFLATION

Inflation is simply the *rate of change in the average level of prices.* Typically we express inflation as the annual rate of change in the average price level. Thus if consumer prices rise by 0.5 percent in a month, we say that consumer price inflation in that month was 6.2 percent (0.5 percent a month compounded for twelve months). If the price level rises by 20 percent over a five-year period, the average inflation rate over that period has been 3.7 percent (the annual rate, when compounded for five years, that generates a 20 percent increase).

Obviously, in calculating the average price level, whose change constitutes inflation, we want to weight the prices of the various goods and services according to their importance in the economy, or in the subsector whose inflation we are measuring. Thus, to measure the change in consumer prices, we give more importance to a 10 percent increase in the price of automobiles than to a 10 percent change in the price of chewing gum.

The Department of Labor (and for some special types of products, other federal agencies) regularly collects prices on a wide range of goods and services. Price indexes are then constructed for all the goods and services included in the GNP (the GNP deflator), for all consumer goods and services at retail (the consumer price index—CPI), and for goods and services at the wholesale or producers' level (the producers' price index—PPI). To construct the price index for the economy as a whole or some subsector within it, the prices of individual goods and services are weighted by their relative importance (that is, according to how much is spent on them), and then averaged. The resulting measures of the average price level—for the whole economy, or for consumer prices, or for any other sector within the economy—are expressed as indexes, with some base year as 100.

The GNP deflator has a base year of 1987; the index for 1987 is 100. In 1991 the GNP deflator was 117.0, which means that the average level of prices for all the goods and services in the GNP was 17.0 percent higher in 1991 than in 1987, amounting to an average rise, or annual inflation rate, of 4.0 percent a year over the four-year period.

To be representative, the expenditure weights used to combine individual prices should reflect current expenditure patterns. It wouldn't be very useful to assume that consumers in 1991 did only as much airline traveling as they did in 1947. And so the base year and the expenditure weights

FIGURE 11-3. A Change in Inflation versus a One-Shot Price Increase

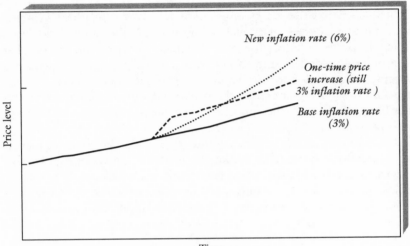

for the different price indexes are periodically updated. Thus, in late 1991, the base of the GNP deflator was moved from 1982 to 1987, and the relative weights assigned to the various goods and services changed to reflect the expenditure pattern of the latter year.

Remember that inflation is the change in prices. Suppose, for example, that a very large rise in crude oil prices occurs, which drives up the price of gasoline, heating oil, and other energy products. That year the inflation rate in the GNP deflator and the CPI will rise. But if oil and oil-related prices stop rising, and if they do not set off sympathetic wage increases and further price increases outside the energy sector, the extra surge of inflation will stop after the first year even if oil prices remain high. Figure 11-3 illustrates the difference between an event that produces a one-shot increase in the level of prices and something that generates a new and higher level of continuing inflation. This distinction will become very important when we discuss the effect of oil price and other price increases on inflation and unemployment.

WHY INFLATION IS UNPOPULAR

By now virtually all except the very poorest nations of the world share two characteristics. First, they are highly specialized. Only a small fraction of the population engages in self-sufficient agriculture and can survive without trade. And second, all economies are monetary economies; within each country prices are expressed in a common monetary unit, and goods and services are exchanged for that monetary unit; barter constitutes only a minute fraction of trade. As a consequence, instability of the price level—the average rate at which goods are traded for money—greatly complicates not only business planning but everyday life. Most of the big decisions in life require some long-term planning, which in turn includes an economic component: deciding when to have children, whether and when to buy a house or a car, whether and when to open a small business, where to attend college, and so on down the list. Planning ahead is made much more onerous and much less efficient when people suffer great uncertainty about the future terms on which goods and services will exchange for money and the rate at which money can be borrowed and lent.

Hyperinflations, with annual inflation rates rising into the thousands of percent, can paralyze society. And even when societies learn how to survive with huge inflation rates, as some of the countries of Latin America have done, their productivity is impaired. The hyperinflation that afflicted Germany after the First World War was so severe and so hated that seventy years later the fear of inflation still dominates German economic policymaking to an extent not approached anywhere else in the world.

But inflation does not have to get close to the hyperinflation stage before it becomes an actual and a psychologically serious problem. When the inflation rate rises sharply, that change is unexpected (if it had been expected, people would have acted accordingly, rushed out to buy goods to beat the higher inflation, and caused it to occur even earlier). Both business firms and households make mistakes in their long-term planning when inflation heats up. Thus, people saving for retirement who bought government or corporate bonds in the mid-1960s and early 1970s earned far less than they had planned, as the rise in inflation starting in the mid-1960s eroded the value of their bonds by much more than seemed likely when the interest rate was initially set and they made their purchases. Borrowers, however, were able to pay off their debts with incomes swollen from inflation. Conversely, those who bought bonds in 1980 and 1981, just before inflation began to fall sharply, ended up with a very high rate of return. Lenders lose and borrowers gain when inflation unexpectedly rises, while the opposite occurs when inflation declines.

Because of these effects, the economy is less productive and individuals feel cheated when the rate of inflation changes markedly. And, as noted earlier, periods of high inflation have generally been marked by variable inflation. One of the marks of civilization is the extent to which individuals feel they have control over their lives. Though inflation is not the only force that weakens that sense of control, it is a prominent one, especially because the entire population feels its effects. It is not just economists and creditors who decry inflation. Some countries seem to tolerate and work well with a higher average rate of inflation than others. Germany has little tolerance, Italy has a good bit more, and the United States is in between. But in all the industrial countries, a significant rise in the rate of inflation almost always translates into a political liability for the incumbent administration. Ultimately, steps are taken to reverse a sharp bulge in inflation. The subsequent cost, in years of higher unemployment, lost output, and higher bankruptcies, is also unpleasant. The widespread realization that a jump in inflation will be followed by a period of recession and contraction adds to its political unpopularity. Hence, voters almost always perceive a significant rise in inflation as harmful, even when wages keep up with prices, so that the average worker does not lose purchasing power.

In theory a steady and predictable rate of inflation, even a high one, should not be a serious problem. If all prices and wages kept the same relationship to each other, if interest rates always fully reflected the proper inflation premium, and if we could be sure that inflation would continue into the future at the today's rate, everyone, with a little arithmetic, could plan accordingly.[2] Over time society would become used to the steady high inflation. But high rates of inflation are never stable. Countries that have had, on average, high rates of inflation have also had highly variable rates of inflation.

It does seem possible, however, for countries to have positive, but low rates of inflation that do not vary much over long periods. Figure 11-4 illustrates this relationship for several industrial and developing countries: it compares the average inflation rates of the past ten years with a measure of the variability of inflation over the same period. Countries like Germany and Japan with low average inflation rates have experienced relatively small volatility in inflation, while countries with high inflation have also had large ups and downs in their inflation rate. It seems that the various economic forces or government policies that lead to inflation are themselves seldom stable. Even countries with a propensity to pursue policies that sporadically get them into serious inflationary troubles find the consequences so unpopular that they periodically introduce programs to reduce

FIGURE 11-4. Annual Average Inflation versus Average Variation of Inflation, Selected OECD Countries, 1961–90

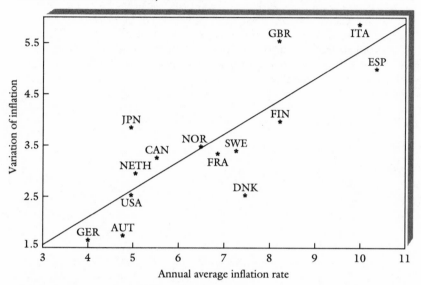

Source: OECD Economic Outlook (GDP deflator).

inflation, but then backslide and repeat the process in subsequent years. In sum, whenever a surge in inflation occurs, subsequent rates of inflation will probably be different—sometimes higher, sometimes lower, but different. The possibility that a high but steady rate of inflation could be fairly harmless may be an interesting intellectual concept, but it has no counterpart in reality.[3]

NOTES

1. The price of energy oil temporarily stopped rising in 1975, and so the overall rate of price increase (that is, the inflation rate) did slow down. But the inflation rate for the rest of the economy, which had risen during 1973 and 1974, did not fall very much during the 1975 recession.

2. To neutralize the effects of inflation, it would also be necessary to re-form the many provisions in the tax code under which tax burdens can change depending on the inflation rate.

3. Even a predictable and steady rate of inflation has some unavoidable costs. It is convenient to keep a significant minimum balance in a checking ac-

count—it avoids the necessity of keeping a daily watch on your bank balance, making frequent trips to the bank, or carrying out frequent transactions to avoid having checks bounce. But business bank balances don't earn interest, nor do the relatively modest balances held by the typical consumer. And so a high inflation rate makes it costly to enjoy the convenience of a reasonably sized cash balance. The purchasing power of that cash balance erodes, and the higher the inflation, the faster it erodes. This cost would exist even if inflation were completely predictable.

To: The President

From: CEA Chairman

Subject: **The Causes of Inflation and the Inflation-Unemployment Trade-off**

To appreciate the nature of the inflationary process, and why its reduction, and in some cases its prevention, usually requires a costly bout of unemployment and economic slack, we need to understand with some precision the relationship between prices, wages, productivity, and raw material costs and how changes in aggregate demand affect these elements.

PRICES, COSTS, AND PRODUCTIVITY

The prices of goods and services in a market economy respond to two kinds of influences—changes in demand and in costs. If the demand for a product rises or falls relative to the existing capacity to produce that product, its price is likely to rise or fall even if costs do not change—profit margins will expand or contract. For products sold under conditions of what economists call "perfect competition" (for example, most farm products, some standard textile products) where there are very many producers selling a standardized product, the price response will be immediate and substantial. In a modern economy, however, most goods are produced and sold by a limited number of firms, each offering a somewhat different brand name product. For these goods the price response to a change in demand is likely to be sluggish and gradual. This sluggishness of response, especially with respect to demand decreases, is a major source of economic problems for market economies. Nevertheless, prices do move, even if sluggishly, to changes in demand.

129

Prices will also change in response to changes in costs. For most firms, the two most important kinds of costs are labor costs and raw material costs. The labor cost of a product depends on two things: (1) the wages, and (2) the productivity (or efficiency) of labor, that is, the output produced per worker.[1] When wages rise, labor costs increase; when productivity rises, labor costs decrease. In industrial economies, productivity typically rises each year, spurred by advances in technology and by new investments that increase the capital available to the work force. Thus wages can rise each year without raising costs and without causing prices to rise, as long as the annual increase in wages doesn't exceed the annual increase in productivity.

If, for example, productivity grows at 3 percent a year, wages can rise 3 percent a year, while labor costs and prices stay constant. If wages rise 5 percent a year, and productivity only 3 percent, then labor costs will grow by 2 percent a year and over time price inflation will settle down at 2 percent a year. Finally, if the annual growth of productivity slows down, while wages keep rising at an unchanged rate, the growth of labor costs will speed up and the rate of inflation will increase. This phenomenon—a slowdown of productivity growth not accompanied by a slowdown in wage growth—is one of the factors that helped boost inflation in the United States and other industrial countries in the mid-1970s.

The growth of wages is principally influenced by two factors. The first is the demand for labor. If the demand for labor by business firms outstrips the supply of workers available to work at going wages, the annual growth of wages will tend to speed up. Conversely, an oversupply of workers relative to demand—as evidenced by a high unemployment rate—will slow the growth of wages. But, as in the case of prices, the response of wages to an excess supply of workers is typically sluggish; only relatively large or long-lasting periods of excess labor supply significantly slow the preexisting rate of wage increase.

The growth of wages also tends to rise or fall along with the rate of inflation in the cost of living—that is, in consumer prices. If wages have been rising at 5 percent and prices at 3 percent, then real wages, nominal wages adjusted for inflation, have been rising at 2 percent. If, for whatever reason, prices now begin to rise at, say, 4 percent annually, nominal wages will have to begin rising at 6 percent to keep the growth in real wages, which is what are really important to workers, growing at the same rate. As long as the demand for labor is unchanged, workers and employers have an interest in maintaining that growth in real wages; workers for obvious reasons, and employers to keep their labor force intact, satisfied, and productive.

Apart from labor, the second principal cost to business firms is raw materials. But, with two important exceptions, the major cost of most raw materials consists of labor costs and other raw material costs. Ultimately, changes in most raw material costs are principally traceable to changes in labor costs.

The two exceptions are very important. The first is the cost of energy. In the past two decades sudden massive changes have occurred in energy costs owing principally to actual or feared disruptions in crude oil supplies from the Persian Gulf and lesser but still important changes in prices owing to the partially effective price rigging of the OPEC cartel of foreign oil producers. The importance in the overall economy of other basic raw materials—iron ore, bauxite, copper, and so on—is small enough, or competition among producers is great enough, or enough possibilities of substituting one material for another exist, that sharp and sudden up-swings in their price, large enough to cause a serious increase in overall prices, have proved just about impossible. But oil and its derived products are such an important input into the production processes of modern nations and the possibility of conservation or of substituting other energy sources is small enough, in the short run, that even relatively modest disruptions in supply can, for a significant period, drive up the costs of producing goods and services dramatically. Thus, the 1973–75 rise in imported crude oil prices from $4.00 to $13.90 a barrel was sufficient to raise costs and prices of consumer goods directly in the U.S. economy by almost 4 percent; and the rise from $14.50 to $37.00 a barrel, which occurred from 1978 to 1981, directly raised the overall cost by some 5.5 percent. And the oil prices not only had these direct effects on prices but indirect ones as well.

The second independent source of upward pressure on costs is a rise in the price of imported goods, either raw materials or finished goods bought by American retailers. In turn, an increase in import prices can occur because prices have risen in countries from whom we import or because the exchange value of the U.S. dollar falls. (When the value of the dollar falls, American importers have to give up more dollars to purchase the marks, the yen, or the other foreign currency with which they have to pay their foreign suppliers; that of course raises the price of imports).

FIGURE 12-1. Major Elements in the Process of Inflation

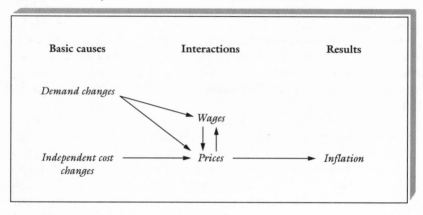

THE PROCESS OF INFLATION

We can now pull these various threads together and look at the several ways in which inflation can arise, be kept going, and also be controlled.

Figure 12-1 provides a schematic view of the various influences on inflation and on how wage and price increases interact. Keep in mind three basic factors affecting inflation: changes in demand, changes in costs arising independently of demand, and the interactions of wages with prices and prices with wages.

Demand

Let's imagine an economy running along steadily at reasonably full employment with inflation steady at a low rate and wages rising faster than prices to the extent allowed by productivity growth. If, for some reason—for example, an expansion of defense spending not matched by a tax increase and accompanied by an easy money, low-interest-rate policy by the Federal Reserve—aggregate demand rises significantly above potential GNP, many firms will find they can raise prices relative to costs and, more importantly, will begin to speed up the growth of wages as they try to expand their work force to meet the new demands and are forced to compete for scarce labor. (A shortfall of demand relative to supply will work in the opposite direction, although as noted, sluggishly.) Having speeded up the growth of wages to attract more employees, employers will of course find that their costs are rising more rapidly, and they will correspondingly increase the rate at which prices are being raised. The extra demand for labor and the availability of higher wages will have reduced the rate of unemployment below the economy's normal full-employment level, but the rate of inflation will have risen to a new level.

It doesn't stop there. Once the pace of inflation has speeded up, workers will find that the purchasing power of the extra wage increases has been dissipated by the higher inflation. If economic policymakers allow the excess demand to persist, employers will have to speed up the growth of wages even further in the competition to secure additional labor or simply to keep their labor force intact, satisfied, and productive. Another upward ratchet in wage-price spiral will occur, and the rate of inflation will rise still further. But again, *as long as the excess demand persists*, this second upward ratchet will not settle things down; workers will again find that the purchasing power of the new round of wage increases has been dissipated, and another upward ratchet of the wage-price spiral will take place. The magnitude and speed of the upward ratcheting of inflation will, at least roughly, depend on how large, relative to the size of the economy, the excess aggregate demand is.

At any time in this process, elimination of the excess demand will halt further upward ratcheting of inflation. Employers will no longer have to find additional labor to meet the extra demand nor to increase the growth of wages simply to keep their current work force intact. But inflation will now be running at the new higher level it reached at the end of the process, with unemployment rising to the point it was when the process started.

To reduce the inflation rate to where it was at the beginning, the whole process must be reversed. The economy will have to be put through a period in which aggregate demand is brought below potential GNP, and unemployment is pushed above the full employment level to produce a falling inflation.

This outline of the interaction of excess demand with wages and prices, and the adjustment of wages to prices and prices to wages is a highly simplified description of a much more complicated process. In real life, wage increases are not so tightly linked to the rate of price increases; prices do not respond in lock step with labor costs; and modest fluctuations in demand relative to supply, especially if they are thought temporary, need

Aggregate Demand and Inflation

The existence of a trade-off between inflation and unemployment does not mean that a country can permanently lower its unemployment rate at the cost of a one-time increase in its inflation rate. As long as aggregate demand is maintained significantly above potential GNP, and unemployment is kept significantly below its full-employment level, inflation will rise. Correspondingly, the maintenance of aggregate demand below potential GNP, and unemployment above the full-employment level, will result in a continuing fall in inflation.

Once the excess (or deficient) demand is eliminated, inflation will remain at the new level it had reached during the inflationary (or deflationary) process.

Thus, the trade-off referred to means that a period of excess or deficient demand, and lower or higher unemployment, moves an economy from one inflation rate to another, leaving the unemployment rate at the end roughly where it was at the beginning. An economy can operate at full employment with different inflation rates.

not trigger the full process just described. Nevertheless, the response of inflation to swings in aggregate demand above and below potential GNP can, with rough accuracy, be summarized as shown in the box. The behavior of inflation, however, may be "asymmetric." The persistent maintenance of even moderate excess demand could well keep inflation rising indefinitely. But the continuing presence of a moderately high unemployment rate is unlikely to push inflation below zero and produce a steadily growing deflation, with prices falling faster and faster. The resistance to absolute cuts in prices and wages, as opposed simply to moderating the rate of increase, is very strong.

Independent Changes in Costs

Earlier we identified three principal sources of upward cost pressures, apart from the rise in wages owing to demand pressures, that can create an inflationary problem: a slowdown in productivity growth, a large rise in energy prices, and an increase in the prices of imported goods (which in turn may occur because of foreign inflation or because of a depreciation of the exchange value of the U.S. dollar). These cost increases, combined with the interaction of wages and prices, can push the economy to a higher inflation rate even in the absence of an initially excessive aggregate demand.

Let's start with the consequences of a substantial fall in the rate of productivity growth. Imagine a fairly stable situation, with an economy at high employment but not overheated relative to its supply potential. Productivity has been growing at 3 percent a year and wages at 7 percent; labor costs and prices have consequently been rising at a 4 percent annual rate (that is, the effect on labor costs of the 7 percent annual wage increase is being reduced to 4 percent by the annual 3 percent gain in labor productivity). Real wage growth—nominal wage increases less inflation— is proceeding at 3 percent a year. Now assume that the growth of productivity falls to only 1 percent a year (which is about what happened to productivity growth in the United States after 1973). As long as nominal wage growth continues at 7 percent a year, inflation in labor costs and prices will escalate to a 6 percent annual rate—only 1 percentage point of the 7 percent gain in wages is now being offset by productivity improvements.

The problem may be even more difficult. Even if workers retain their annual 7 percent wage increases, they now find that inflation is eating up 6 percent of it; the annual growth in their real wages is only 1 percent a year compared with the 3 percent they were used to. To the extent that workers aspire to continue those real wage gains, and to the extent employers meet those aspirations—to maintain labor peace and to avoid the lower productivity that might accompany worker dissatisfaction—the 7 percent nominal wage growth will have to be raised. But that will increase the growth of labor costs still more, and inflation will ratchet up even further. As long as workers and employers keep trying to achieve the historic rate of real wage increases, inflation will keep rising. In turn, to prevent this course of events, economic policymakers will have to engineer a reduction in aggregate demand and a rise in unemployment to moderate wage growth.

A fall in the rate of productivity growth requires a slowdown in the rate of growth in real wages.[2] If workers and firms try to avoid this slowdown, upward pressure on inflation will continue, which in turn will bring on restrictive demand policies and a rise in unemployment. In the late 1970s and during much of the 1980s, unemployment in most European countries rose sharply and remained high (figure 12-2). Some economists have attributed that rise in unemployment to the failure of

FIGURE 12-2. Unemployment in the United States and Europe, 1960–90

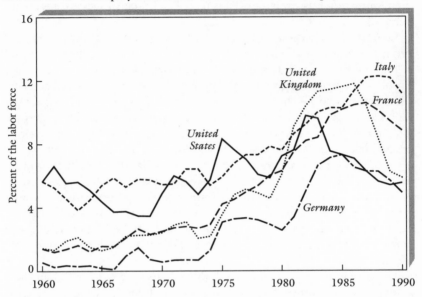

workers to accept the necessity of reducing their real wage aspirations in the face of slowing productivity growth. To avoid mounting inflation, monetary and fiscal policies had to be very restrictive for a long time. Although this explanation cannot account for all of the unemployment increase, nor for its persistence for so many years after the mid-1970s, the failure of European workers to trim real wage aspirations did contribute significantly to the problem. The failure of growth to adjust to the fall in productivity growth after 1973 also helps explain some of the rise in U.S. inflation in the mid-1970s. But apparently, U.S. workers accepted the inevitability of a slowdown in real wage growth more promptly than was the case in Europe. Although initially important, failure to make such an adjustment does not seem to have been an important factor in explaining movements in U.S. unemployment in the 1980s.

Energy Prices

Three times in the past twenty years, large increases in the price of crude oil have destabilized the American economy, leading simultaneously to

FIGURE 12-3. Inflation and Energy Prices, 1970–90

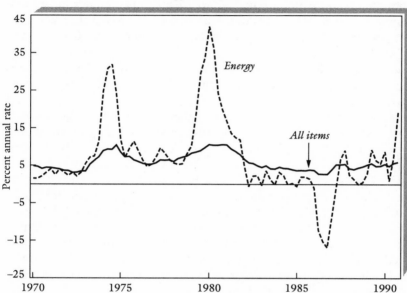

higher inflation and higher unemployment. The magnitude of the resulting energy price increases can be seen from figure 12-3. It has already
been noted why oil and its derived and related energy products are so
important to the economy. A large rise in crude oil prices has three
economic effects. Most obviously, the U.S. economy and U.S. consumers
suffer a loss in living standards since we now have to pay more for our oil
supplies. But if that were all, if a $10 a barrel rise in oil prices occurred
gradually over, say, a decade, it would be a regrettable but a less than
traumatic event, lowering the annual growth in living standards over that
period by less than 0.1 percent a year. There need be no increase in
unemployment or inflation.

If the rise is a sudden one, however, then two other effects are present.
First the increase in oil prices sets in motion recessionary forces. Because
consumers suddenly have to pay more for gasoline, heating oil, and
other energy products, they have less money available to spend on other
consumer goods; sales, production, and employment in the consumer
goods industries decline. About half of the additional sums paid out by
consumers for their oil products goes to domestic producers mainly in

Texas, Oklahoma, Alaska, and other oil-producing states. The other half goes abroad to foreign producers. Eventually most or all of these funds are respent in the United States—through higher investment and consumption in the oil-producing states and greater purchases of U.S. exports by foreign oil producers. But these increases in demand by oil producers occur more gradually than the decreases in demand by U.S. consumers. A temporary decline occurs in aggregate demand, pushing the economy toward recession.

If this were all, the problem would be manageable. The Federal Reserve could intervene temporarily with easier money, pushing down interest rates and creating additional demand in interest-sensitive industries, thereby avoiding the recession. But here, the third and final problem created by the sudden increase in oil prices rears its head. As noted earlier, the rise in oil prices pushes up the cost of living. But this direct increase in the consumer price index is not the problem; it would simply be a one-time jump in the price level, not a higher continuing rate of inflation. However, the initial increase in the consumer price level will get incorporated, in part at least, into higher wage settlements, which in turn will lead to further price increases in sectors outside of energy, and so generate a new and higher level of inflation.

The only means available to economic policymakers to insure that the initial, oil-induced, price increase does not get reflected in higher wages, and hence in a new wage-price spiral, is to allow some or all of the recessionary forces to prevail, using the rising unemployment as a damper on wage increases. That of course is painful and unpopular. And so during the major oil price shocks of the 1970s, in Europe and the United States, we had some of both—higher inflation and higher unemployment.

In the end there is no option for workers but to accept the lower real wages that the higher oil prices force on society. If they are accepted quickly, without any effort to offset them with higher money wages, the only pain will be the fall in real wages. But if the growth of money wages is speeded up, in an effort to avoid the reduction in real wages, then the adjustment process will include some period of higher unemployment and additional inflation. In the first two oil shocks of 1974 and 1979–81, the growth of money wages did rise here and abroad, as workers and their employers sought to avoid some of the reduction in real wages. Inflation rose, and eventually the central banks of all countries were forced to crack down with very restrictive monetary policies, leading to the severe recession of 1981–82. During the run-up in oil prices in the last half of 1990, after the Iraqi invasion of Kuwait, the growth of money wages did not accelerate. And once the outbreak of the war in January 1991 demonstrated that Saddam Hussein could not interrupt the supply of oil out of the Persian Gulf, oil prices fell to their earlier level. We do not know what would have happened to wage inflation had this last rise in oil prices been permanent.

A fall in the price of oil of course works in a benign direction for oil-importing countries, tending to raise aggregate demand and reduce inflationary pressures.

Since it is the disruption accompanying sudden large oil price increases, not the long-term effect on living standards, which causes the most serious problems to the major oil-consuming countries, the accumulation of a large strategic oil stockpile makes a lot of sense. If the major oil-using countries have a large stockpile and an agreed-on strategy of gradual releases in case of an interruption in Middle East oil supplies, the simultaneous but temporary recessionary and inflationary effects of the oil shock can be greatly moderated. In the 1980s the United States, Japan, and Germany had together acquired a governmentally owned stockpile of more than 900 million barrels of crude oil, enough to replace more than a 20 percent cut in OPEC production for almost half a year. Though the three governments seemed slow in using the stockpile to meet the run-up in oil prices, which occurred when Iraq invaded Kuwait, some releases were finally made, and the mere existence of the stockpile probably helped hold down prices. An accumulation of a still larger stockpile by all of the OECD countries would be good insurance against yet another repeat of an oil-induced recession with inflation.

Because it simultaneously sets in motion both recessionary and inflationary forces, a sudden disruption of oil supplies accompanied by a large run-up in oil prices is virtually impossible for economic policymakers to handle. Measures that ease the recessionary problem exacerbate the inflation problem, and vice versa. This means that U.S. policymakers, in concert with other major oil-consuming nations, have a vital stake in avoiding such disruptions. At the present time no one country, not even Saudi Arabia, controls a large enough share of the world's oil supplies that it can exercise monopoly power over world oil supplies; no one country, through cutting its production, can raise the world price of oil enough to increase its revenues. But if any one country could directly or indirectly dictate oil supply decisions for all of the Persian Gulf, it would acquire such power. It should be U.S. policy to prevent any one country from acquiring that power.

Import Prices

A sharp rise in prices of imported goods has the potential of setting off a rise in inflation. The increase in import prices could come from a substantial and widespread inflation originating abroad, unaccompanied by any change in the exchange rate for the dollar. That would translate into a big jump in the prices of goods we import. Alternatively, and more likely, import prices could rise because of a depreciation in the value of the U.S. dollar relative to the currencies of U.S. trading partners, which would make it more expensive for U.S. importers to buy imported goods. In either case, just as would happen if oil prices rose, some fraction of the rise in import prices would threaten to get into wage settlements, turning a one-time jump in the price level into a new and more rapid wage-price spiral. And, unlike the case of an increase in oil prices, an upsurge in foreign inflation or a depreciation of the dollar would, after a time, boost aggregate demand and increase the probability that the import price increases would be passed on into higher wage settlements. Restrictive monetary or fiscal policy would have to work even harder to squelch the problem of inflation. A fall in foreign inflation or an appreciation of the dollar will of course work in the opposite direction, as the lower import prices lead to wage moderation.

The Experience of the 1970s and the Reversal in the 1980s

Economic history during much of the past twenty years was dominated by the direct and indirect effects of cost inflation. In the 1970s the economy was staggered by the inflationary effects stemming from a large slowdown in productivity growth, two large oil shocks (1974 and 1979–81), a big run-up in food prices in 1972–74 and 1978–79, and an uneven but serious depreciation in the exchange value of the dollar during the five years after exchange rates were freed in 1973. Inflation (in consumer goods prices) rose from 4.6 percent in 1970 to almost 11 percent in 1980. Princeton economist Alan S. Blinder, in a study of the rise in inflation during those years, attributes the bulk of it to the direct and indirect effects of cost shocks, and especially food and oil price increases.[3]

Just the opposite occurred in the early 1980s. As noted in memo 10, the large rise in interest rates accompanying the huge U.S. budget deficits, however harmful on most grounds, made dollar securities an attractive investment for foreigners, and as a result, the overseas exchange value of the U.S. dollar soared. After 1981 the price of oil stabilized and in 1985 fell precipitously. The disinflation started by the tight money and the recession of 1982 was helped along substantially by this unwinding of the cost increases of the 1970s induced by oil shocks and depreciation of exchange rates.

NOTES

1. As will be discussed in part 3, the productivity of labor depends on a host of factors, including not only the skills, education, and attitudes of the work force but also the quantity and quality of the capital it works with, the state of technology, the abilities of management, and many other conditions. Although we call the efficiency with which labor operates labor productivity, that does not imply that the quality of labor alone is what determines labor productivity.

2. Employers could for a while pay the extra wages out of their profits and not increase the rate of price inflation. But without a fall in aggregate demand they are unlikely to do so, and even if they did, profit margins are not high enough to allow more than a temporary postponement of the problem. In the end, workers would still have to settle for a lower growth in real wages.

3. Alan S. Blinder, "The Anatomy of Double-Digit Inflation in the 1970s," in Robert E. Hall, ed., *Inflation: Causes and Effects* (University of Chicago Press, 1982), pp. 261–82.

To: The President

From: CEA Chairman

Subject: **The Stubbornness of Inflation
          and Its Consequences**

Once inflation has gotten under way, it is devilishly hard and very painful to expunge. For one thing, wages and most prices do not respond sensitively to changes in the demand for goods or labor. When the markets weaken, firms are not quick to shave margins and reduce prices relative to costs. And it takes a fairly large and sustained fall in the demand for labor and a considerable rise in unemployment to moderate the ongoing rate of wage increases. Consequently, whenever inflation gets out of hand and rises to a new level, it takes a substantial bout of reduced demand, economic slack, and unemployment to pull it down again. Instead of resulting in a fall in wage and price inflation, with little loss of output and employment, the drop in aggregate demand, initially at least, depresses inflation very little and output a lot. Even though a proportional reduction in the growth of wages and prices would harm neither workers nor firms, the reduction in inflation is resisted.

THE SLUGGISHNESS OF INFLATION
AND THE SACRIFICE RATIO

Imagine an economy in which inflation was running at 7 percent a year. Suppose, contrary to fact, that a 5 percent reduction in the value of aggregate spending below the level of potential GNP, maintained for one year, would produce a 4 percent reduction in the growth of prices and wages. Since, of the 5 percent drop in aggregate spending, 4 percent would occur because of lower inflation, only 1 percent would represent a drop in real purchases and production. Inflation could be lowered from 7 to 3 percent in a year at a cost of only 1 percent in lost output. (And that 1 percent drop in output would produce a rise in unemployment of only 0.3 to 0.4 percent.) The sacrifice ratio—the ratio of the loss of output to the drop in inflation—would be very small, about 1 to 4.

But suppose, in a situation closer to reality, that the response of prices and wages to a drop in demand and spending was much more sluggish, so that a 5 percent reduction in demand below potential GNP for one year would yield only a 1 percent moderation in the growth of wages and prices and a 4 percent fall in output. Then it would take four years of output remaining at 4 percent below potential for inflation to fall from 7 to 3 percent. The sacrifice ratio would be 4 to 1. And that would mean four years of extra unemployment amounting to about 1.5 percent of the labor force.

How large in fact is the output and employment cost of disinflation and is it relatively stable? Professor Robert Gordon of Northwestern University conducted several studies during the 1980s to measure the cost.[1] Early in the decade his analysis of the prior three decades of economic history in the United States led him to conclude that a permanent reduction of 1 percentage point in the inflation rate "costs" about 6 percentage points of lost output; to reduce inflation by 1 percentage point, the economy must be run for one year at 6 percent below potential, or three years at 2 percent below, or any other combination of years and economic slack that equals 6; the sacrifice ratio is about 6 to 1. In a later study, he concluded that reduction in inflation and the loss of output during and subsequent to the recession of 1981–82 followed this pattern, allowing for the favorable effects of the appreciation of the dollar and the collapse of oil prices in 1985.[2] However, one group of economists, the "flexible price, rational expectations" school, strongly disagree with these conclusions, and indeed argue that there is no inevitable "trade-off" between changes in inflation and unemployment.

REAL WAGE STICKINESS

The sluggishness of the wage response to changes in aggregate demand shows up in another way. Whenever consumer prices jump—say because of some cost increase such as a rise in oil prices or a falloff in productivity— workers and firms attempt to keep the real value of wages from falling by increasing money wages and thus, as described above, starting a new round of inflation. And here also, it takes a big dose of reduced demand and higher unemployment to moderate the wage increases. When government policymakers attempt to head off the new threat of inflation by restricting aggregate demand, the initial reduction in real wage demands is relatively small, and so again the demand restraint necessary to avoid a cost-based inflation results in a period of below-normal output and employment.

If the growth of money wages and prices responded sensitively to changes in demand, and if real wage aspirations were similarly sensitive to demand changes, the control of inflation would be far less difficult for policymakers, at least economically. Mistakes might be made; a boom might be allowed to get out of hand by a policy of excessively easy money so that inflation began to rise sharply. But a modest application of demand restraint would quickly eliminate the unwanted inflation at small cost in output and employment.

Even more important, it would be possible to avoid the inflationary consequences of large oil shocks while simultaneously offsetting, through easy money or expansive fiscal policy, most of its recessionary effects. It would take only a small dose of recessionary medicine to get workers to swallow the reductions in real wages that an oil price rise or other large cost increase necessitates. The villain in the piece, then, which causes all the trouble for governments trying to stabilize the economy, is the sluggish adjustment of wages and prices.

Wages and prices respond only slowly to changes in demand in either direction. They are slow to fall when demand declines, but they are also slow to rise when demand increases. The United States and other major industrial countries do not have a hair-trigger inflation process; inflation does not start to rise sharply with the appearance of small amounts of excess demand. The chief problem posed by inflation is not so much that it starts easily, but that once started, it is very costly to reverse. Sometimes government policymakers are tempted to let inflation creep up slowly rather than impose the unpopular medicine of higher interest rates or budget restraint needed to curb economic overheating. They should resist the temptation. The later cost of reversing a series of small upward movements will be substantial.

THE CAUSES OF WAGE AND PRICE STICKINESS

The term "wage and price stickiness" conveys the idea that in response to changes in demand conditions, wages and most prices are not completely rigid; they do adjust but only slowly and reluctantly and with far less speed than in those few industries, for example, agriculture, which are characterized by thousands of producers and completely competitive conditions. Stickiness is easily observable. Wages are the most obvious example. In a recession, millions of additional workers are unemployed, but employers, while moderating wage increases to some extent, do not start paring wages and bringing in the unemployed to take the place of those who refuse to accept wage cuts. One can observe stickiness in most prices as well—the price of newspapers, for example, is virtually never cut, and even when auto firms offer discounts during a sales slump, they never do so in the amounts necessary to get their plants back to prerecession production.

While stickiness can be taken for granted, economists have for many years tried to find an answer to the question of why wages and prices are sticky, and in particular how to explain stickiness in light of the concept of rational behavior by workers and employers.[3] The problem is especially important for wages; if wages were flexible, small changes in demand could achieve large gains in lower inflation even if the markup of prices on costs remained constant. Clearly, many of the unemployed, especially those who had been unemployed for a long time, would be willing to replace currently employed workers at a significantly lower wage. Why don't employers take advantage of this willingness and use the threat of hiring the unemployed to wring wage concessions from their workers—which would allow them to reduce prices and expand sales, output, and employment?

On the surface there are two kinds of wage stickiness to explain: first, when demand falls, why don't wages and prices fall together? No reduction in real wages is required, only that both wages and prices fall, leaving workers and firms in the same relative position. Second, why won't workers and their employers allow real wages to be eroded promptly and significantly when faced with a reduction in the demand for labor? If they would do so, then the economy could absorb cost-raising price increases without the need for a period of reduced output and employment.

INDEXING WAGES: WHY THAT'S NOT THE ANSWER

The first kind of wage stickiness can be likened to the situation at a football game. When everybody is standing, no single person or small group can see when sitting down. If only everybody would sit down, everyone would have the same ability to see the ball game; everybody would be better off. Similarly, for wages, if all wages and prices were cut simultaneously and proportionately, nobody's relative position would change. Inflation could quickly be brought down without a rise in unemployment, and everybody would be better off. But without some coordinator, any one firm's decision to cut wages looks to that firm and its workers like a loss in real wages not only absolutely but relative to the wages of other workers.

Suppose wages were fully indexed to prices so that every 1 percent change in prices would automatically trigger an equal change in wages. In some cases that would be a partial help; any reductions in the rate of inflation would automatically be transformed into wage moderation. If prices were somewhat sticky, and if the wage indexing took place infrequently, say once a year, disinflation, though not costless, would be less painful than under current arrangements. But with full indexing, the economy would be out of the frying pan and into the fire. Whenever any independent cost increase took place, such as a rise in oil prices, the rise would be fully and automatically reflected in higher wage increases, and then into further price increases as the higher wage costs were passed along, leading to further wage increases, and so on into a new wage-price spiral. And that would require even stiffer demand restrictions. In 1979 through 1982, Brazil, with its highly indexed wage system, was devastated by the induced effects of the large oil price increase, resulting in a huge wage-price spiral. In the U.S. economy, automatic cost-of-living clauses have often been incorporated into union contracts. But full indexing was seldom provided (that is, a rise in the consumer price index was only partially offset by an automatic wage increase), and in any event indexed union contracts never covered more than a fairly modest proportion of the U.S. labor force.

WHY DON'T WAGE AND PRICE INCREASES MODERATE PROMPTLY WHEN UNEMPLOYMENT RISES?

The question then becomes why, in response to actual or threatened unemployment, wage settlements in individual firms aren't more flexible in response to changes in the demand facing that firm. This question is still the subject of much research and heated debate in the economics profession, and a complete discussion would be far beyond this memo. But several important aspects of the answer can be addressed. In the first place, economic research has only recently begun to appreciate the striking prevalence of continuity of association between workers and firms, and between customers and suppliers. While young people typically switch jobs several times before finding a niche, the typical full-time job for mature workers lasts a surprisingly long time. Professor Robert E. Hall has calculated that 50 percent of the work done in the United States is performed by workers who can expect to stay at least fifteen years in their job, and if one confines attention to adult male workers, 50 percent of the work is done on jobs that last twenty-five years.[4]

There is obviously a tremendous gain to worker and firm for continuity of association. Screening and training workers is costly, and in many jobs, skills are acquired that are peculiar to the particular firm. It's hard to detect shirking at work, or to know in advance who is likely to be a frequent absentee and who is not. A firm with a large core of workers whose attitudes and abilities have been tested by long experience can save a great deal in costs. Workers who pass the test of experience are worth more than a replacement about whom much less is known; long-time workers can be paid more—seniority premiums. Workers learn about a firm and about the characteristics of their fellow workers; and to a certain extent, like attracts like through word-of-mouth referrals. Severing that connection is to lose those advantages. In Japan, with "lifetime" employment arrangements for many (though not all) workers, continuity of association has been carried further than in the United States, and in Europe job tenure is also longer than in the United States. Nevertheless, in the United States as elsewhere, the labor market has developed over the years to foster and reward long-term employment with a particular firm. Simple-minded slogans to the contrary, smart employers have never treated workers, including blue-collar workers, as homogenous and interchangeable commodities, to be hired and discarded indiscriminately. And the growing skill content of jobs has undoubtedly strengthened the advantages of continuity over the past half-century.

Besides macroeconomic fluctuations, individual firms face all kinds of vicissitudes and fluctuations in markets, tastes, technologies, competition, and the like. Nevertheless, it makes no economic sense for firms to cut wages sharply whenever the situation facing the firm becomes temporarily worse. Nor do workers quit to gain a slight wage advantage in another firm. Wages do sometimes have to change in particular firms relative to other firms in order to deal with long-term alterations in the conditions facing the firm. But for eminently sound reasons grounded in rational self-interest, wage changes are far more gradual and wages are far stickier than would be the case if worker-firm relationships were the impersonal and ephemeral connection envisaged in simple texts.

To an important extent, therefore, the wage stickiness that is so troublesome from a macroeconomic standpoint is a by-product of relationships that are reasonably efficient when viewed from the microeconomic standpoint of an individual firm. In a decentralized market economy, an individual firm responds very slowly and cautiously with wage changes to temporary fluctuations in its demand and sales relative to those of other firms. And that is a desirable economic arrangement for society. But when the society as a whole is trying to reduce an existing inflation or to prevent a cost increase from creating a new inflation, it wants a prompt and sizable response in reduced wage increases. Unfortunately, society has to send the same signal to individual firms—a drop in demand and sales. The economy gets the right response at the wrong time—wage stickiness, leading in turn to a loss of output and employment.

A somewhat similar analysis can be made about the stickiness of prices, stressing the disadvantages to consumers of having to cope with the large and frequent price changes that would occur if firms literally changed their prices to get the maximum advantage or to minimize the loss from increases and decreases in demand. When buying a car or taking an airplane trip, it is good for the consumer to be able to bargain for discounts or take advantage of a various prices and terms of sale. Even here some standardization and continuity of terms from month to month is helpful. But suppose all purchases had to be made by bargaining and auctionlike procedures to reflect changes in demand-supply conditions? Suppose the prices at the supermarket were changed hourly to reflect the demand at the time? Or what if the prices of hotel rooms were changed daily to reflect the state of occupancy? What would be the possible range of prices for a left front brakeshoe on a 1985 Chevrolet in Peoria, Illinois, on a Saturday morning if prices were continually set in an auction-type market to reflect the current state of demand?[5] For prices, as for wages, daily life is made easier and more efficient by some stickiness in prices.

A further reason for the stickiness of wages stressed by some economists and labor specialists is that workers are likely to respond to what they perceive as a cut in their wages relative to other workers with dissatisfaction that takes the form of lower productivity. The firm may lose through a drop in efficiency any cost saving from the wage cut. In a general disinflationary cut in demand, it may be true that eventually everyone shares in the reduction in the money wage increase and suffers no loss of real wages. But in a decentralized market system, that is not likely to be fully apparent to groups of workers as the wage cuts occur firm by firm.

In sum, the stickiness of wages and prices in response to changes in demand, which causes such problems for the economy in light of controlling inflation, essentially stems from labor market practices and institutions that represent an efficient and desirable way for firms and workers to behave.

THE "RATIONAL EXPECTATIONS" VIEW OF INFLATION

One group of economists, prominent in the 1970s and 1980s, holds a much different view of the inflation process. Essentially this group argues that wages (and prices) are quite flexible in response to perceived changes in demand. In this view, if people are convinced that aggregate demand is going to fall in the near-term future, they will respond with significant wage and price moderation, believing that other firms and workers will be doing the same thing.

Workers and firms, they argue, make their decisions about wage settlements on the basis of fully rational forecasts of future events; they look to the future, taking into account all the information available, including the lessons of experience. In particular, they forecast what they think the actions of the Federal Reserve and other government institutions are going to be. And here lies the nub of the problem, according to the proponents of this view. Firms and workers have learned from postwar history, they say, that the government quickly moves to bail out the economy once it looks as if recession will occur and is likely to finance an employment-creating boom with additional money and credit. Consequently, workers and firms do not really believe that any demand restraint will last, and they set prices and wages accordingly. What looks like sticky wages and prices is simply the rational response of individuals and firms to their own rational forecast that whatever the government says, it will, in the end, accommodate the failure to moderate wages and prices with the appropriate dose of additional money and credit. Why, then, moderate wage and price behavior?

The lack of credibility of aggregate demand restraint produces the apparent stickiness of wages and prices and generates the high "sacrifice ratio." If only workers and firms could be convinced that the government would not finance inflationary behavior—that is, the failure to moderate wage and price increases—the problem would disappear. Wages and prices would moderate in the face of credible demand restraint; workers would absorb the inevitable loss of purchasing power brought about by a large oil price increase without trying to recoup with higher money wages. And some politicians carried the rational expectations approach well beyond what the economic theorists had in mind. As David Stockman described the views of his colleagues in the administration during the early 1980s, if there were established a determinedly restrictive monetary policy, "the inflation premium would melt away like the morning mist."[6]

The economists of the rational expectations school do not believe that the government can be trusted to resist the temptations of easy money and credit. And hence many of them advocate that monetary policy should be guided not by the discretionary decisions of the Federal Reserve but by a firm rule under which the Federal Reserve would maintain a constant growth of the money supply, regardless of circumstance.

When it comes to financial markets, rational expectations about future events, including expectations about future government policy, greatly help to explain the prices of stocks, bonds, and the like, which—unlike the prices of most goods and services—are highly flexible. Moreover, expectations about the future also influence wage and price decisions in the markets for goods and services. But that influence is much less strong than in financial markets and in the economic models of the rational expectations theorists. To start with, individual prices and wages do not behave with the flexibility of the Chicago wheat pit—they are truly sticky, and that stickiness is not an irrational aberration but, as we have seen, is fully consistent with rational behavior in a world where continuity of relationships is very important. Though in a general disinflation, workers and firms wouldn't lose from a universal and proportional moderation of wage and price increases, wage decisions are still made firm by firm. Even if a policy of demand restraint announced by the government were fully believable, individual groups of workers and their employers are not going to abandon their normal caution in making wage reductions because they forecast that everyone else will also forecast a general disinflation and match their move. Indeed they would be irrational to believe that everybody's forecasts and wage response would be the same, given that even among the best-trained, most objective, and fully rational individuals, the future remains murky and forecasts often vary widely.

The evidence of history is not friendly to this rational expectations view of inflation. Several studies have shown, for example, that in the nineteenth century, when there was no countercyclical government monetary policy and no "bailout" from recession, prices and wages even then moved sluggishly in response to cyclical changes in aggregate spending. And in 1982, when there seemed to be widespread acceptance of the fact that the Federal Reserve would stick by its guns in disinflating the economy, it still took the largest recession and the highest unemployment of the postwar period to do it.

The rational expectations approach has performed an important service in reminding economists that expectations play a significant role in influencing wage and price decisions, and that the credibility of the government's announced policy stance can help determine how sensitively wages and prices will respond to demand restraint.[7] But the main picture that emerged in these last three memos on inflation still remains valid:

> Wages and prices respond sluggishly to changes in aggregate demand. Although this means that inflation is not on a hair trigger, the sacrifice ratio is high. Inflation does not surge sharply in response to moderate overheating in the economy. But it takes a disturbingly large amount of unemployment and output loss to achieve disinflation or to suppress the inflationary potential of a large independent cost increase.

NOTES

1. See, for example, Robert J. Gordon and Stephen R. King, "The Output Cost of Disinflation in Traditional and Vector Autoregressive Models," *Brookings Papers on Economic Activity* 1: 1982, pp. 205–42. (Hereafter *BPEA*.)

2. Robert J. Gordon, "The Phillips Curve Now and Then," Working Paper 3393 (Cambridge, Mass.: National Bureau of Economic Research, June 1990), p. 17, n.5.

3. As I have already noted, much of economic theory is built around the use of the concept of the rational maximizing individual to explain economic behavior. Economists tend to be very reluctant to accept at face value explanations for economic behavior that appear to be inconsistent with rational maximizing behavior. One of the reasons that the Keynesian approach to macroeconomics lost so many adherents in the 1970s was that it had for years simply assumed wages and prices to be sticky without offering any explanation that could be made consistent with the body of microeconomic theory which dealt with the behavior of firms and workers and was based on the assumption of rational maximizing behavior.

4. Robert E. Hall, "Employment Fluctuations and Wage Rigidity." *BPEA* 1: 1980, pp. 90–123.

5. This example is adapted from the one given by Robert J. Gordon, "A Century of Evidence on Wage and Price Stickiness in the United States, the United Kingdom, and Japan," in James Tobin, ed., *Macroeconomics: Prices and Quantities* (Brookings, 1983), pp. 85–133, esp. p. 113.

6. William Greider, "The Education of David Stockman," *Atlantic Monthly*, December 1981, pp. 27–54.

7. Indeed it has been a most useful contribution to economic theory to have worked out, as the rational expectations theorists have done, the full implications of how the economy would behave *if* wages and prices were highly flexible and *if* wage and price setters based their decisions on fully "rational" expectations of the future. By contrasting actual economic outcomes and economic behavior with what is predicted by these models we can begin to isolate exactly what it is about price and wage decisions and expectations formation that makes the real world behave the way it does.

14

To: The President

From: CEA Chairman

Subject: **Unemployment: Who, How Long, Why**

Earlier memos have referred to the concept of full employment. But how would we know full employment if we saw it? As figure 14-1 shows, the unemployment rate in the United States, even in years of prosperity, has seldom fallen below 4 to 4.5 percent, and when it did for several years during the Vietnam War, inflation started rising steadily. Perhaps more disturbing, even a cursory look at figure 14-1 shows that unemployment rose during most of the 1970s and early 1980s, with unemployment higher at each successive recession and recovery (until the last few years of the 1980s). Do these figures mean that the amount of unemployment consistent with full employment has grown over time and if so, why? And who are the unemployed that remain even in times of prosperity? What proportion do not represent a serious social problem, being young people entering and wives newly returning to the labor force, unemployed for short periods as they seek the job they want? At the other extreme, what proportion are family breadwinners out of work for long periods, whose inability to find a job means real social distress and economic loss?

This first of two memos on unemployment sketches a picture of the nature of unemployment; who the unemployed are; how evenly or unevenly unemployment is distributed among various groups by age, sex, race, occupation; how many people are short-term unemployed, how many long term; how many are engaged in a productive job search and how many cannot find jobs even at lower wages. The second memo deals with the more difficult issue of determining how high the full-

FIGURE 14-1. The U.S. Unemployment Rate, 1948–91

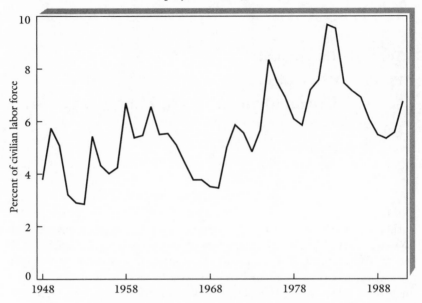

employment level of unemployment is—a most important fact for economic policymakers to be aware of.

DEFINITIONS

The Census Bureau undertakes a monthly survey of some **68,000** households from which data on employment and unemployment are collected and published by the Bureau of Labor Statistics (BLS). According to the official definition, a person is unemployed if he or she is not employed during the week of the survey but tried during the past month to find a job and was available for work during the survey week. To be defined as unemployed, a person cannot just say that he or she has been looking for work; the person must report specific actions (such as applying to an employer).

Like any single characterization of a complex phenomenon, this definition can be criticized as being too tight and too loose. On the one hand, a person who quit a job a week ago and finds a better one the next week

TABLE 14-1. Alternative Measures of Unemployment, Third Quarter, 1990

Measure	Unemployment rate (percent)
Persons unemployed 15 weeks or longer	1.3
Unemployed persons 25 years or over	4.4
Total unemployed (official measure)	5.6
Full-time jobseekers + 1/2 part time + 1/2 persons working part time who want full-time jobs + discouraged workers	8.3

is counted, during the week of unemployment, equally with someone who has been trying to find work for six months. On the other hand, a person who has worked only part time and would like to find full-time work is counted as employed. Even more important, many workers, after a long period of a fruitless job search, stop searching at least for a while. These "discouraged workers," however, are not counted as unemployed but are classified as "out of the labor force," the same category as full-time housewives or students.

Table 14-1 shows several different possible measures of unemployment for the third quarter of 1990, a period in which unemployment was just beginning to increase after a long period of relative prosperity and high employment. Some 7 million people, 5.5 percent of the labor force, were unemployed. But only 1.1 percent of the labor force had, at the time of the survey, been unemployed for fifteen weeks or more (although that is a deceptively small number; some of those workers would wait a long time before finding jobs). And young people accounted for a large fraction of this short-term unemployment. Many of them were, as is especially true of the U.S. economy, moving from job to job to find their niche in the labor force. The unemployment rates for workers twenty-five years of age and older was a good bit lower than the total, at 4.4 percent. However, many people had been put on part-time work by their employers because of slack work, or they were otherwise working part time because they couldn't find full-time jobs. And some 800,000 discouraged workers dropped out of the labor force. Adding these categories to the official numbers raises the total unemployment rate to only a shade below 8 percent of the labor force.

CHARACTERISTICS OF THE UNEMPLOYED

The unemployment rates normally reported are a snapshot in time. They show what proportion of the labor force is unemployed at a particular moment—technically during the week in which the monthly sample survey is taken. The unemployment rate quoted for a year is the average monthly value for that year. But the number of people who are unemployed at some time or the other during the year is a much higher number. Thus, in 1990, the average unemployment rate was 5.5 percent. But 14.7 percent of the labor force were unemployed at some time during that year. Many people who are unemployed at any one moment find jobs or drop out of the labor force fairly quickly. Of the 14.7 percent who experienced some unemployment during 1990, almost half were unemployed twelve weeks or less. But one-third had two or more spells of unemployment, and one out of seven was unemployed three times or more. In short, during any extended period, for example, a year, the fraction of the labor force experiencing some unemployment is much higher than indicated by the widely cited average unemployment rate. For most people, however, unemployment lasts only a relatively short time.

The average unemployment rate is unevenly distributed among different demographic groups in the population. Some of the big differences are shown in table 14-2. As already mentioned, young people have much higher unemployment rates than older people, partly because young people, even more so in the United States than in Europe, move from job to job during their early years in the labor force, trying to better themselves. Typically they spend some time between jobs. Unemployment among black teenagers, however, is two to two and a half times that of their white counterparts, indicating that even in reasonably good times, something more is at work than voluntary unemployment during the normal job search.

Several decades ago, female unemployment was typically about 1 percentage point above male unemployment, but in recent years rates have been approximately the same. Black unemployment has been higher than white unemployment throughout the postwar period, and because of discouraged workers, the situation may be worse than this statistic suggests. Finally, the higher the skill content and professional status of an occupation, the lower its unemployment rate.

Only during the Second World War and the Vietnam War, when the

TABLE 14-2. Selected Characteristics of the Unemployed,
October 1990

	Characteristic	Unemployed rate (percent)
Age	16–19	16.2
	20–24	9.6
	25 +	4.4
Sex	Male	5.7
	Female	5.6
Race	White	4.9
	Black	11.8
	(Black aged 16–19)	(31.8)
Occupation[a]	Managerial and professional	2.2
	Technical, sales, admin.	4.3
	Craft, repair	6.5
	Operators and laborers	8.0

a. Not seasonally adjusted.

economy was stretched drum tight and employers were short of labor everywhere, was the black unemployment rate pushed down closer to the white one. There is nothing more effective than a large excess demand to open up opportunities for those workers at the bottom of the labor market. Unfortunately, we do not know how to run the economy in such a superheated way without generating accelerating inflation or regimenting it as we did temporarily during the Second World War. And although a regimented economy can probably be made for a time to produce vast quantities of standard goods, it will not generate innovation and progress nor can it respond sensitively to changing consumer needs and tastes.

THE UNEVEN DISTRIBUTION OF UNEMPLOYMENT

As already mentioned, the typical spell of unemployment is short. In the BLS surveys, the average length of time people report they have been out of work is close to two months. But paradoxically, most of the nation's unemployment is suffered by people who can expect to be unemployed for a relatively long period of time. How can this be possible? I'll use an example. Imagine an economy in which each January one person starts a long, twelve-month spell of unemployment. And each month one person starts a short spell of unemployment, finding a job at the beginning of the next month and being replaced on the unemployment rolls by another person with a similar one-month's spell of joblessness. Each month the BLS would report two people unemployed, one short term and one long term. Over a year, however, there would be a ratio of twelve short spells to one long spell. The average spell of unemployment—averaging together the twelve one-month spells and the one twelve-month spell—would be a little less than two months. Yet half of the time spent in unemployment in this economy would come from the one unfortunate person who remained out of work for twelve months.

The real world is not so far from this imaginary economy. In a well-known 1979 paper, Harvard Professors Kim B. Clark and Lawrence H. Summers demonstrated that the average completed spell of unemployment in 1974 was only 1.9 months—most spells of unemployment are indeed short.[1] But they estimated that 42 percent of the unemployment was suffered by people who could expect to be out of work for six months or more. Further, they pointed out that an important fraction of the unemployed do not leave unemployment for another job—many of them become discouraged by their long fruitless search. If these "out-of-the-labor force" people are also counted as unemployed, then it turns out that 67 percent of the time spent in unemployment in the country is accounted for by those out of work for six months or more, and over 40 percent by unemployment lasting forty weeks or more. Later research suggests that something like two-thirds of the *increase* in joblessness that was evident in figure 14-1 is concentrated among those with unemployment lasting more than six months.

In sum, most spells of unemployment suffered by American workers are short ones, typically arising as those people newly entering the labor force or laid off from their jobs search for and find work relatively quickly. And many of these short spells of unemployment are accounted for by young people trying to find the long-term job that suits them. Nevertheless, even in relatively good times, a very sizable fraction of the time lost to unemployment in the United States does not represent a relatively benign and even efficient search for the right job, but stems from lengthy periods of economically wasteful and socially distressful joblessness.[2]

In the past fifteen years, joblessness has become increasingly concentrated among that part of the labor force with low skills and education.

Chinhui Juhn, Kevin M. Murphy, and Robert H. Topel have estimated that the lowest paid 10 percent of male workers (who had some work experience) spent on average 31 percent of the time out of work in 1987–88 compared with 15 percent in 1967–69.[3] Among the next lowest paid 10 percent, joblessness rose from 8 to 21 percent over the same twenty-year period. But among the top 40 percent of the work force, ranked by pay, the jobless rate stayed virtually the same, at 5 percent. Later I will discuss how these facts are related to evidence about the deterioration in the quality of American elementary and secondary education, and the consequences for American productivity and growth.

NOTES

1. Kim B. Clark and Lawrence H. Summers, "Labor Market Dynamics and Unemployment: A Reconsideration," *Brookings Papers on Economic Activity* 1:1979, pp. 12–60. (Hereafter *BPEA*.) The example in the prior paragraph was adapted from one in this paper.

2. In most large European countries during the 1980s and at the present time, not only is the average rate of unemployment higher than in the United States, but the fraction of unemployment accounted for by relatively long-term joblessness is much greater than it is here.

3. Chinhui Juhn, Kevin M. Murphy, and Robert H. Topel, "Why Has the Natural Rate of Unemployment Increased Over Time?" *BPEA* 2:1991, pp. 75–126.

To: The President

FROM: CEA Chairman

SUBJECT: **The Full-Employment Level
          of Unemployment**

Full employment is the minimum rate to which unemployment can be pushed without creating an excess demand for labor and setting off a continuing rise in wage and price inflation. That is perhaps the most useful definition. Economists have given this level of unemployment a mouth-twisting title, "the nonaccelerating inflation rate of unemployment" (the NAIRU).

There is a problem with this definition. As noted in memo 11, when a large independent jump in costs occurs, for example, a major surge in oil prices, economic policymakers must keep the initial rise in prices from setting off a new wage-price spiral. The only way they can do so is by temporarily creating additional economic slack and unemployment. If one defines full employment simply as the level of unemployment necessary to keep inflation from rising, one would have to say that the NAIRU, or the full-employment level of unemployment, has suddenly risen. But that would be misleading. Better, therefore, to define full employment as the minimum noninflationary level to which unemployment can be pushed in periods not marked by major independent cost increases. If unemployment is greater than this minimum, an expansion of spending and aggregate demand for goods and labor can fruitfully be set in motion, lowering unemployment without leading to continuing inflation pressures. But if unemployment has already been pushed to the full-employment level, then attempts to lower it by further increases in demand will be inflationary.

WHY SHOULDN'T FULL EMPLOYMENT BE ZERO UNEMPLOYMENT?

Modest unemployment is not only unavoidable, it is the consequence of beneficial activities. Young people seeking their first job or switching jobs to better themselves need time to search for the best position they can find. Housewives returning to the labor force after a lengthy absence during early child-rearing years may spend some time finding the job they want, even in the healthiest labor market. And in any dynamic economy, where patterns of production continually alter to meet changing consumer preferences or to exploit new technologies, some jobs are constantly being destroyed while others are being created, and often the new jobs are at different firms than the ones where the jobs were destroyed. It takes time for the displaced workers from the old jobs to match up with the newly created job vacancies. Sometimes a new job can be located before the old one disappears, but often not. It is better for the worker and the economy that displaced workers take at least a reasonable time to seek out the most advantageous niche for themselves. National productivity will be higher if they do. That is one reason why a reasonable system of unemployment compensation is desirable not only as a social safety net but as a productivity-enhancing measure.

One of the reasons, although not the sole one, why the planned economies of Eastern Europe could have such low unemployment was that they were not very dynamic—the pattern of employment and production was not sensitively altered to meet changes in consumer preferences and in technology. The low unemployment was to some extent purchased at a steep cost in lower living standards.

Even in a prosperous and well-functioning economy, some unemployment and some unfilled job vacancies will simultaneously exist as the search and match between individual worker and job goes on. Trying to reduce unemployment below that level by raising aggregate demand and creating more unfilled job vacancies may temporarily succeed in lowering unemployment—some workers will find the jobs they are looking for more quickly. But an excess of unfilled jobs over unemployed workers to fill them will recur; labor will become scarce; firms will begin bidding up wages; and inflation will start rising. If there are many unemployed workers relative to the number of unfilled jobs, however, even an efficient job search will not pay off. Unemployment is higher than the minimum, and an increase in aggregate demand can open up new job

vacancies and provide more employment without setting off new inflationary pressures.

WHAT DETERMINES THE FULL-EMPLOYMENT LEVEL OF UNEMPLOYMENT?

Several different factors, economic and social, determine the full-employment level of unemployment. And since those factors can change over
time, so can the full-employment level of unemployment.

Demographics help determine the full-employment level. A work force
with a high proportion of very young people, who are typically frequent
job changers, will, everything else equal, have a higher minimum level of
unemployment than a work force of predominantly experienced workers
and relatively few young people. Similarly, an increase in the number of
married women reentering the work force after a substantial absence will
raise the minimum level.

A wide divergence between the location or skill requirements of new
jobs and the skills and locations of the unemployed will raise the minimum
level of unemployment. If, in the process of economic change, the location of new jobs and destroyed jobs is widely and jointly dispersed around
the country, matches between jobs and unemployed workers are likely to
be fairly quick and the minimum level of unemployment low. But if a
disproportionate number of the new jobs are in the Southwest and the
displaced workers are in New England, the match will take much longer
and unemployment will be higher. Similarly, if the new jobs are principally
for skilled and professional workers and the lost jobs are among the less
educated and unskilled, the minimum level of unemployment will be
high. If employers cannot find workers with the skills they want, they
will eventually "downskill" some of their jobs (at the cost of reduced
efficiency), relieving some, but not likely all, of the higher unemployment.

The nature of a country's labor market and work training institutions
can help determine the noninflationary level of unemployment. In the
United States, young people find jobs mainly by trial and error, resulting
in a relatively high level of "search" unemployment. In Germany, formal
apprenticeships and other training arrangements, with direct transition
from apprentice training to long-term career jobs, is much more common;
as a consequence, search unemployment among new entrants to the labor
force is much less frequent. Correspondingly, unemployment in most
European countries is much more heavily concentrated among the long-

term unemployed—the short-term unemployed constitute a smaller fraction of total unemployment. There are advantages and disadvantages to the two systems, and evaluating them is not the point of this memo. But this picture is a good example of how the nature of labor market institutions can affect the minimum level of unemployment. Effective training programs for unemployed workers can help retool workers for new jobs, improve the match between unfilled jobs and the unemployed, and reduce the minimum level of unemployment. The trick of course lies in the word "effective." Government funds for public training programs have been sharply cut over the past decade, and there is a large literature and much controversy about how effective such programs were. The evidence is mixed; some increase in federal support for training programs might well pay off, but the resultant reduction in the minimum level of unemployment is unlikely to be dramatic.

The aspiration wages of the unemployed also determine the minimum level of unemployment. The higher the wage that new labor force entrants or displaced workers insist on before accepting a job, the larger the number of jobs that will be turned down, the longer the period of search, and the higher the average level of unemployment consistent with full employment.

The generosity of the unemployment compensation system has some effect on the full-employment level of unemployment. The higher the benefits and the longer the duration of eligibility for unemployment compensation, the less costly it is for an unemployed worker to hold out for a higher wage before accepting reemployment. A difficult economic trade-off must be considered in designing a country's unemployment compensation system. As noted earlier, some unemployment compensation improves economic efficiency, providing workers displaced from their jobs the means to sustain themselves and their families while seeking a job opportunity most nearly matching their skills and abilities. As the system is made more generous, however, it can keep reservation wages unrealistically high and encourage longer spells between jobs than is warranted by search requirements.

The unemployment compensation system of the United States usually supplies twenty-six weeks of unemployment benefits for workers laid off their job, extended to thirty-three weeks in states with very high unemployment rates. For a worker earning the average wage, who was employed long enough before layoff to qualify for full benefits, the benefit is now about 35 percent of the prior wage.

U.S. unemployment compensation is less generous in eligibility requirements, duration of benefits, and wage replacement than in most European countries. In recent years, states have generally tightened up eligibility requirements, and the scope of the extended unemployment insurance program has been cut back. In 1989 fewer than one-third of the unemployed were receiving unemployment compensation compared with roughly 40 percent in nonrecession years of the 1960s and 1970s.

Economic studies of the U.S. unemployment compensation system on the unemployment rate do not agree on how much the system increases the wage aspirations of laid-off workers and raises the unemployment rate consistent with full employment. It surely has some effect—but as we have seen, at least some of the search time induced is probably economically beneficial. And since the generosity of the system did not on average increase much after 1970, it cannot have played a major role in causing the rise in unemployment in the United States since then.

HOW HIGH IS UNEMPLOYMENT AT FULL EMPLOYMENT?

Economists use two approaches in trying to determine the full-employment level of unemployment below which inflation starts to mount. First, they look directly at conditions in the labor market, and second, they try to discern from the historical record the level of unemployment at which inflation began to rise.

Labor Market Conditions

Under very favorable conditions, when the skills of the unemployed closely match those being sought by employers to fill job vacancies, when the new jobs are distributed in roughly the same locations as the unemployed, when unemployed workers do not hold out very long for a higher wage, and when the proportion of job-changing young people and other new entrants into the labor force is low, then unemployment can be pushed down to a very low level without bringing on an aggregate excess demand for labor in the country. Under those circumstances, neither unfilled job vacancies nor spells of unemployment last long; there are not many of either. An overheated boom will create many unfilled job vacancies for which there are unemployed job searchers, and a recession can create more unemployed workers than job vacancies. But when

FIGURE 15-1. Unemployment versus the Help-Wanted Index, 1971–89

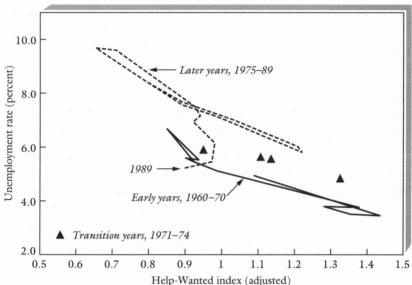

neither recession nor overheated demand is present, the economy will experience low unemployment and low job vacancies.

If, however, these favorable conditions are not present—if new entrants are a large share of the work force, if there is a substantial mismatch between the skills and location of the unemployed and the skill requirements and location of the job vacancies, and so on—then, job vacancies and unemployment will be high at the same time. And because of the mismatch, the full-employment level of unemployment will be high. Thus, by observing the relationship between job vacancies and unemployment, we can get some insight into whether the full-employment level of unemployment has risen or fallen.

The United States does not have any decent figures on nationwide job vacancies. But reasonably good data on the volume of help-wanted ads exist, and Katherine Abraham of the University of Maryland has converted these data into a consistent series that can be used as proxy for the missing vacancy statistics.[1] Figure 15-1 shows the changing relationship between unemployment and help-wanted ads in the United States.

During the 1960s the relationship between the volume of help-wanted ads and unemployment was stable: in recessions, unemployment rose while the volume of help-wanted ads fell; in recovery, unemployment declined and the volume of help-wanted ads rose. But in the early 1970s the level of *both* unemployment and want ads began to rise. And by 1975 a new relationship existed in which both unemployment and help-wanted ads were higher than they used to be. (The early 1970s seem to be transition years as the economy moved from one set of relationships to another.) To the extent that want ads are a good proxy for unfilled job vacancies, this changing pattern of relationships implied a greater mismatch between unemployment and vacancies than had existed in the 1960s. The full-employment level of unemployment had risen.

In about 1985 the relationship between unemployment and job vacancies began to fall back toward the more favorable situation that had existed in the 1960s. Though one cannot draw firm conclusions from just a few years of data, it seems that the full-employment level of unemployment has fallen.

This pattern confirms the rough visual evidence from the unemployment data shown in figure 14-1 (see memo 14). During the 1970s and early 1980s each succeeding recession had higher unemployment; and at the end of each recovery, unemployment was higher than at the end of the previous recovery. But after 1985, for the first time in fifteen years, the continuing recovery pulled unemployment below its best level in the prior recovery. And except at the tail end of the recovery, the drop in unemployment was not accompanied by rising inflation.

Why did the full-employment level of the unemployment rate rise during the 1970s and apparently fall after 1985? For one thing, in the 1970s and at least the first half of the 1980s, unemployment was less equally distributed among the various states and regions of the country than it had been earlier. There was a bigger difference between low-unemployment and high-unemployment states in those later decades. Under these conditions, the mismatch between the location of job openings and the location of the unemployed had probably become greater. However, no long-term increase took place in the inequality of economic conditions among industries (which might have suggested a worsening match between the skills of the unemployed and the skill requirements of new jobs).

Demographic changes did contribute to the shift. In particular, as the baby boomers entered the labor force in large numbers during the 1970s and a growing number of women reentered the labor force after some years' absence, the amount of voluntary "search" unemployment rose

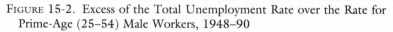

FIGURE 15-2. Excess of the Total Unemployment Rate over the Rate for Prime-Age (25–54) Male Workers, 1948–90

significantly. But by the mid-1980s the proportion of such new entrants to the labor force had started to decline, and the full-employment level of unemployment began to fall. A rough and ready measure of this phenomenon is given simply by the difference between the total unemployment rate and the unemployment rate for male workers between the ages of twenty-five and fifty-four. Adult male workers are not generally new entrants or reentrants in the labor force and are not changing jobs in large numbers. When the total unemployment rate is high compared with the unemployment rate for those adult male workers, that implies a large voluntary search component to unemployment and, everything else being equal, a high full-employment level of unemployment. Of course, when the ratio is reversed, the full-employment level falls. As figure 15-2 shows, this demographic indicator of the minimum level of unemployment rose to a peak in the 1970s and receded in the 1980s. On the other hand, this changing demographic pattern is almost surely not the only factor at work; the ratio of total unemployment to that of adult males begins to rise earlier and fall much sooner than suggested by the relationship between unemployment and job vacancies discussed earlier.

Identifying the Level of Full Employment by Analyzing Inflation

So far, the evidence suggests that the full-employment level of unemployment rose in the 1970s and then fell back somewhat in the 1980s. But that still doesn't tell the policymaker what the level of the full-employment level is. Granted that the number is not a precise one, what is the level of unemployment below which economic policymakers should fear to push the economy because of the inflationary consequences? Many economists have sought to tease this number out of the historical data, essentially by trying to determine the level of unemployment below which inflation starts rising and above which it starts falling.

This is far from a simple task. The economy has suffered several serious, independent cost shocks—oil price increases, productivity slowdowns, exchange rate changes, food price rises, and the like—which boost inflation even with unemployment higher than the full-employment level. The analyst has somehow to control for these developments. Moreover economic developments don't take place instantaneously; they develop over time, and assigning an inflationary effect that takes place in one period to an event that occurred sometime earlier introduces possibilities for error. And the rational expectations theorists (see memo 12) constantly remind us that the wage-setting reactions of firms and workers to changes in the demand for labor depend on what they believe the monetary authorities will do in the near future. These are some of the reasons why various economic studies disagree on the full-employment level of unemployment, even though agreement is widespread that it was significantly higher in the 1970s and at least part of the 1980s than it had been earlier.

Perhaps the most systematic and continuing research on this topic has been carried out by Robert Gordon of Northwestern University.[2] His studies suggest that the full-employment level of unemployment was about 5 percent in the early 1960s and rose to about 6 percent by the mid-1970s. The Congressional Budget Office, relying in part on Gordon's work, has also estimated a full-employment level that follows roughly the same path as Gordon's in the 1960s and 1970s but starting in the early 1980s declines to 5.6 percent by the end of the decade.[3] Figure 15-3 shows the CBO estimates of the full-employment level of unemployment compared with the actual unemployment rate.

These estimates seem like a reasonable assessment of where the economy begins to run into the danger zone of rising inflation. One can clearly

FIGURE 15-3. The Actual and Full-Employment Level of Unemployment, 1956–90

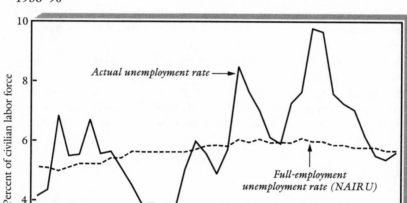

see in figure 15-3 the substantial excess demand during the Vietnam War period, which pushed the unemployment rate well below its full-employment level and gradually boosted inflation from a 1.5 percent rate in the early 1960s to 5 percent by the decade's end. A much smaller period of excess demand is also visible in 1972–73, as are the huge recessions of 1974–75 and 1981–82. The CBO estimate of the level of unemployment consistent with full employment for the beginning of the 1990s is 5.6 percent, which seems roughly in accord with economic developments in 1989–90. In those years, the unemployment rate fell into the range of 5.2 to 5.3 percent. And, by late 1989 and early 1990, careful scrutiny reveals an upward creep in the rate of wage and price inflation.

The assessment that the full-employment rate of unemployment is probably a little over 5.5 percent does not mean that unemployment can never be brought below this level. Rather that estimate tells us how far down unemployment can be pulled through the expansion of aggregate demand without setting in motion a new bout of rising inflation. When unemployment is much higher than 5.5 percent, monetary or fiscal measures to expand demand can bring unemployment down without generating rising inflation.[4] But beyond that point, the remaining unemployment is structural. It clearly is higher than necessary for the efficient working of the economy. But it cannot be conquered on a long-term basis by demand stimulation, and even temporary improvement will be purchased at the cost of rising inflation.

Reducing structural unemployment requires improvements in the internal workings of the nation's labor markets—better information, training, education, perhaps assistance for moving to distant new jobs, and so forth. An evaluation of potential public and private measures of this nature is an important topic but outside the scope of these memos.

SOME CONCLUSIONS

We have attempted to explain and document five important points in these last two memos:

—Most *spells* of unemployment are short, often representing efficient job search. But much of the time spent in unemployment is accounted for by those workers suffering from long periods of unemployment that provide no economic benefits.

—Unemployment is unevenly distributed and concentrated among lower-paid, less skilled, and less educated workers and among minorities.

—Periods of heavy unemployment are caused by the insufficiency of aggregate demand and spending. Unemployment in those periods can be reduced by policies to stimulate demand. But there is a full-employment level of unemployment. If unemployment is pushed significantly below that level by demand expansion, inflation will start rising. And unemployment above that level will produce falling inflation.

—The full-employment level of unemployment is importantly determined by the demographics and the structural characteristics of the labor market. Large numbers of new entrants or reentrants into the labor force produce high levels of full-employment unemployment. The greater the regional or skill mismatch between the jobs destroyed and the jobs created in an ever-changing economy, the higher the full-employment level of unemployment.

—The full-employment level of unemployment was probably in the neighborhood of 5 percent, or perhaps even lower, in the 1950s and early 1960s; it rose to something like 6 percent in the 1970s; and it may have fallen a little below 6 percent in the 1980s.

NOTES

1. Katherine G. Abraham, "Help-Wanted Advertising, Job Vacancies, and Unemployment," *Brookings Papers on Economic Activity* 1:1987, pp. 207–48.

2. Robert J. Gordon, *Macroeconomics*, 3d ed. (Little Brown, 1984) pp. xiv–xvi, app. B, table B-1; and Robert J. Gordon, "The Phillips Curve, Now and Then," Working Paper 3393 (Cambridge, Mass.: National Bureau of Economic Research, June 1990), pp. 7–8.

3. Gordon, however, does not interpret the evidence of the 1980s to warrant any fall in the NAIRU below 6 percent. Because of the violent movement in oil prices and exchange rates during the 1980s, disinterested and competent observers can easily come to somewhat different conclusions about the NAIRU, especially when the differences are only in the range of about 0.5 percent of unemployment. See Robert Gordon, "U.S. Inflation, Labor's Share, and the Natural Rate of Unemployment," in Heinz Konig, ed., *Economics of Wage Determination* (Berlin: Springer-Verlag, 1990), pp. 1–34; and Congressional Budget Office, *The Economic and Budget Outlook: Fiscal Years 1993–1997* (Washington, 1990), p. 113.

4. Be careful about what this statement implies for public policy. As the later memos on monetary and fiscal policy will discuss, it takes some time for those policies to take effect in changing demand and GNP. Even if the unemployment rate is currently above the full-employment level, there must be good reason to believe that it is going to remain above that level for some time before launching policies to expand demand and lower unemployment. The same caution holds true, in reverse, when the unemployment level seems too low relative to full employment.

To: The President

From: CEA Chairman

Subject: **Monetary Policy: The Tools**
         of the Federal Reserve

The power to coin money, together with the power to levy taxes and assemble armies, has always helped define a sovereign government.[1] Modern governments, with paper currency and widespread use of checking accounts to make transactions, have far more power to create (or destroy) money than their otherwise autocratic predecessors of many centuries ago whose subjects would accept only coins they felt had some "intrinsic" worth.

Over the very long run, creating more or less money in a country won't change its productive capacity. Real per capita income in the United States in 1990 was almost three times what it was in 1929, and the increase would have been about the same whether the average growth in the supply of money over the intervening years had been more or less plentiful than it was. But in the shorter run, how the government sets the monetary dials can seriously influence, for good or for ill, the course of aggregate demand and through that route influence year-to-year changes in national output, employment, and inflation.

Sometimes countries get themselves into a dizzily accelerating inflation, reaching thousands of percent a year, because they have for all practical purposes lost control of the money-creating mechanism. This misfortune often happens because, for political reasons, they run massive budget deficits to maintain highly popular subsidy programs, cannot sell their bonds to private investors, and must therefore "print" money (actually create bank deposits for themselves) at an ever-expanding pace to keep up their spending. Much can be learned from an examination of such incidents, but in these memos I will concentrate on the more moderate, but still sometimes difficult, monetary issues and problems facing the United States and other advanced industrial countries.

MONEY IN A MODERN ECONOMY

Money is what individuals and firms use to make transactions. It includes currency (and coins) and checking account checks (also called demand deposits). Economists call this definition of money M1. A somewhat broader definition of money, M2, is also in use; it includes, besides what is in M1, savings accounts and small time-deposits in thrift institutions, both banks and savings and loans, as well as money market funds. Until the early 1980s, the law and banking regulations allowed no interest to be paid on checking accounts; holding some of one's financial assets in the form of money (M1) was convenient but costly since the opportunity of earning interest on that portion of holdings was given up.

In the past fifteen years, financial deregulation, competition among various institutions, and computers have vastly complicated this simple picture. Financial institutions can now pay interest on personal checking accounts, and one can write checks on savings accounts and, in a limited way, on holdings in money market funds, a recent addition to the array of liquid assets that people can hold. For the moment, let's concentrate on two facts about money that are central to an understanding of what monetary policy is all about.

> One, the central bank—in the United States, the Federal Reserve—can create money.
> Two, the initial holders of the newly created money, usually commercial banks, will not normally hold onto it but will seek to lend it out or buy securities with it.

HOW THE FEDERAL RESERVE CREATES MONEY

Commercial banks and other depositary institutions solicit deposits from individuals and business firms and use those deposits to make loans, originate mortgages, or buy securities. They are required to keep a fraction of their deposits as a reserve with the Federal Reserve (as of 1991, 3 percent of the first $42 million and 12 percent of all additional checking account and similar deposits). If a commercial bank (say, with current deposits of more than $42 million) receives a new $1 million deposit, it first sets aside 12 percent of that deposit to add to its required reserves at the Fed and then is free to make loans or buy securities with the remaining 88 percent.

If the new deposit came from a check drawn on another bank, the paying bank would lose $1 million in deposits, reduce its reserves with the Fed by $120,000, and have to contract its loan or security portfolio by $880,000.[2] The banking system as a whole would have gained no reserves or deposits; the same aggregate amount of reserves and deposits would simply have been shuffled among various depositors and banks, as is done every day by the trillions of dollars as the country goes about its normal but vastly complex economic life.

However, if the new deposit in the first bank was not simply a reshuffling of deposits and reserves among banks, but a net addition of deposits to the system, then total deposits and total bank loans or other investments in the economy could expand. The Federal Reserve can inject new deposits into the system. It does so simply by purchasing for its own account, government securities on the open market. When the Fed buys Treasury securities from various government bond dealers who are in the business of buying and selling such securities, the Federal Reserve pays them with checks written on itself. When those checks, totaling, say $100 million, are deposited by the government bond dealers in banks around the country, those banks "collect" from the Fed. Consequently, they now have on their books $100 million in new deposits and $100 million in new reserves available at the Fed. *The Fed has just created $100 million in new reserves for the banking system and $100 million in new money (in checking accounts).* The process of creating the new reserves is called the open market operations of the Fed. How the initial injection of reserves leads to a process of deposit and loan expansion throughout the banking system is illustrated in table 16-1.

The process of money creation doesn't stop there. The banks who have the $100 million in new deposits and new reserves can now make more loans with their extra resources. They set aside a fraction of the new reserves to meet the reserve requirements on the new deposits and then lend out the rest. The loans are made, the funds are disbursed to the borrowers, and they use them for various purposes. Those who receive the money from the borrowers deposit most or all of it in other banks, who now have more deposits (in checking or savings accounts) and more reserves. They set aside a fraction of the new reserves and lend out the

TABLE 16-1. How the Federal Reserve Creates Money

Federal Reserve action and consequence	Initial reserves acquired by receiving bank	Deposits	Loans	Required reserves (held at Fed)
Fed injects $100 million:				
Bank A	100	100	. . .	. . .
Expansion of deposits and loans:				
Bank A	100	100	90	10
Bank B	90	90	81	9
Bank C	81	81	73	8
Bank D	73	73	66	7
	~	~	~	~
Total	1,000	1,000	900	100

rest. And by this means, the initial injection of new deposits and reserves by the Federal Reserve leads to an increase in the money supply—deposits in checking and savings accounts—amounting to a multiple of the initial reserve addition. (How big a multiple depends on a complex mix of factors, including the magnitude of the Federal Reserve's reserve requirements).

To simplify the explanation, assume that the entire $100 million from the Fed purchases of government securities has been deposited in Bank A. With the $100 million in new deposits, Bank A will keep the required fraction of those deposits (again, for simplicity, 10 percent) on reserve with the Federal Reserve. But it can now loan out or otherwise invest the remaining $90 million in earning assets; usually banks will not want to hold any more in idle reserves earning a zero return than they have to.

The new reserves that started the process of money creation were created out of thin air by the central bank. When the Fed wrote the initial $100 million in checks for the government securities it purchased, and those checks were turned in for "collection" by the receiving commercial banks, the Federal Reserve simply made a computer entry in its books crediting those banks with an additional $100 million in reserves. The process can of course be reversed. When the Federal Reserve sells on the open market some of the government securities in its portfolio, the purchasers write checks from their bank accounts to the Fed; the Fed then "collects" the funds by simply erasing equivalent reserves from the reserve accounts held at the Fed by the paying banks.

Not all of the Federal Reserve's responsibilities pertain to the grand realm of national monetary policy. It is also constantly injecting and withdrawing reserves from the banking system to meet the seasonal ebb and flow of business activity, pumping in additional funds, for example, to meet the surge of Christmas transactions and withdrawing them in the succeeding weeks.

HOW THE ADDITIONAL BANK RESERVES AND DEPOSITS AFFECT AGGREGATE DEMAND

The process of money creation and destruction just described is intimately connected with the credit-lending-borrowing transactions of the economy. Additions to the money supply do get spent and thereby add to aggregate demand. But the new money passes into the economy through the operations of the credit system; the Federal Reserve doesn't scatter money over the land from the bomb bays of B-52 airplanes.

When the banking system receives a fresh injection of reserves from the Federal Reserve, the supply of funds available for lending increases. If, before the Fed acts, the demand and supply of funds is in balance with each other, the additional supply of loanable funds will create an excess supply looking for borrowers: interest rates should be driven down. The most immediately affected rate will be the "federal funds rate." This is the rate at which banks lend funds to one another, usually on an overnight basis. With thousands of inflows and outflows of funds each day, banks are often in need of immediate funds to make payments or have a temporary surfeit of funds to lend. The federal funds rate is a sensitive barometer of the tightness or looseness of the supply of funds in the banking system relative to the demand for them.

An increase in the supply of bank reserves, and the consequent increase in the money supply, will also drive down other short-term interest rates as more funds become available for lending or investing in securities; for example, the rate on ninety-day Treasury bills will decline. The rate that banks charge for loans is somewhat sticky and not changed everyday like the federal funds rate, but that rate too will come under downward pressure. If the drop in market interest rates seems long lasting rather than temporary, the bank "prime rate" will fall. The prime rate used to be a reasonably good indicator of what banks charged their best customers, but individually negotiated rates have become so common that the prime rate no longer measures the rate at which good customers can borrow. Nevertheless, many rates are set as so many tenths of a percentage point "on" or "off" the prime rate, so that a movement in the prime rate does signify a change has occurred in what business firms are paying for their funds.

The effect of Federal Reserve open market operations on long-term interest rates is more attenuated and variable over time than their effect on short-term rates. As discussed in memo 8, long-term lenders and borrowers must consider the state of the credit markets during the whole maturity of the loan. It doesn't pay the lender to get locked into making a long-term loan at substantially reduced interest rates if the current interest rates are likely to change soon. Borrowers, however, would quickly take advantage of any substantial fall in long-term interest rates and refinance their old higher-interest loans at the lower rate, especially if they think the current situation is a temporary one. And so the demand and supply for long-term loans will tend to moderate the decline in long-term interest rates. But if short-term rates were plummeting, while long-term rates remained completely unaffected, many potential long-term borrowers would instead begin looking for temporary short-term loans. And so a fall in short-term rates can be expected to exert some downward pressure on long-term rates. Pragmatically, an examination of past relationships suggests that on average about one-quarter to one-third of the cyclical fluctuations in short-term rates find their way into long-term rates, although this relationship is quite variable.

There is one more complication. If there is a widespread belief that the Federal Reserve is pushing monetary ease too hard or too long, threatening a subsequent period of excess demand and higher inflation, then a fall in short-term rates, induced by the Fed's creation of additional bank reserves, may not be reflected at all in lower long-term rates. Indeed, under these circumstances, long-term rates could rise, as long-term lenders projected higher inflation and higher interest rates in the future. Some financial commentators, who consistently argue that the Federal Reserve is spineless and too prone to ease monetary policy, often issue dire warnings that long-term rates will rise every time the Fed takes action to lower interest rates. They are often wrong. Nonetheless, they are occasionally right; under the circumstances described, monetary easing could conceivably lead to a rise in long-term rates.

CREDIT RATIONING AND CREDIT AVAILABILITY

When the supply of loanable funds becomes scarce relative to demand, banks and other lenders (for example, insurance companies) react not only by raising interest rates but also by screening potential borrowers more stringently and by tightening the terms of the loans. Borrowers who earlier would have been accepted for a loan at the going interest rate will be turned down. Maturities of loans may be shortened and more restrictions placed on the borrowers' ability to borrow money elsewhere. In other words, tight money works not only by dissuading some individuals and business firms from borrowing because of higher interest rates, but also by inducing lenders to ration credit, turning down loans even to potential borrowers willing to pay the higher rates. The opposite phenomenon occurs when the Federal Reserve eases credit through adding to bank reserves. Thus the tightness or ease of monetary policy cannot be assessed solely by what has been happening to interest rates, but also by the harder-to-gauge rigor of credit rationing. One prominent series of studies argued that the Great Depression of the 1930s was brought on not so much by a lack of availability of money and bank reserves, but through the introduction of extremely cautious and rigorous credit rationing by lenders who had become so gun-shy and afraid of losses that they were turning away potential borrowers despite a relatively plentiful supply of excess bank reserves available for lending.[3] In all probability, the mistaken contraction of money supplies initially produced the Great Depression, and the subsequent "gun-shy" rationing of credit helped keep it going so long.

My emphasis on the role of the Federal Reserve in influencing interest rates and altering the terms of credit definitely does not imply that over the longer run the Federal Reserve can set whatever interest rates it wants to have. If national saving is very high—or to say the same thing another way, consumption is low—relative to investment demand, as was true for many years in Japan, interest rates will be low. And in a high-saving–low-consumption environment, if the central bank wants total demand and spending high enough to keep the economy near full employment, it will have little choice but to provide sufficient bank reserves to keep interest rates low so as to generate a high level of investment. Conversely, if public and private consumption rise sharply and national saving correspondingly falls, as happened in the United States in the 1980s, interest rates will rise. The Federal Reserve, to prevent inflation, will find itself forced to restrict investment and other interest-sensitive spending with tight money and high interest rates. Thus, in the long run, the level of saving relative to investment demands is the fundamental determinant of interest rates. And as international capital becomes more mobile, interest rates in a particular country are increasingly influenced by the worldwide level of saving relative to world investment demands.

OTHER TOOLS OF MONETARY POLICY

Although the Federal Reserve's principal weapon is the use of open market operations to increase or decrease bank reserves, two other measures are at its disposal to alter credit conditions and interest rates: changes in the discount rate; and changes in the reserve requirement ratio.

The discount rate is the interest rate at which banks can, temporarily, borrow from the Fed. When the discount rate is low, relative to other interest rates, banks will keep few "excess" reserves on hand to meet sudden demands for cash. Except for required reserves, they will lend or invest all their funds, since they can borrow cheaply from the Fed to get through periods of temporary cash shortage. Lowering the discount rate thus effectively makes more reserves available for loans and investments. At one time, manipulating the discount rate was an important instrument of monetary policy. In recent decades, however, the Fed has kept the discount rate more or less in line with market interest rates, rather than using it as an independent tool. Since the Fed doesn't move the discount rate up and down frequently, a change in the discount rate can sometimes be used to send a signal to financial markets that a recent change in the federal funds rate is not a temporary blip but a more fundamental shift in monetary policy that can be expected to last for some time.

The Federal Reserve can change the amount of bank reserves available for lending and investing by raising or lowering the reserve requirement ratio, that is, the fraction of their deposits that banks must keep on reserve with the Fed. Although the Fed may occasionally change the required reserve ratio to achieve some objective relating to the structure of the banking system, it no longer does so as a means of conducting monetary policy. If the Fed wants to change the volume of reserves available for bank loans or investments, it does so by engaging in open market operations.

THE EFFECT OF CHANGES IN BANK RESERVES, MONEY SUPPLY, AND INTEREST RATES ON THE ECONOMY

Earlier memos on consumption, investment, and the trade balance have already identified the sectors of aggregate demand most sensitive to changes in interest rates and credit conditions. In general, where the "up front" cost of expenditure is highest, the changes in interest rates brought about by monetary policy will have their greatest effect. If the initial expenditure is large relative to the annual flow of services expected from that expenditure (the cost of a house is very high relative to the annual rent it produces), then the interest costs of borrowing the money to make the expenditure will be a large share of total costs. And even if the purchase is made without resort to borrowing, the interest earnings being sacrificed to pay for the good in question will be sizable relative to the stream of services. And so, the level of interest rates will loom large in making decisions about the expenditures, and changes in interest rates can be a potent factor in altering spending.

Residential Construction

Residential construction has typically been the sector most favorably affected by changes in interest rates and credit market conditions. This is not surprising since, as noted in memo 7, interest costs are a big part of the monthly payments that a potential homebuyer has to consider when deciding whether and when to purchase a home. For example, on a thirty-year mortgage, a drop in the interest rate from 10 percent to 8 percent reduces the monthly payment by 16 percent. The opposite of course occurs when interest rates rise.

The sensitivity of the residential construction industry to changes in credit conditions is a bad thing for the construction industry since it makes homebuilding a highly volatile business, which probably militates against more efficient construction practices. New homes probably cost more than they would if homebuilding were a stable industry. The interest sensitivity of the demand for new homes, however, helps stabilize the aggregate economy. When recession gets under way, its depth and length are reduced by the responsiveness of housing to declines in interest rates, both those that naturally occur in recession and the deeper cuts resulting from an active policy of monetary ease. And when the economy threatens to overheat, some of the pressure is taken off by reduced housing construction. Though the relationship is far from perfectly synchronized, more houses are built when idle resources become available, and construction is cut back when the demand for resources is particularly great elsewhere. It's not a bad outcome.

Recently, a growing share of home mortgages have been of the adjustable rate type (ARMs)—the mortgage interest rate is adjusted periodically in line with interest rates generally, rather than remaining fixed for the life of the mortgage. The declines in interest rates that characterize a recession or the rise that occurs when the economy is straining at its potential will no longer be quite as important to would-be new homebuyers. They will expect that lower interest rates offered when the economy is in recession will be raised again when the economy recovers—and vice versa when mortgage rates are unusually high.

Despite the developments in financial markets and mortgage finance over the past decade that reduce the interest sensitivity of residential construction, it remains true that changes in interest rates and credit conditions affect residential construction proportionately more than other forms of investment.

Consumer Purchases of Durable Goods

Because of losses from defaulted loans, and the fact that administrative expenses are large compared with other forms of lending, the interest rates which consumers pay to banks and finance companies for loans to purchase automobiles and other durable goods are usually quite high. But they are also relatively stable and don't move up and down over the business cycle as much as other interest rates. During periods of recession when the supply of credit is plentiful relative to the demand, lenders relax their terms and are a little less rigorous in screening potential borrowers. Sales of consumer durables are modestly affected by lower interest rates and a greater availability of credit.

Business Investment in Plant and Equipment

Memo 7 noted that business investment will be encouraged by reductions in the cost of capital—which lower interest rates do provide—but that it has been hard to pin down through empirical research how large an effect lower interest rates might have.

One result does seem to emerge from many of the studies. The changes in business investment brought about by changes in interest rates occur slowly. A recent study by the staff of the Federal Reserve Board, for example, estimates that a 1 percent drop in short-term interest rates, maintained indefinitely, would in the first year induce only a tiny rise in business investment in plant and equipment, about one-fifth the size of the induced increase in residential construction. By the end of three years, however, the rise in business investment would have grown much larger and would be about equal in dollar value to that of residential construction.[4]

The Trade Balance

Memos 9 and 10 described the mechanism by which changes in interest rates induce changes in the exchange rate of the dollar and, by that route, affect the volume of exports and imports. Those memos also reported on some recent studies that concluded that changes in the U.S. trade balance are a much more important component of the aggregate demand response to changes in interest rates than was the case several decades ago (while residential construction is somewhat less responsive).

NOTES

1. The currently planned establishment of a money-creating central bank for the countries of the European Community, who will still retain most other attributes of sovereignty will, if realized, represent a new kind of political creature.

2. In fact, the normal way banks settle up with each other is by a transfer of reserves from one to the other on the books of the Federal Reserve.

3. See, for example, Ben Bernanke, "Non-Monetary Effects of the Financial Crisis in the Propagation of the Great Depression," *American Economic Review*, vol. 73 (June 1983), pp. 257–76.

4. Eileen Mauskopf, "The Transmission Channels of Monetary Policy: How Have They Changed?" *Federal Reserve Bulletin*, vol. 76 (December 1990), pp. 985–1008.

To: The President

From: CEA Chairman

Subject: **Monetary Policy: What It Can and Cannot Do**

As discussed in memo 16, the Federal Reserve may use several tools to influence the course of aggregate demand, in the process affecting various sectors of the economy. In the real economic world of constant change and uncertainty about the future, difficult choices must be made and great skill is required from the Federal Reserve.

—Choosing interest rate targets. As a practical means of operating monetary policy from month to month the Fed sets an interest rate target (for the federal funds rate) and injects or withdraws enough bank reserves to hit the target. But in doing so, it has to be very careful not to end up being counterproductive. Memo 8 pointed out that even in the absence of action by the Fed to supply additional bank reserves to the system, interest rates would naturally tend to fall during periods of recession when spending declines and saving is plentiful relative to investment opportunities. And interest rates naturally rise when booms are under way. But those increases and decreases in interest rates are not enough by themselves to stabilize the economy against the forces of inflation and recession. The Federal Reserve needs to supplement the "natural" interest rate response with additional upward or downward pressure on rates to generate an interest rate change larger than the natural one.

When the Fed sets an interest rate target to combat recession or inflation, the target may not be ambitious enough. Suppose, for example, that a recession gets under way of a size sufficient, even without action by the Fed, to push down interest rates by, say, 2 percentage points. If the Fed sets an interest rate target that yields a reduction in rates of only 1.5

percent and provides bank reserves just enough to reach that target, it would have made things worse, not better, and supplied too little bank reserves to the economy.

The same problem crops up in a period of inflationary pressure, but then the Fed has to be careful it isn't pursuing an interest rate target that is less ambitious than what the natural forces of the economy would have produced. In this case, the Fed would be unwittingly oversupplying the economy with bank reserves at the wrong time.

—Setting a fixed path for money growth. Economists of the monetarist persuasion have emphasized the problems with interest rate targeting as an important reason why the Federal Reserve should *not* pick an interest rate target. Instead they say the Fed should provide a fixed growth of bank reserves or money supply and let interest rates change in response to fluctuations in aggregate demand. The monetarists argue that a close and stable relationship exists between the quantity of bank reserves and money supply on the one hand and the level of aggregate demand (and GNP) on the other. However complex the process that links changes in the money supply and changes in GNP—working through effects on interest rates and credit availability—the end result is that aggregate demand tends to change in a relatively fixed and predictable relationship to changes in the money supply.

By setting a fixed path for the growth of the money supply, the Federal Reserve could, according to the monetarists, achieve a relatively stable path of growth in aggregate demand and insure against large inflationary or recessionary fluctuations in GNP. They realize the relationship between money and GNP isn't perfectly fixed so that not all fluctuations will be avoided. But the practical difficulties of trying actively to manage bank reserves and interest rates to anticipate and counteract fluctuations in GNP are so great that in attempting to do so the Federal Reserve is likely to exaggerate rather than smooth those fluctuations.

There are several difficulties with the monetarists' recommendation. First, while a monetarist approach might insure that the Fed was never actively counterproductive, it would also insure the Fed's inability to supplement the natural rise and fall of interest rates and act as a positive countercyclical force.

Second, the monetarists must grapple with the troubling fact that the proportion of assets that individuals and business firms want to hold in the form of money can change significantly from period to period. Changes in the demand for money have been especially pronounced during the past fifteen years of financial deregulation and innovation. Banks now pay interest on checking accounts. And the public now has an array of highly liquid assets it can hold apart from money, such as mutual stock and bond funds, from which it can transfer funds quickly and cheaply. Consequently, the difference between money and other liquid assets has narrowed significantly, and the public switches preferences among them depending on the structure of interest rates and the availability of new kinds of financial instruments.[1]

The Fed controls the supply of money; the total volume of checking deposits and other forms of money that is outstanding at any one time is, as mentioned in memo 16, limited by the bank reserves made available by the Fed. But the demand for money—the fraction of their assets that people desire to hold in the form of money—can change according to their wants and needs and the pattern of interest rates. If the public should increase the fraction of liquid assets it wanted to hold as money, while the Fed stuck to its monetarist target for the supply of bank reserves and money in the economy, an unwanted rise in interest rates and a reduction in credit availability would occur. Individuals and business firms would seek to lend less or borrow more in their efforts to shift their portfolio toward holding fewer nonmoney assets and more money—the supply of which had not increased. If interest rates had been appropriate before the switch in asset preferences they would be too high, and aggregate demand too low, afterward. And of course if the demand for money suddenly falls, the same forces will work in reverse to generate an unplanned drop in interest rates and a surge of aggregate demand, just when that may not be wanted. But by setting an interest rate target and varying the quantity of bank reserves to meet it, the Fed will automatically react appropriately to switches in asset preferences by the public and supply more or less money as needed.

In short, if the Fed targets interest rates, it must take account of the danger of under- or overreacting when aggregate demand begins to deviate seriously from potential GNP. If the Fed targets a specific growth in the money supply, it must remember that the public's demand for money can change unpredictably, an increasingly important consideration in recent years.

In a complex and uncertain world, no monolithic approach is likely to be appropriate. In the late 1970s and early 1980s, a period of apparent monetarism, the Federal Reserve set and tried to stick with a fixed target for the growth of the money supply. More recently, the Fed has followed an eclectic policy. Although it announces annual targets for the growth of the money supply (several of them to accommodate alternative definitions of money), the Fed has been willing to violate those targets to achieve its more fundamental objectives for restricting or stimulating aggregate demand. For its month-to-month operations, the Fed now sets a target for the federal funds rate and supplies the bank reserves necessary to nudge rates up or down to meet the target. It is aware of the danger of being insufficiently active on either count. It tries to choose, and when appropriate, revise interest rate targets to move the economy in the direction it seeks. The Fed pursues a pragmatic course, the best one can hope for in a rapidly changing world.

—Taking account of long lags between Fed actions and economic results. Changes in credit conditions and interest rates are indeed a potent device to alter demand and spending in various sectors of the economy. But their effects occur only gradually, with the speed of the response varying from sector to sector. For example, the staff of the Federal Reserve, using the Fed's own large econometric model, recently estimated the effects on various sectors of aggregate demand of a 1 percentage point decline in the federal funds rate, with the new rate then being sustained indefinitely. Most of the (rather small) effect on inventory investment would be felt quickly. According to the Fed staff, about two-fifths of the effect on residential construction, for instance, would occur in the first year, and three-quarters of the effect would take place by the end of the third year. However, in the first year after the change in the federal funds rate, only one-quarter of the effect on net exports and only one-twentieth of the effect on business purchases of plant and equipment would have occurred. For aggregate demand as a whole, less than one-third of the stimulative effect would have been felt by the end of the first year and less than half by the end of the second year.

To make matters more difficult, different studies give different estimates of the length of the lags (although they agree that lags are rather long for some important types of spending). It is extremely difficult for the empirical studies to ascertain exactly how strongly and how rapidly some sector of the economy has responded to a change in interest rates when, during any given historical period, a host of other economic factors affecting that sector were also changing. And the length of the lags almost certainly changes depending on the circumstances.[2]

For all of these reasons, the Federal Reserve must forecast an uncertain future in the process of conducting monetary policy. When it pushes the monetary policy buttons, the consequences will be felt for a long time ahead. If, for example, the economy is in a shallow recession, about to begin recovery, a large dose of easier money today may push next year's aggregate demand into the inflationary zone. And the opposite danger crops up near the end of a boom. The economy may be about to turn down, and an additional dose of restrictive monetary policy would further depress an economy already in recession.

LEANING AGAINST THE WIND

In a pragmatic way, the Federal Reserve typically acts to reduce the chances of making serious mistakes by practicing a policy of "leaning against the wind." Essentially, if the economy is clearly suffering from recessionary problems, the Fed will take stimulative action but never enough, at any one time, to close the full gap between the lagging aggregate demand and potential GNP. If recovery is closer at hand or more vigorous than forecast, such a partial response will be much less likely to backfire by proving later to have been too large. But if, after the passage of time, the economy doesn't seem to be getting any better, the Fed can take further stimulative action. Occasionally, circumstances may argue for the abandonment of this gradualist approach and the adoption of a radical shift in the stance of monetary policy. Starting in 1980, and intensifying its efforts in 1981 and 1982, the Fed under Chairman Paul Volcker instituted a draconian policy of monetary tightness to wring out the double-digit inflation that had become embedded in the economy after the oil price surge of 1979. But these situations are the exception rather than the rule.

Given the uncertainties of forecasting, the Fed doesn't, and shouldn't, micromanage the economy by trying to keep aggregate demand precisely in line with potential GNP. The Fed will not try to offset moderate deviations from full employment. However, in light of the difficulties of reducing inflation once it has gotten under way, the Fed is likely to operate a bit conservatively. It will be quicker to drain bank reserves from the system and drive up interest rates because of a forecast that the economy is about to drift into inflation than it will be to intervene early because of a forecast that the economy is about to sag.[3]

As you can appreciate by now, the conduct of monetary policy requires the mastery of an array of technical skills but is also an art. On certain decisions, reasonable people, who share the same fundamental objectives, can sometimes disagree. In the exercise of monetary policy, it is wise to eschew the advice of the monetarists who would set a fixed target for the growth of the money supply and tell the Fed to keep hands off, as well as the urgings of the activists who want the Fed to intervene at the slighted deviation from the path of full employment.

THE BANKING CRUNCH OF 1990–91

Some very special problems confronted monetary policy in the late 1980s and early 1990s, stemming from the financial situation of the commercial banking system at that time. Bank regulatory authorities require a bank to have ownership capital equal to a fixed fraction of the bank's assets. If a bank's capital falls below the requisite amount, it must either raise capital, for example, by selling stock in the bank, or contract its portfolio of loans and investments. Beginning in 1989 or thereabouts, many American banks ran into shortages of capital that caused them to be unwilling or unable to expand their loan portfolios, even when the Federal Reserve was supplying additional bank reserves to the system. A number of developments produced the capital shortage. Banks began suffering large losses from soured loans for real estate and corporate takeovers that had been made during the 1980s, and these losses impaired their capital. Second, the United States, in concert with other major industrial countries, was increasing the capital requirements of the banking system in an effort to improve its financial soundness. Third, the bank regulatory authorities, reacting to the savings and loan fiasco, toughened their loan evaluation criteria and forced banks to write down the value of many loans.

The capital-short banks responded in two ways. When additional reserves became available, they put a larger than usual share into relatively safe securities (for example, Treasury bonds) and less into loans, since the capital requirement against such securities is lower than against business loans. And many of them lowered the interest rates they paid to depositors to discourage new deposits and shrink their deposit base to fit the capital available.

Some observers suggested that such developments rendered Reserve policy impotent; when the Fed added reserves to the system, additional credit would not become available to business firms, homebuyers, and others. That is not correct—although the reluctance of the banks to lend did cause a problem. When instead of making loans, a bank buys Treasury securities with the reserves added to the system by the Fed, those funds do not disappear from the credit stream. Whoever sold the Treasury securities to the bank—for example, a pension fund, or an insurance company—now has additional funds that won't be held in cash but will be put back into the credit markets. And the deposits that were discouraged from going into the banking system were not put under a mattress, but found their way into the credit market in other forms, for example, by way of mutual funds or through direct purchases of bonds and other securities. In other words, part of the flow of funds from savers to investors, which normally would have gone through the banking system as loans, was diverted into other credit channels.

This bypassing of the normal (bank-related) channels through which funds are transferred from savers to investors is a less efficient and more expensive way of getting the job done. Two consequences emerge: first, smaller and less creditworthy firms, whose bank sources of credit dry up, have a hard time tapping into the other channels of credit where funds have been diverted, and sometimes such firms cannot find willing lenders. Second, the alternative channels of credit are not as efficient as the older ones; for example, the network of information about old customers' creditworthiness possessed by banks is not available to potential new lenders. Consequently, the spread widens between market interest rates and the effective rates that business and other borrowers have to pay for credit.

In this situation the Federal Reserve is not impotent. By expanding bank reserves, it can increase the availability of credit. But the Fed has to work harder to do so. More particularly, the Fed has to lower market interest rates further than it might otherwise have had to do to provide the necessary antirecession stimulus. Because the spread between market interest rates and the rates charged to borrowers widens, market rates have to come down further to achieve any given reduction in loan rates. And since some sectors of the economy are especially affected by banks' reluctance or inability to lend, other sectors, who do have access to nonbank lines of credit, have to be stimulated even more than normally. The delay in economic recovery, after what was otherwise a rather mild recession in 1990–91, may well have occurred because the Federal Reserve was late in realizing that the shortage of bank capital required it to ease money and reduce interest rates more aggressively than dictated by experience.

THE RECENT RECORD AND PROSPECTS FOR THE FUTURE

The economic history of the United States since the Second World War has been characterized by much milder fluctuations in economic activity than was typical of the nineteenth and early twentieth century. Many factors contributed to this improved record, but one of them was the Fed's policy of leaning against the wind. Mistakes were made; sometimes the Fed leaned too hard and too long and at other times not enough. Monetary policy was not tight enough to counteract the inflationary stimulus of the large Vietnam War deficits nor the overheated boom of 1972–73. A premature tightening of monetary policy in 1959 brought the ongoing economic recovery to a premature halt and pushed the economy into the mild recession of 1960. And, as just noted, the Federal Reserve was, possibly, slow in 1991 to grasp the special need for an especially aggressive monetary easing in the face of the recent capital shortage in the banking system. Nevertheless, compared with the era between the Civil War and the 1940s, when the U.S. banking system freely increased the money supply to prolong booms and sharply contracted money supplies once recession got under way, monetary policy in the postwar period was, on balance, an important stabilizing influence.

The conduct of monetary policy in the 1980s, during the long recovery from the recession of 1982, was quite good. The economy enjoyed the longest peacetime recovery in history, despite sustained budget deficits unlike any the country had ever seen, fluctuations in exchange rates of unprecedented magnitude, a stock market crash second only to the Great Depression, and widespread failure and massive losses in the savings and loan industry.

After wringing out much of the high inflation that dominated the late 1970s—at the cost of the 1981–82 recession, the worst since the Great Depression—the Federal Reserve has pursued two objectives. Its primary goal has been preventing the excessive aggregate demand that might generate new inflation. Since 1983 this aim has meant offsetting, with tight money and high interest rates, the potential inflationary stimulus of the huge and continued federal budgets that characterized the period. Thus, in May of 1983, only five months into the fledgling recovery from the 1982 recession, the Fed, fearful that the massive budget deficits beginning to unfold would expand aggregate demand too far and too fast, began to restrict the growth of bank reserves. Over the following fifteen months, the Fed pushed up short-term interest rates by about 2.5 to 3 percentage points.

To begin tightening up so soon into recovery was unprecedented. But the prompt tightening was necessary to balance the excessive stimulus to aggregate demand, from the 1981 tax cut and the large growth of defense

FIGURE 17-1. Real Interest Rates, 1951–90

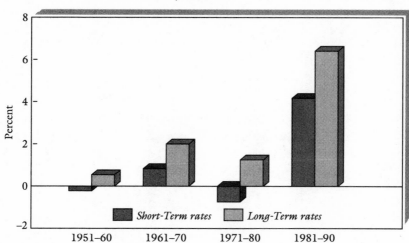

spending, with the restraining effects of higher interest rates on spending for domestic investment and net exports. And although the strength of aggregate demand fluctuated during the 1980s, leading to variations in Federal Reserve policies, the need to contain the potential inflationary stimulus of the high budget deficits produced real interest rates that fluctuated around an average level higher than any the United States has experienced on a sustained basis in the twentieth century (figure 17-1).

Though its first objective was to make sure that aggregate demand did not at any time become excessive, the Federal Reserve apparently had no intention, once the 1982 recession was over, of pushing the economy, or allowing external events to push it, into another recession in order to wring out the remaining 3 to 5 percent inflation. While it might have erred a bit on the side of caution, the Fed seemed willing to live with that remaining inflation. Consequently, whenever aggregate demand began to slacken substantially, the Federal Reserve moved fairly aggressively to furnish additional bank reserves and drive interest rates down. Figure 17-2 shows the changes in short-term interest rates during the 1980s as the Fed moved back and forth from fighting excessive aggregate demand to providing antirecession stimulus.

Starting at the end of the 1970s, the Fed gained the political freedom to engineer sharp increases in interest rates whenever they were needed

FIGURE 17-2. Changes in Real Short-Term Interest Rates in the 1980s

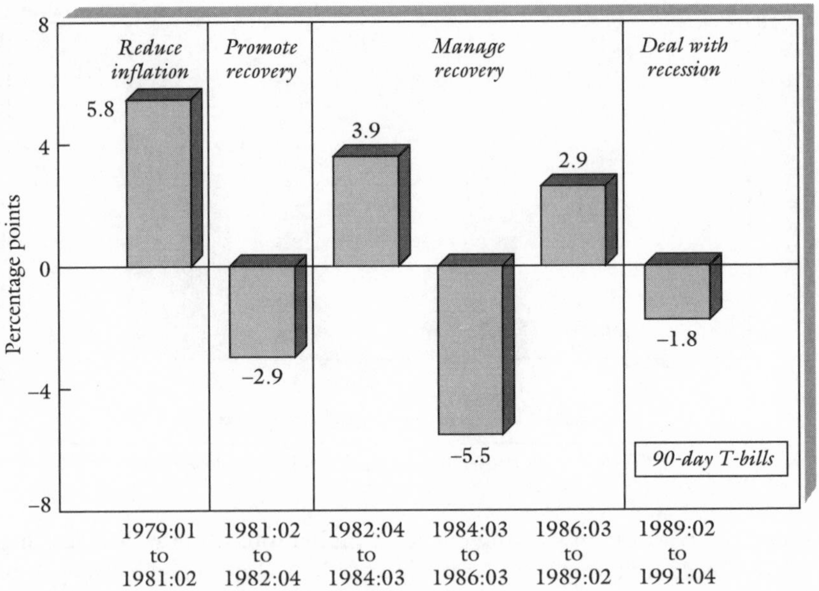

	Reduce inflation	Promote recovery	Manage recovery		Deal with recession
5.8		-2.9	3.9	2.9	-1.8
			-5.5		90-day T-bills

Percentage points

| 1979:01 to 1981:02 | 1981:02 to 1982:04 | 1982:04 to 1984:03 | 1984:03 to 1986:03 | 1986:03 to 1989:02 | 1989:02 to 1991:04 |

to ward off excessive aggregate demand. That is one reason the Fed did so well. In earlier decades, it was a popular sport for many in Congress to attack the Fed for even small increases in interest rates, implicitly threatening that too sharp an increase in rates might provoke legislation restricting the Fed's freedom to act. But since the experience of the 1970s, when inflation several times exceeded 10 percent a year, the American people and their representatives in Congress have given the Federal Reserve much greater leeway to administer the unpleasant medicine of tight money and high interest rates. Similarly, the administrations of Presidents Reagan and Bush, while occasionally muttering that the Fed has been too slow to ease policy when the economy weakened, have usually kept their criticisms muted. Presumably, the Fed could lose this political trust, for example, by driving the economy into a deep recession in a campaign to bring inflation down from its current 3 or 4 percent to zero. But given a continuation of the objectives and methods that the Fed has adopted in recent years, it will probably retain the political freedom to pursue a flexible and mainly successful stabilization policy.

MONETARY POLICY AND EXCHANGE RATES

Memos 9 and 10 pointed out the link between interest rates and exchange rates. Thus a rise in U.S. interest rates relative to those abroad will raise the value of the dollar as foreign investors buy dollars to take advantage of the higher yields; and a fall in U.S interest rates will reduce the dollar's value. Changes in monetary policy, producing changes in interest rates, can thus affect exchange rates. But you should not take too much comfort from this fact. Changing monetary policy to achieve some exchange rate objective may sometimes damage other domestic economic objectives. Thus, given the huge budget deficits of the 1980s, an easing of monetary policy in those years in an effort to produce lower interest rates, a fall in the exchange value of the dollar, and a decline in the American trade deficit would have also meant excess aggregate demand and higher domestic inflation. Only if the budget deficit could have simultaneously been reduced through spending cuts or tax increases—to offset the decline in aggregate demand—would it have been wise to have reduced interest rates in the interests of a lower dollar and more competitive American exports. But achieving the political consensus necessary to reduce the budget deficit was impossible. The administration and Congress put a higher value on avoiding major tax increases and spending cuts than they did on accomplishing the other objectives that would flow from a reduced budget deficit.

MONETARY POLICY AND THE BUDGET DEFICITS OF THE 1980s

In the late 1970s, if one had polled a large sample of economists and politicians on what would happen if the federal government year after year ran budget deficits in excess of $200 billion, most of them would have predicted soaring inflation followed by substantial recession. And if they had also been told that during this period consumers would begin consuming a much higher share of their incomes, they would have been even more confident of their predictions of inflation. In fact, as everyone knows, that did not happen. During much of the period of huge budget deficits and declining private saving, the inflation rate fell, as did the unemployment rate. The deficits did not lead to economic instability. Why? As just discussed, the Federal Reserve gained the political leeway to pursue a monetary policy that restricted the growth in bank reserves and offset the demand-stimulating effects of a large tax cut, a rapid defense buildup, and a fall in the consumer saving rate with the demand-repressing effects of unprecedentedly high interest rates. In the 1980s the United States learned it could muddle through a period of massive budget deficits without the consequences of the terrible inflation predicted earlier.

But the successful stabilization of the economy emphatically did not mean that the budget deficits had no economic consequences. The Fed put a lid on the expansion of total aggregate demand. The burgeoning growth of public and private consumption, fed by the federal budget deficits, had to come out of the hide of the other two major categories of aggregate demand—net exports and domestic investment. And that's exactly what the Fed's high interest rates did, namely, restrict sharply those two forms of spending. The high interest rates directly restrained the growth of domestic investment. And as discussed in memo 10, the high rates made dollar securities an attractive buy for foreign investors whose demand for dollars drove up the dollar's value relative to other currencies, making American exports more expensive and imports cheaper. American exports were depressed while imports soared, and on both counts aggregate demand for American-made products was reduced. Given the successful Fed stabilization policy, the consequences of the budget deficits (greatly exacerbated by the fall in private saving) were not to alter the level of aggregate demand but to change its composition— toward consumption and government spending and imports and away from domestic investment and exports.

Notes

1. Then why not simply expand the definition of money to include the new instruments, and have the Fed stabilize the growth path of the newly defined money supply? That's really no solution. While the newly defined money supply might indeed maintain a somewhat more stable relationship to GNP, the money supply itself, including as it does the new instruments, would now tend to fluctuate more sharply relative to the level of bank reserves, which is, after all, what the Fed controls. The link between money supply and GNP would be tighter but the link between the Fed's open market operations and the size of the money supply would be looser.

2. The rational expectations theorists (see memo 13) emphasize that the speed and magnitude of the responses would depend critically on the expectations of individuals and business firms about the future. What, for example, did they believe the Fed would be doing in a year? Although the variety of po-

tential responses is often overstated, nevertheless, differing expectations do contribute to the uncertainty faced by the Fed's policymakers.

3. Some people believe the Federal Reserve should go even further in its anti-inflationary stance. They would have the Federal Reserve set a goal of zero inflation and conduct monetary policy to reduce gradually the inflation rate, which has fluctuated between 3 and 5 percent in recent years, to zero. But as discussed in memos 12 and 13, it takes a significant period of economic slack and high unemployment to reduce the ongoing rate of inflation. The Federal Reserve could follow several patterns to achieve the zero inflation goal; for example, by failing to intervene vigorously each time a recession came along, or by tightening up monetary policy very early in recoveries to prevent the economy from returning to the neighborhood of full employment. In that way, the inflation rate could be ratcheted down over many years. But any pattern that produced such a result would entail several years of subpar economic performance and high unemployment rates. Despite much lipservice to the goal of zero inflation, Federal Reserve policymakers probably do not give it high priority.

Memorandum 18

To: The President

From: CEA Chairman

Subject: **Fiscal Policy: The Federal Budget and Its Stabilizing Features**

Public spending in the United States by federal, state, and local governments is equal to 35 percent of GNP. Although public spending in the United States constitutes the smallest fraction of GNP of any of the major industrial countries except for Japan, the budgets of the public sector are enormously important in shaping the American economy.

Fiscal policy is the term typically used to emphasize the effect of government decisions about spending and taxes on the overall economy, as opposed to the many other aspects of budget policy, such as its impact on certain groups and regions of the country, its effect on the environment or on national security, the efficiency with which government programs are run, and so on.

Government spending and taxes influence the overall economy through their effect on aggregate demand. Government spending adds to aggregate demand, either because the government is buying something (a tank or a computer or a mile of road construction) or because it is writing checks to people (a social security recipient or a family on welfare) who will buy something with it. Government taxes reduce aggregate demand primarily because they take purchasing power out of the hands of individuals and firms, but also to a smaller extent, because some taxes reduce the return that can be realized from investing in tangible assets and thereby reduce the demand for plant, equipment, housing, and the like.

Government tax and spending policies also influence the level and growth of potential GNP, that is, aggregate supply. The level and structure of taxes affect incentives to work, to save and to invest, and govern-

TABLE 18-1. The Different Kinds of Government Spending
  Billions of dollars

Type of spending	All governments	Federal	State and local
Purchases of goods and services	1,043	425	618
Transfer payments	675	511	164
Net interest	122	176	−64
Net subsidies	5	25	−20
Grants-in-aid to state and local governments	. . .	132	. . .
Total	. . .	(1,269)	(698)
Total (excluding grants-in-aid)[a]	1,910	1,139	(698)
Total as percent of GNP	33	20	13

a. Grants-in-aid excluded to avoid double counting. See p. 199.

ment spending for infrastructure, education, and research and development influences the long-term growth of productivity and real income. I have stressed repeatedly the importance of the distinction between those economic developments and policies that affect spending, or demand, and those that affect supply. Both are important, but they are not the same. Major policy mistakes can occur from confusing the two effects.

THE DIFFERENT TYPES OF SPENDING PROGRAMS

Several kinds of government expenditures affect aggregate demand (table 18-1). For instance, federal and state and local governments made direct purchases of goods and services, amounting in 1990 to more than $1 trillion. Of that amount some 50 percent was accounted for by the payments of wages and salaries for the services of government employees—teachers, police officers, members of the armed forces, government clerks, and so forth. (Of the nonmilitary personnel, 80 percent work for state and local governments.) Another 18 percent of government purchases was paid out to business firms by the Pentagon for construction, procurement of weapons, research and development, and the like. And governments paid the remaining 27 percent to business firms for the purchase of civilian goods and services—constructing roads and dams, computers, space vehicles, taking delivery of crops for farm price support programs, and a myriad of other purchases. These purchases are a direct use of national output and along with consumption, investment, and exports are a major component of aggregate demand and GNP.

A second major category of government expenditures is transfer payments. Money is paid to individuals, not for their services, but as cash or in-kind benefits to which they are "entitled" under a wide range of public programs. Social security retirement, disability, and medicare payments constitute a major component of these payments, but there are also payments to veterans, civil service retirees, welfare recipients, the unemployed, and many other smaller categories of beneficiaries. Three characteristics of all of these transfer, or entitlement, programs are important.

First, unlike government purchases of goods and services, transfer payments do not represent a direct use of national output by the government. Rather the individuals who receive the transfer payments from the government will use the funds, or at least a large share of them, to make purchases themselves, chiefly consumer goods and services. And so when the government increases or decreases transfer payments, it indirectly adds to aggregate demand by inducing increases or decreases in private consumption spending.

Second, almost all of the transfer programs represent money that is automatically paid to individuals who meet the eligibility requirements set in the laws governing the programs. Whereas Congress (and the various state legislatures) each year appropriate sums to buy military aircraft or space vehicles, or to hire a larger or smaller number of police officers, the amount spent on transfer programs will be automatically determined by events outside the control of the executive or the legislature, such as the number and prior wages of people retiring and claiming social security benefits, the number and prior wages of the unemployed eligible for unemployment insurance, the extent to which the elderly use medical services under medicare, and so on. The basic laws can be modified, but until that is done, outside events, not government decisions, determine spending on transfer programs.

Third, spending for some transfer programs is closely determined by macroeconomic developments. I have already mentioned the countercyclical role of unemployment insurance. Many other benefit programs do not respond to unemployment but are indexed to the consumer price index, and thus their growth depends on the rate of inflation.

Net interest payments are the next principal category of public spending. Interest payments by the government are like transfer payments—

they increase the income of the recipients and thereby induce more consumption spending. Various agencies of the government pay interest to one another, and these intragovernmental payments are netted out, thus revealing the net payments from the government as a whole to the public. Within the federal government, the social security trust funds have recently been taking in far more revenues than were being paid out in benefit payments and have been accumulating a large surplus that is invested in Treasury securities. As a consequence, the Treasury pays substantial interest each year to the trust funds ($62 billion in 1990), which have to be subtracted from the gross total of interest payments in calculating net interest. State and local governments have large retirement funds for their employees, which are annually running very large surpluses ($64 billion in 1990 alone). These surpluses are also invested in Treasury securities, and the amounts are so large that the interest receipts on these funds exceed state and local interest payments on their own obligations, which explains the negative entry for net interest in the state and local column of table 18-1.[1]

Both federal and state and local governments provide subsidies to business enterprises of one kind or another—federal subsidies for housing, agriculture, and the merchant marine, for example. The operating profits of government-owned enterprises of a businesslike character are subtracted from these subsidies, leaving a single figure for net subsidies. State and local governments own and operate many water and other public utilities, and their earnings are larger than the subsidies they provide to business, so their entry for the net value of subsidies in table 18-1 is negative.

Finally, the federal government makes grants-in-aid to state and local governments, which they in turn spend for various programs. Although this item of the federal budget bore the lion's share of the cutbacks in budget spending during the 1980s, it is still a substantial sum, more than $130 billion in 1990. To avoid double counting, these grants-in-aid are not included when federal, state, and local budgets are added together.

Total government spending is equal to 33 percent of GNP. Three-fifths of that spending is accounted for by the federal government and two-fifths by state and local governments (table 18-1). In this accounting, expenditures are assigned to the unit of government that actually does the spending; spending financed by federal grants-in-aid is assigned to the states and localities. When spending is categorized by who finances it, grants-in-aid are assigned to the federal government, and the federal share of total government spending then rises from three-fifths to two-thirds.

TAXES

As Justice Oliver Wendell Holmes wrote, "Taxes are the price we pay for a civilized society." In the more prosaic language of economics, taxes are the principal way governments acquire the resources they need to carry out their business. In an economy in which aggregate demand is already equal to potential GNP, an increase in government spending must be matched by a decrease in demand and spending elsewhere if inflation is to be avoided. The chief means of doing so is to levy additional taxes, thereby reducing private demand. (But, as noted in memo 17, another way to do it is to drive up interest rates and tighten credit, forcing a reduction in interest-sensitive private spending).

However, in an economy operating at less than full employment, with aggregate demand below potential GNP and idle resources available to be reemployed, government spending can be raised relative to taxes, or taxes cut relative to spending, and the consequent rise in aggregate spending in the economy need not create excessive demand and rising inflation.

The chief way in which taxes depress aggregate demand is through their effect in reducing the income of taxpayers, leading to a reduction in consumption. Personal income taxes directly lower household income. The employee share of social security payroll taxes directly reduces worker income, and economists conclude that most of the employer share of the payroll tax, while initially paid by the employer, eventually comes out of the pocket of the workers since wages are lower than they otherwise would be. (And to the extent that the employer passes the cost of the payroll tax forward in higher prices to consumers, then households—as consumers rather than workers—also bear the burden.) Sales taxes are principally passed forward to consumers, whose real purchasing power is thereby reduced, also leading to a smaller volume of consumer purchases.

Since personal income taxes are levied on interest and dividend income and on capital gains, they lower the rate of return to individuals from their saving and may therefore reduce the share of income devoted to saving and to direct investments by small entrepreneurs. We will look more closely at these incentive effects in later memos dealing with 'supply-side' issues. But at the moment it is sufficient to know that the major effect of general changes in personal income taxes is likely to be on consumption demand.

Business income is also subject to taxation. Here the effects on aggregate demand are more complicated. Ultimately, all taxes on business firms are borne by indivduals, either directly or as the taxes are passed on in the form of higher prices or lower wages. The corporate tax reduces the after-tax income of corporations. In the short run, the owners of capital bear the tax; there is some reduction in dividends and some cut in retained earnings, and presumably these consequences are reflected in a lower price for common stocks. The demand for investment goods—plant, equipment, and inventories—is likely to suffer because the cost of capital has been raised (see memo 7) and because those firms who have a limited access to the capital market and depend heavily on retained earnings to finance their investment now have lower retained earnings. But the cut in dividends and in stock prices will also have some effect in reducing consumption.

Off and on over the years, provisions designed especially to reduce the effect of corporate taxes in discouraging investment have been added to the tax laws and sometimes later removed. The investment tax credit, first introduced into the tax code in 1962, and removed in the tax reform of 1986, provided business firms with a credit against taxes of 10 percent of the value of any new equipment and machinery purchases. Under accelerated depreciation, business firms could, for tax purposes, depreciate plant and equipment faster than the actual rate at which those assets actually depreciate, thus enabling them to delay the payment of taxes on the income earned from those investments. The degree of allowable accelerated depreciation changed from time to time during the postwar period, but in the 1986 tax reform, accelerated depreciation was eliminated. Devices such as investment tax credits and accelerated depreciation probably achieve a greater increase in investment demand than would an equivalent loss of revenues devoted to a general reduction in the corporate tax rate. Such provisions, however, alter the pattern of investment from that determined by market forces, because they favor some forms of investment over others. Changes in taxes that alter the volume of investment have a dual effect on the economy: they change aggregate demand, since investment is a component of GNP, and they gradually have an effect on aggregate supply, since it is through investment that the nation alters the stock of capital that is itself a major factor of production.

Table 18-2 shows the relative importance of the major tax sources for the federal and for state and local governments. Over the past several

TABLE 18-2. The Major Types of Federal, State, and Local
Income Taxes, 1990

Percent of GNP

Type of tax	All governments	Federal	State and local
Personal income	11.2	8.7	2.5
Payroll	9.1	8.1	1.0
Corporate income	2.4	2.0	0.4
Sales	5.2	1.2	4.0
Property	2.7	. . .	2.7
Total	30.7	20.0	10.7

decades, corporate taxes have become a much smaller fraction of the total tax take, partly because corporate tax rates have been reduced but mainly because corporate profits declined as a share of GNP. In turn, the decline in the corporate profit share reflects not principally a lower return to the capital invested in corporations, but an increase in the share of that capital financed by debt rather than by equity and a corresponding increase in interest payments and reduction in profits.

Except for the United States, most countries rely importantly on the value-added tax as a revenue raiser. A value-added tax is like a sales tax, but instead of being levied on the final sale of a product, it is levied on the value added to a good or service at each stage of the production process. Typically, if a good is used for investment purposes or is exported, the value-added taxes paid at the earlier stages of production are rebated to the seller. In effect, therefore, a value-added tax is a tax on consumption only.

Most of the tax changes likely in the foreseeable future will have their main effects on consumption spending. Changes in sales or payroll taxes would affect consumption almost exclusively, as would the introduction of a new value-added tax. And unless a change in income taxes were heavily concentrated among the very highest income groups (in which case it wouldn't raise a lot of money), most of its effect would also be on consumption.

As already noted, taxes not only affect aggregate demand, they also change the incentives of firms and individuals to work, to save, to invest, and to take business risks. While I will discuss the supply side of taxation in later memos, one important point should be made here. The effect on aggregate demand of a tax reduction of given size will be much larger than its effect on aggregate supply. Suppose, for example, that a reinstitution of a generous investment tax credit raised the annual volume of business investment by $55 billion. That will directly add $55 billion to aggregate demand (equal at the present time to 1 percent of GNP). Through the multiplier, it will indirectly increase aggregate demand still further (the magnitude of that indirect effect will depend on what happens to monetary policy). Over time, the new investments will produce additional output more than equal to their $55 billion cost, that is, they will earn a profit. But the annual increment to potential GNP will be much smaller than $55 billion, on average something like $6 billion a year, or one-tenth of 1 percent of GNP. If the economy was already at full employment, the tax change would push aggregate demand above aggregate supply and either be inflationary or require a dose of tight money and high interest rates, reducing investment spending in areas not favored by the tax incentive (for example, housing construction).

This analysis does not imply that supply-side tax policies are undesirable. But once the economy is performing at a full-employment level, there is no free lunch. The reduction in tax revenues and the increase in aggregate demand occasioned by the supply-side tax cut must be matched by government spending cuts, by tax increases that depress consumption, or by a tightening of monetary policy to insure that the increase in investment spending is offset, or nearly offset, by cuts in demand elsewhere. Similarly, given a realistic evaluation of the work-incentive effects of income tax cuts, which tend to be quite modest, the effect of personal income tax cuts in raising the demand for consumer goods will swamp its effects in raising aggregate supply. Failure to appreciate this lesson was a serious mistake made by those who launched the supply-side revolution of 1981.

AUTOMATIC STABILIZING CHARACTERISTICS OF THE FEDERAL BUDGET

Two kinds of changes in government revenues and expenditures are important: automatic and discretionary. Budget revenues and some budget expenditures automatically rise and fall with increases and decreases in GNP. How do those automatic changes in the budget help smooth out fluctuations in aggregate demand?

The revenues from most kinds of taxes automatically rise and fall as GNP rises and falls. State and local property taxes are an exception; although assessed property values are ultimately influenced by economic conditions, they don't closely follow the ups and downs of the economy. But receipts from income, payroll, and sales taxes, which constitute most other government revenues, do rise and fall with national income and output. Unlike most other sectors of aggregate demand, however, the outlays of the federal government do not decline when the federal government's income falls. (State and local governments are typically forced by budget-balancing requirements in their constitutions and by other obstacles to pare spending when revenues decline.) Indeed, some forms of federal spending, especially outlays for unemployment insurance and to a lesser extent for welfare programs, rise when economic activity and government revenues fall off. And so the federal budget automatically moves heavily toward deficit as aggregate demand, output, and employment decline.

The Congressional Budget Office has estimated that, under current tax laws and entitlement programs, every $1.00 decline in gross national income and product produces a $0.25 fall in federal revenues and an $0.08 rise in federal spending for interest payments and for unemployment compensation and similar benefits. Altogether, therefore, the government absorbs about one-third of any decline in private income, leaving the private sector to absorb only two-thirds. To think of it another way, the income of the federal sector of the economy shares in the decline of gross national income that occurs when aggregate demand and output drop, thereby reducing the fall in spendable private income. But unlike the private sector, the federal sector does not cut spending and indeed increases it somewhat. The same reactions occur, with the opposite sign, when GNP and income rise.

These changes in federal revenues and spending in response to changes in GNP help to stabilize the economy—they are called *automatic stabilizers*. They reduce the size of the multiplier—the secondary, induced, changes in income and expenditure that occur when a change in spending and output initially occurs somewhere in the economy (see memo 5). When output falls and workers lose income because of unemployment or short hours, their tax payments also decline, and they may receive unemployment compensation. As a consequence, their consumption spending doesn't change as much as it would have in a world with much smaller government or one in which tax revenues and spending did not depend on the level of economic activity. Note, however, that the stabilization works in both directions. When recessionary forces appear, the stabilizing characteristics of the federal budget fight recession. But once the economy starts to turn up, tax revenues begin rising and unemployment compensation declines, slowing the pace of the recovery.

The automatic stabilizing characteristics of the federal budget are one reason why GNP and employment have fluctuated less sharply in the years after the Second World War than they did in earlier eras. In the nineteenth and early twentieth centuries, federal revenues were too small a fraction of income to matter much, and unemployment insurance was nonexistent.

Necessarily, the sensitivity of federal revenues and expenditures to the state of the business cycle means that the federal budget moves strongly toward deficit when recessions occur. Passage of a constitutional amendment rigidly requiring a balanced federal budget under all economic conditions would require tax increases or expenditure cuts during recessions to avoid the prohibited deficits, thus eliminating this stabilizing element of the current economic system.

APPENDIX: ADJUSTING NEW INTEREST PAYMENTS FOR INFLATION

Part of the interest that government bondholders receive represents a payment simply to keep their investment whole against inflation. Thus, if inflation is running at 5 percent a year, a government bondholder receiving an 8 percent annual interest payment experiences a 5 percent annual erosion of the purchasing power of his or her investment and enjoys a real return of only 3 percent. Bondholders do not treat the inflation component of their interest payments as income to be spent; rather they add it to their saving in order to keep the purchasing power of their real bondholdings intact.[2] The inflation component in interest payments, therefore, does not add to aggregate demand. As a consequence, Robert Eisner of Northwestern University has argued, a fraction of government interest payments, equal to that inflation component, should be subtracted from the reported value of government spending and, correspondingly, from the deficit. If that were done, the economically relevant size of the government deficits, especially in years of high inflation such as 1973–74 and 1979–82, would have been much smaller.

Indeed in most of these years, big budget deficits would have been turned into surpluses.

Eisner's argument has much merit. But the implications are not as important as they seem at first glance. If it is true, as Eisner suggests, that the interest income of federal bondholders is overstated, so also must be their saving as reported in the national income and product accounts. Saving is equal to income minus consumption. If the official accounts overstate income, then, since reported consumption is not affected, the official estimates of private saving must be corrected downward by exactly the same amount as federal interest payments and the federal deficit are reduced. Thus, the Eisner adjustment makes no difference to national saving, which is equal to private saving minus the government budget deficit. If it is true that the federal deficit situation has been better than we thought, private saving has been worse than we thought, and the economic picture for national income and saving was no different than reported. The same reasoning would apply to future years if the Eisner adjustment were adopted as the basis for calculating the federal deficit and the national income accounts.

NOTES

1. The aggregate budget balance shown for state and local governments in the national income accounts includes these surpluses, a practice which if not recognized, can give a very misleading impression. Thus in 1990 the national income accounts show an overall surplus of $26 billion for the aggregate of state and local governments. In fact this surplus consists of the $64 billion of retirement fund surpluses mentioned in the text partly offset by a $38 billion deficit in state and local operating and capital budgets. The $64 billion surplus is actuarially required to meet future retirement obligations and is not available to use for supporting the operations of these governments. Their true fiscal condition is better mirrored by the $38 billion deficit in their operating and capital budgets. In later memos, when dealing with the effect of government budgets on national saving, I reclassify these surpluses and treat them the same way that private employer pension funds are treated—as part of private saving.

2. Robert Eisner, *How Real Is the Federal Deficit?* (Free Press, 1986).

To: The President

From: CEA Chairman

Subject: **Fiscal Policy: Using the Budget to Influence GNP**

By changing tax laws and the legislation spelling out eligibility conditions in transfer programs and by voting appropriations for purchasing goods and services, federal and state and local governments can make discretionary changes in their budgets. And these changes can increase or decrease aggregate demand. In general, discretionary policy changes that raise the budget deficit—tax cuts or expenditure increases—will expand aggregate demand and those that lower the deficit will produce a reduction in aggregate demand.

Let's concentrate on the federal budget. I have already noted the automatic stabilizing characteristics of the federal budget system, stemming from the fact that when GNP falls, the deficit rises and vice versa. But changes in the budget deficit from year to year can also reflect discretionary budget policies as well as other developments (for example, a larger number of social security recipients) not caused by changes in national income and employment. These changes in the budget also affect aggregate demand and GNP. To understand how budget policies are influencing the economy, we need to separate those year-to-year changes in the budget deficit that are the automatic response of the budget to changes in GNP from those that reflect discretionary budget policy decisions and other developments. Thus, if the fall in actual GNP below potential GNP during a recession year were large enough to have produced a $70 billion increase in the budget deficit, but the deficit fell only $40 billion, we would know that changes in tax laws and expenditure policies in the "wrong" direction had offset some of the automatic stabi-

FIGURE 19-1. Alternative Measures of the Federal Budget Deficit

lizing effects of the budget and had a contractionary effect on aggregate demand and GNP.

THE HIGH-EMPLOYMENT BUDGET

To help sort out changes in the budget deficit that are automatically produced by fluctuations in income and output from those that are the result of discretionary policy changes and other developments, economists have concocted a measure called "the high-employment budget deficit." It is an estimate of what the budget deficit would be each year, given existing tax laws and budget policies, if actual and potential GNP were equal (in which case actual unemployment would equal the high-employment level of unemployment, the NAIRU). Thus, any change in the high-employment budget deficit from one year to the next is because of changes in discretionary budget policies and other developments but not because of cyclical fluctuations in GNP.

The relationship between the actual and the high-employment budget deficit is shown in figure 19-1. During the recessions of 1975 and 1982 the budget deficit rose sharply, far more than could be accounted for by the fall in income and the rise in unemployment; the high-employment deficit increased sharply in both years. Discretionary budget policy—cuts in taxes and increases in expenditures—supplemented the automatic stabilizers in fighting the recessions. (The main budgetary effect of a recession typically occurs in the subsequent fiscal year—the 1975 recession in fiscal 1976, the 1982 recession in fiscal 1983, and so on—partly because of lags in tax collections and partly because the federal fiscal year starts in the prior calendar year.) Figure 19-1 also shows that the large budget deficits of the Vietnam War were worse than they seemed on the surface; they occurred despite extremely low unemployment rates and levels of GNP temporarily above potential GNP; the high-employment deficits were larger than the actual deficits.

Figure 19-1 also shows the high-employment budget deficit further adjusted to remove the effect of inflation in eroding the real value of bondholder's debt—the Eisner adjustment (see the appendix to memo 18). Because there has been at least some inflation throughout the postwar period, the inflation-adjusted deficit is at all points below the high-employment deficit. But because the inflation premium in government interest payments was particularly high from 1974 through 1982, removing that premium markedly reduces the deficits of those years. The large deficits of the subsequent years then appear to be much more of a break with the past and less a continuation of an uptrend that began much earlier.

The estimates of the high-employment budget deficit can also be used for a related but slightly different purpose, namely, to ask whether the budget deficits of a particular period are structural or not—would they persist even if the economy were operating in a period of normal prosperity? As shown in figure 19-1, even when unemployment was still relatively high in 1983 and 1984, the rapid increase in the high-employment budget deficits confirms that the emerging large budget deficits were the result of budgetary policy not a weak economy.

THE EFFECT OF DISCRETIONARY BUDGET POLICY ON AGGREGATE DEMAND

Changes in government purchases of goods and services directly change aggregate demand. Changes in transfer payments or reductions indirectly change aggregate demand by raising private incomes and stimulating additional spending (principally consumer spending). Memo 5 noted that any initial increase in spending and demand is likely to be magnified by the multiplier and the accelerator, as the income and consumption spending of the newly hired workers comes into play along with the induced investment spending of business firms undertaken to build new capacity. But Memo 8 explained that part of those secondary effects will be canceled by the increases in real interest rates and the more stringent credit rationing that will accompany the rise in the budget deficit and the increase in aggregate demand. There will be some "crowding out" of business investment. All of this assumes that the Federal Reserve is not accommodating the increased budget deficits with the creation of new money, and that it is sticking to an unchanged path of growth in bank reserves and the money supply.

To state this point another way, an expansion of aggregate demand through the budget deficit will be more or less effective in raising aggregate demand depending on the reactions of the Federal Reserve. By reducing the growth in bank reserves, the Fed can push up interest rates and induce sufficient credit rationing to offset completely the stimulative effects of the budgetary policy. If the Fed leaves the growth of bank reserves unchanged, interest rates will still rise and credit rationing will grow but not by enough to offset fully the demand-expanding consequences of the budget deficits. And finally, if the Fed, in the face of an increase in the high-employment deficit, provides enough additional bank reserves to keep interest rates and the credit rationing unchanged, the full multiplier and accelerator effects will be effective, and the deficit increase will generate a large expansion in aggregate demand. All of the foregoing holds, in the opposite direction, for a fall in the budget deficit.

Although estimates of the magnitudes involved vary, the essential point is clear: under current economic conditions and institutions, the extent to which a change in the budget deficit will expand or contract aggregate demand will depend on the reactions of the Federal Reserve, which can accommodate, be neutral, or actively offset the process.

One particular application of these points is important; I raised it briefly at the end of memo 8, but it's worth repeating. If Congress and the executive take further action in the years ahead to raise taxes or cut spending to eliminate or substantially reduce the federal budget deficit, those actions by themselves will reduce aggregate demand and employment. To keep the economy on an even keel, the Fed would have to provide additional bank reserves to generate declines in interest rates over and above those that would in any event occur, sufficient to keep aggregate demand and employment more or less unchanged. This is not to say that the Fed could successfully stabilize against a massive change in the budget deficit, say by 2 to 3 percent of GNP, that took place all in one year. There is a limit to how fast monetary policy could provide offsetting aggregate demand stimulus.[1] However, the danger that Congress and the executive will make excessive cuts in the budget deficit is something that should rank very low on anyone's list of worries.

THE USE OF FISCAL POLICY TO STABILIZE THE ECONOMY: PROS AND CONS

In the depths of the Great Depression, monetary policy could not be effective in recharging the American economy. Although for many years during the depression, short-term interest rates remained below 0.5 percent, long-term rates stayed a good bit higher, with corporate bonds yielding 3 to 4 percent. After several years of perversely contracting the money supply when the economy was collapsing, the Federal Reserve began to pump bank reserves into the system. But it did no good. Banks, badly burned in the crash, piled up excess reserves and wouldn't lend them out. Business confidence had been so shaken and excess capacity was so great that even if long-term rates had come down somewhat further, it is questionable whether that would have stimulated much investment.

These were the days in which John Maynard Keynes wrote *The General Theory of Employment Interest and Money*, the book that was the beginning of Keynesian economics. It urged the government to use large budget deficits, specifically public works spending, to create additional aggregate demand and get the economy moving again. Keynes told President Franklin D. Roosevelt in a letter that if the U.S. government ran emergency expenditures of $200 million a month, the American economy would see little recovery. But with a $400 million emergency outlay, the economy would recover nicely. (In 1936, $400 million a month was equal to 6 percent of GNP.)

In the postwar era, acceptance of the Keynesian approach of seeking to use the federal budget as a countercyclical stabilizing device gradually spread through much of the economics profession and, more slowly, into government. Its heyday came in the early 1960s when the Keynesian economists around Presidents Kennedy and Johnson designed and watched their bosses push through Congress several major tax cuts explicitly aimed at raising aggregate demand and pushing unemployment down to a lower level. And the U.S. economy in the 1960s did expand nicely. By the late 1960s, however, it became too much of a good thing, as expenditures on the Vietnam War and the Great Society programs were added to the stimulus of the tax cut, and President Johnson refused the advice of his economists to raise taxes. Aggregate demand was pushed beyond potential GNP, unemployment fell well below the NAIRU, and inflation accelerated. In the recession of 1975, Congress, over the objections of President Ford, pushed through a major temporary tax cut and a large extra spending program as antirecession medicine. And finally, as the economy came out of the 1981–82 recession, the large tax cuts and defense spending increases of the Reagan administration, while not adopted for Keynesian reasons, nevertheless gave such a major upward thrust to aggregate demand that very early in the recovery the Federal Reserve found it necessary to apply some monetary brakes to keep the expansion from becoming too vigorous.

While there is not much doubt that tax and spending changes can stimulate or retard aggregate demand, the question remains about their suitability for managing demand to help stabilize the economy. In particular, what should be the relative roles of monetary policy and fiscal policy as economic stabilization tools?

One of the central problems of using budget policy to stabilize aggregate demand against recessions that are moderate in extent and duration is that it is hard to devise countercyclical fiscal policy that is simultaneously effective and reversible (when the recession is over). Most government expenditure changes are ponderous. Although Congress was for many years enamored with the political attractiveness of "accelerated public works" programs, the sad fact is, by the time an increased volume of public works gets under way, the economy is approaching high employment. Further, it is inefficient to take programs that may be desirable in themselves—support for research and development, space exploration, or bridge repairs—and sharply expand or contract them as the business cycle dictates.

In the abstract, public employment programs under which the government hires the unemployed might be a useful device during recessions. But in practice all sorts of difficulties crop up. Unions and others exert a great deal of political pressure to set the wages in such programs relatively high, in which case they attract large numbers not only of the unemployed but of those employed at low-wage jobs. And there are severe difficulties in periodically setting up and then abandoning an administrative apparatus to identify real jobs to be done, provide supervision, and otherwise run a major program. And finally of course there is always big political pressure to keep the program going once the recession is over; the mayors and local groups who, in practice, typically administer the employment funds and hire the workers are loathe to give up the funds, and they fight hard to retain them.

Usually, the discretionary expansion and contraction of government spending programs is not an attractive and effective tool of countercyclical policy during moderate recessions, since the added expenditures may only begin to come on line after the economy begins to approach full employment. In the face of a deep and long-lasting recession, however, when it will be some time before the economy approaches high employment again, additional expenditures can prove useful, as long as they are truly temporary.

What about tax changes as a countercyclical device? Once Congress passes them, they can take effect quickly and are also likely to have relatively quick effects on consumption. But all is not rosy. We may want lower taxes and increased high-employment deficits when the economy is weak, but we don't want those deficits to persist past the recession. And so unless we believe that government spending in the years after the recession is going to be lowered, we do not want any recession-oriented tax cut to be permanent. But as discussed in memo 6, changes in income that are thought to be transitory induce less consumption spending than changes thought to be permanent. This is not to say that a temporary tax cut will have no effect. It will. However, it is likely to take a large tax cut and a big increase in the deficit to produce modest results unless the tax cut is believed to be a lasting one.

The statistical studies of past episodes of temporary tax changes are not completely consistent with one another on how big a consumption response one could expect from a temporary tax change. But the evidence is solid enough to raise some doubt about how reliable temporary changes in personal taxes can be as a countercyclical device.

Finally, it is impossible to apply fiscal policy gradually, testing the wind each month and then, as is the case with monetary policy, leaning against it. Fiscal policy is much more ponderous, requiring a great gathering of effort to shape a political consensus and then to produce a piece of legislation. It is suited for the occasional big effort rather than a continually monitored application of force.

On balance, there is good reason to rely on the use of the monetary tools of the Federal Reserve for economic stabilization policy, saving countercyclical fiscal policy for major and longer-lasting cyclical problems. Monetary policy is also plagued by the problem of long lags between the time action is taken and the time the economic consequences occur. There is indeed no perfect set of countercyclical tools available. But unlike fiscal policy, monetary policy can be applied in gradual doses and reversed quickly, which is a great merit when dealing with an uncertain future. Even though many of its consequences take a long time to occur, some of them take place more rapidly, and timely changes of monetary policy can help overcome surprises or counteract mistaken moves of the recent past.

Despite its limitations, the countercyclical use of fiscal policy is not a weapon to be discarded. While it is not suitable to deal with moderate recessions, its availability is important insurance in the event of some unexpectedly large crisis.

The very large structural budget deficits of the 1980s have cast a shadow over use of countercyclical fiscal policy. Because GNP grows over time, running zero deficits, or very small ones, will lead to a gradual decline in the ratio of the federal debt to GNP. If the United States runs zero or small deficits in good times, it is then possible to have occasional very large budget deficits during a recession, without any long-term increase in the debt-to-GNP ratio, with its consequent rise in the taxes necessary to cover interest on the debt. But if the federal government runs very large budget deficits even during periods of prosperity, as it has done in recent years, then incurring even larger deficits and debt increases during a recession exacerbates the long-term upward drift in interest payments and tax rates. In a very deep or long-lasting recession, it might still be wise to apply countercyclical fiscal stimulus. But there will be a long-term cost in the rise in interest payments and taxes as a share of GNP.

SUMMARY

At the risk of oversimplifying, memos 16–19 carry two main messages for the economic policymaker:

One, the Federal Reserve should be the principal active agent in stabilizing the economy against fluctuations in aggregate demand, supplementing the automatic stabilizing features of the federal budget. The intelligent application of monetary policy will not enable the economy to avoid recessions completely, but, barring major supply shocks, recessions should be infrequent and relatively mild. In a very large disturbance to demand, it may be necessary to adopt deliberate countercyclical fiscal measures. But in choosing them, bear in mind that permanent tax reductions or new spending programs, while helpful in a recession, will add to long-term budget deficits and lower national saving and investment unless offsetting tax increases or expenditure cuts are subsequently enacted.

Two, over the longer term, economic stability can be maintained with various combinations of monetary and fiscal policy. The nation can have full employment with a combination of loose budgetary policy and tight money—large budget deficits and high interest rates—as recurred throughout most of the 1980s. Through that combination we can emphasize the present rather than the future and have a GNP featuring high current consumption (public and private) and low national saving and investment. But we can also have full employment with the opposite mixture—restrictive budget policy with budget balance or even surplus, coupled with easy money and low interest rates. That combination will tilt the structure of the economy toward a more future-oriented shape, with a GNP that has less current consumption but more investment. In other words, with appropriate variations in monetary policy to preserve economic stability and to keep the level of aggregate demand in the neighborhood of potential GNP, we can use fiscal policy principally to influence the composition of demand, that is, consumption and investment, with important consequences for the long-term level and growth of potential GNP, that is, for aggregate supply.

NOTE

1. It isn't that the Fed couldn't offset a large reduction in the budget deficit with an appropriately massive injection of bank reserves. Rather, the problem is that the lags between policy action and economic consequences are different for the two policy instruments. Any action by the Fed big enough to offset fully the first-year consequences of a very large deficit reduction would, by the second year, be too big, forcing a major reversal of Fed policy in the second year, followed by still another reversal in the third year, and so on.

PART 3

Increasing Supply

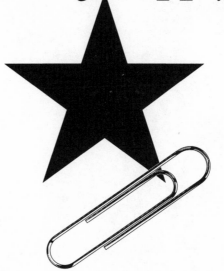

To: The President

From: CEA Chairman

Subject: **The Supply of GNP: The Fundamentals of Long-Term Growth**

This memo signals a major change in subject matter. Memos 5 through 19 focus on managing demand, keeping aggregate demand in the neighborhood of potential GNP to avoid large unemployment and inflation. This perspective is essentially short or medium term, concentrating on problems of economic instability. But potential GNP and aggregate supply grow over time, though slowly. And while the rate of growth in potential GNP attracts far fewer headlines than joblessness or rising prices, it is the chief source of rising living standards for the nation. In this memo, I begin to examine what government policies can and cannot do to increase the long-run growth of national output and income.

Changes in aggregate demand can raise or lower GNP relative to potential. Thus, after a recession, GNP can expand rapidly in response to increases in aggregate demand as unemployed workers, idle factories, and underutilized distribution facilities are put back to work. In the first two years after the low points of the deep recessions of 1975 and 1982, for example, GNP grew at 4.7 and 5.8 percent a year, respectively, much higher than the 3 percent growth of GNP that at the time was sustainable over the long run. But once rising aggregate demand has pulled output in the economy back up to the neighborhood of its potential—once the demand for GNP has risen to equal its long-term supply—then the economy cannot expand any faster than is allowed by the growth of potential GNP. And if a country tries to exceed that speed limit, it will generate pressures driving up the rate of inflation. Changes in aggregate demand can explain the short-run fluctuations in GNP, but over the long term, the growth of GNP is determined by how fast supply rises.

While the economic fortunes of a country can fluctuate, the living standards of its people can improve over the long run only as the supply of economic goods and services increases.

SUPPLY-SIDERS WERE WRONG, BUT THE SUPPLY SIDE IS IMPORTANT

The supply-side "revolution" of 1981 failed to achieve its goal of speeding up long-term national growth through tax cuts. After the deepest recession of the postwar period in 1982, the GNP did rise rapidly for some years, but this change reflected a period of aggregate demand catching up to potential GNP. The growth of potential GNP itself, and in particular, the growth of productivity—that is, output per worker—did not speed up during the 1980s. The growth of productivity between 1980 and 1990, while better than in 1973–79, remained disappointing.[1]

The supply-siders, who became prominent in the early 1980s, vastly exaggerated the efficacy of supply-side policies, and what lower taxes and deregulation could accomplish. That does not mean the government should neglect the supply side. The federal government ought to be deeply concerned with the effects of its various fiscal, tax, and regulatory policies on the level and the growth of potential GNP. Reducing budget deficits can increase national saving and lead to more investment. That federal tax policies can affect the growth of supply through their influence on saving, investment, work habits, and the like is widely appreciated although there is far less agreement on the magnitude of these effects. Almost all of the other domestic policy measures generate some supply-side consequences. They affect, however slightly, the output the economy can produce.

There is a common thread running through this and the subsequent memos dealing with the supply side. It's devilishly difficult for the federal government to raise the growth rate of potential GNP by substantial amounts. The things government can do, at least in principle, such as balancing the budget to raise the national saving rate, have modest effects on the growth rate, measured in a few tenths of 1 percent a year. Many other things could be important for growth in the long run, for example, improving the quality of American education or increasing the rate at which new technology is discovered and put into practice. But it is far from clear exactly what the federal government should do to achieve those goals.

The fact that we cannot expect large and dramatic payoffs from supply-side measures is not a reason to neglect them. Precisely because nudging the growth rate up is difficult, the federal government ought to avoid policies, such as the large budget deficits of the 1980s, that nudge it down. When output per worker is advancing at less than 1 percent a year, as it now is, policies that add or subtract one or two tenths of 1 percent a year loom large in the scheme of things. If, on each policy issue, the federal government ignores supply-side effects, the consequent small, individual erosions of national efficiency can cumulate over the years into government policies that greatly reduce potential GNP. Precisely because the growth effects of individual policies are so small, political concerns made it easy to allow the economy to drift into a large cumulative loss of national growth potential.

The culture, historical background, work habits, and entrepreneurial drive of a nation's citizenry also greatly influence its capacity for sustained economic growth. The discipline of economics has little to say about these fundamental characteristics of a country. That Japan, Taiwan, Korea, Singapore, and often but not always in postwar history, Brazil, grew so rapidly while Guatemala, Bangladesh, and Zaire languished is not explainable solely on grounds that fit easily into the usual categories of economics. Economics is most useful in explaining things at the margin—somewhat more or somewhat less. Nonetheless, there is a large body of organized economic knowledge to draw on in studying the factors that can raise the level of productivity or cause its growth to speed up or slow down.

CHANGES IN THE LEVEL AND IN THE RATE OF GROWTH OF PRODUCTIVITY

There are two kinds of improvements in productivity: increases in its level and increases in its rate of growth. Anything that increases the efficiency with which the economic system operates, for example, a dismantling of regulations that have been misallocating resources to low-productivity uses, will raise the level of productivity. But then productivity will settle down on the new higher path, and except for the transition period, will grow at the same rate as earlier, as illustrated in path B of figure 20-1. Many things that might help explain the level of productivity that a

FIGURE 20-1. Two Kinds of Changes in Productivity

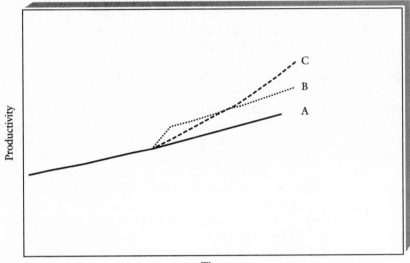

country enjoys in comparison with other countries—such as the flexibility of markets, the mobility of its labor force, or the average quality of management—are not the focus of these memos. Rather I am concentrating on those developments in the economy and in society that can produce a sustained growth in productivity, as illustrated in line C of figure 20-1, for example, a growing stock of productive capital, continuing improvement in the skills and educational attainments of the labor force, and advancing technology.

PRODUCTIVITY GROWTH: THE HISTORICAL RECORD

Table 20-1 records economic growth in the United States over the past 120 years. GNP grew most rapidly in the first half of the period, from 1870 to 1929, slowed during the next two decades when the Great Depression and the Second World War intervened, sped up again after the Second World War, and finally, after 1973, receded to the much slower pace we are now experiencing. Sometimes the growth rate of a country's total GNP is at issue, for example, when the nation is considering overall military power. But for ascertaining how well a country per-

TABLE 20-1. GNP Growth since 1870
Average annual percent change

Period	GNP	Employment	GNP per worker
1870–29	3.9	2.3	1.6
1929–48	2.4	1.3	1.1
1948–73	3.7	1.4	2.2
1973–90	2.5	1.9	0.6

forms in long-run improvements in living standards, the advance of GNP per worker is the most relevant measure.

IMPROVEMENTS IN PRODUCTIVITY AND LIVING STANDARDS

At the deepest philosophical level, a nation's living standards could be said to depend on a wide array of elements including the national culture, the quality of family life, the absence of crime, and so forth. But economics confines its scope to the material well-being of a society. From that narrower perspective, advances in a nation's living standards can be measured as the per capita or per worker level of goods and services that it furnishes its citizens.[2]

Over any sustained period there are only two ways in which a country's workers—including those who are self-employed—can provide themselves with an increased flow of goods and services: first, and overwhelmingly the most important, the country can increase the output and income that each worker can, on average, produce. The country has more goods and services available to enjoy, by using them directly or by trading them abroad to acquire goods and services produced elsewhere. Second, for the relatively modest share of most country's living standards that do depend on trading exports for goods imported from abroad, the country can improve its terms of trade. It can get more imports for a given quantity of exports.

PRODUCTIVITY AND LIVING STANDARDS

I will use the term "productivity" to stand for output per unit of labor input—output per worker. As stressed earlier, each dollar's worth of production generates a dollar's worth of income. When, for the economy as a whole, the amount of output produced by the average worker rises, an equal increase in the amount of income per worker is generated. Real wages—wages, including salaries and fringe benefits, adjusted for inflation—will rise proportionately with the rise in productivity as long as the distribution of income remains unchanged between the earnings of capital (profits, interest, dividends, and rent) on the one hand, and the compensation of employees on the other. During recessions and booms, the shares of income going to profits and wages do fluctuate, but over the long run, the distribution of income shares between returns to capital and returns to labor has not changed very much. And so, averaged over long periods, real wages have grown more or less in line with productivity.

The growth in income will be our rough and ready measure of the growth in living standards. After adjustment for inflation (as are all the data in this memo) a person's income is a measure of the goods and services he or she can acquire. It makes some difference whether one looks at the growth in income per worker, or average family income. But as figure 20-2 shows, the slowdown in productivity growth that occurred in the United States after 1973 was accompanied by a marked decline in the growth of family income and of real wages, including fringe benefits.

THE SOCIAL IMPORTANCE OF RISING AVERAGE INCOMES

The catch phrase, "a rising tide lifts all boats," is sometimes used to rationalize opposition to federal social programs for the poor. Nevertheless, it contains an important truth—a healthy pace of economic growth not only raises average incomes, but greatly eases the lot of the poor and those who might otherwise be hurt severely by economic disruptions. In any economic society marked by change, a minority of firms, workers, and communities suffer as tastes alter and technologies change, perhaps leaving them behind. But when growth in productivity and real wages is rapid, most of the "losers," after a short adjustment period, end up as well off as they were not too many years earlier. If, for example, average wage incomes are growing at, say, 3 percent a year, a displaced worker who has to take a job paying 20 percent less than his or her old one will typically catch up to the earlier wage after six years. But if the annual

FIGURE 20-2. The Growth of Real Wages and Family Income, 1955–90

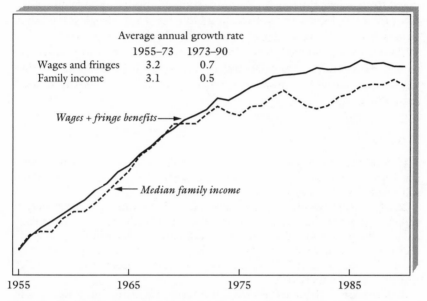

Note: By showing the data in logarithms, equal space is given to equal percentage changes. Thus a rise in income from 1.00 to 1.10 (10 percent) shows up as equal to a rise from 1.50 to 1.65 (also 10 percent).

growth of productivity and average wages slows to 1 percent, that worker will take almost twenty years to catch up.

During the past two decades, the slowdown in economic growth was not shared evenly. The bottom half of the income distribution was hit harder than the top half. And young male workers with high school or less education were particularly affected. Frank Levy of the University of Maryland has estimated that between 1970 and 1987, this group of less-educated workers suffered a 16 percent income loss.[3] As demand in the labor market increasingly called for workers with higher skills and educational backgrounds, the supply of lesser-skilled and lesser-trained workers continued to grow.[4] Consequently, their wages fell relative to the average. The same shifts in demand might well have occurred in an economy growing faster than the U.S. economy did. But the fact that it occurred in an environment of generally slow growth meant that those who fell behind suffered with particular severity. Even with relatively favorable assumptions about how this group will fare over the next twenty years, for the first time in American history an important segment of the labor force can look forward to having incomes at age forty less than their fathers had at the same age. In short, the productivity slowdown after 1973 not only produced slow gains in average incomes, but was accompanied by absolute income losses for a significant part of the nation's work force. Growth is more than a luxury, even for an already well-off society like ours.

NOTES

1. After the first oil shock, the rate of productivity growth did temporarily fall sharply to almost zero. It then recovered somewhat, but to a growth rate still well below the rate before 1973.

2. Most people would also judge a society by how widely the rise in output and income is distributed among its members. If growth bypasses a large segment of the population, that country has not improved its living standards as much as the country whose income distribution is more equitable. These memos do not focus on income distribution. But that does not reflect a belief that the issue is unimportant.

3. Frank Levy, "Incomes, Families, and Living Standards," in Robert Litan, Robert Z. Lawrence, and Charles L. Schultze, eds., *American Living Standards: Threats and Challenges* (Brookings, 1988), pp. 108–53.

4. Memo 27 examines this phenomenon in more detail and relates it to the American educational system.

MEMORANDUM **21**

To: The President

From: CEA Chairman

Subject: **The Sources of Economic Growth
and How Important Each One Is**

Public discussion about productivity seems to concentrate almost exclusively on productivity improvements in the manufacturing workplace. That's a mistake. A big part of the past century's improvement in American living standards came about because of the massive reduction in the costs of transportation. Otherwise it would have been impossible to develop efficient large-scale production and nationwide markets. Similarly, the development of large and sophisticated retail and wholesale distribution increased the volume of goods that any given number of employees could deliver to consumers. And the early development of a network of banking and thrift institutions, which could channel the nation's savings into a wide variety of productive uses, also promoted American economic growth.

The average Japanese worker in manufacturing is probably about as productive as his or her American manufacturing counterpart. But the average Japanese worker has a living standard about 20 percent lower than the American worker, principally because the nonmanufacturing sectors of the United States are so much more efficient than those in Japan. In short, the increases in total national output per worker can come from all sectors of the economy, not just the one-fifth of the GNP produced in manufacturing establishments. Indeed, the recent decline in U.S. productivity growth arose not because of events in the manufacturing sector, where productivity seems to be advancing at a reasonably good clip, but rather because of a virtual cessation of earlier substantial gains in productivity in trade, service, financial, and other sectors of the economy.

GROWTH ACCOUNTING: IDENTIFYING
THE SOURCES OF ECONOMIC GROWTH
AND MEASURING THEIR EFFECT

Besides some general background characteristics, a host of specific factors
determines a country's rate of productivity growth. Chief among these
are (1) the amount that the country saves and invests in equipping its
labor force with productive capital—tools, machinery, transportation
equipment, and other manmade means of production; (2) improvements
in the education and skills of its work force; and (3) the pace at which new
technology and improved techniques are introduced into the production,
transportation, and distribution of goods and services.

There are two ways a country can acquire new technology: discover it,
that is, push out the technological frontier; or adopt new technology
from someone who has already discovered it. In the earlier postwar years,
America was the preeminent technological leader; industry was at the
technological frontier; the level of productivity and living standards was
correspondingly far ahead of anyone else's. However, because it is difficult
to push out the technological frontier, the growth of American productivity was slower than in most other industrial countries. Those countries
started far behind the United States but were then able to adopt American
technology. By now the incorporation of advanced technology into the
workplace is more nearly equal among the major industrial countries, and
differences in growth rates are less pronounced.

Other influences on economic growth are at least partially measurable;
for example, the influence of demographic shifts. Everything else being
equal, young and inexperienced workers are likely to have lower productivity than more experienced workers, so that a rising fraction of young
people in the labor force will reduce productivity growth. Other important influences on productivity, for example, the quality of management, are much more difficult to measure.

All of these factors and others have changed over time, making some
contribution to economic growth, or in a few instances, retarding growth.
But how is one to sort out each influence's contribution to growth and,
more important, how can we exploit the historical record to estimate
the potential growth-promoting (or growth-retarding) effects of various
government policies?

In 1957 Robert Solow of the Massachusetts Institute of Technology,
in a study that was heavily responsible for his later selection as a Nobel

Prize laureate, first worked out a defensible technique for quantitative measures of the individual contributions to economic growth of several major factors.[1] (The Appendix to this memo briefly describes the essence of that technique.)

Solow initially applied his method to isolating the contributions of labor and capital to the growth of output in the United States between 1929 and 1956. He found that economic growth had been much greater than could be explained simply by increases in the quantities of labor and capital used in production. The large unexplained increment of growth, the Solow residual, has been taken to reflect the productivity-raising effects of technological progress and other advances in human knowledge. This result confirmed common sense. After all, if America had accumulated capital and added to its labor force as it did between 1929 and 1956, but had adhered slavishly to 1929 technology, production in 1956 would clearly have been far less abundant than it was.

Edward Denison greatly expanded Solow's work, estimating for the United States and for other industrial countries the contribution of several other elements to the growth of output and output per worker. Among other things, he separated the contribution of labor to economic growth into two parts: the increase in the number of people employed and the rise in the average education of the work force. A slightly modified version of his results, explaining the growth of output per worker in the United States during the postwar period, before and after 1973, is shown in table 21-1. Although Denison's estimates end in 1982, the table gives a quick overview of the chief factors that have contributed to American productivity growth since the Second World War and the reasons for the decline in productivity growth since 1973.[2]

SUMMARY

Americans have taken a significant part of their increased productivity out in the form of more leisure—that is, fewer working hours—rather than in higher income. Annual output per worker, and the income that went with it, grew about 0.5 percent a year less than it might have, as the average work week fell, the number of holidays rose, and vacations lengthened. This trend has been continuing since the nineteenth century. Americans were not alone; the same developments occurred in other industrial countries. Indeed, taking into account the length of the work week and the high proportion of American women who work outside the

TABLE 21-1. Sources of American Productivity Growth, 1929–82
Percent

Item	Average annual growth	
	1948–73	1973–82
Output per worker	2.3	0.2
Owing to changes in:		
Average weekly working hours	−0.4	−0.5
Quantity of education	0.4	0.4
Quantity of capital	0.5	0.3
Economies of large-scale production	0.3	0.2
Other identifiable factors[a]	0.4	−0.3
Residual (advances in technology and other unknown factors)	1.1	0.1

Source: Based on Edward Denison, *Trends in American Economic Growth, 1929–82* (Brookings, 1985), p. 114, table 8-4.

a. A major factor included in this category is the productivity gain that results when underemployed workers leave farms and self-employment and find employment at higher-productivity jobs. The contributions of this factor fell from 0.3 percent in the early period to less than 0.1 percent in the later one.

home, Americans spend more time on the job than do citizens of most other industrial countries outside of Japan.

Even after considering improvements in education and other factors affecting productivity growth, about half of the growth in output per person during the postwar years comes from sources that cannot be identified (that is, the residual). As I noted earlier, the chief one of these unidentified sources of growth is assumed to be advances in technology and human knowledge. If that identification is correct, then it turns out that the intellectual, nonmaterial elements of our productive system—the combined effects of increased education of the work force and advances in knowledge (lines 2 and 6 in table 21-1)—are overwhelmingly the main sources of American growth in productivity and living standards. According to Denison, over the whole period 1948-82, the intellectual factors have accounted for more than 75 percent of the growth in output per worker.

National saving and investment have traditionally been sufficient to equip the nation's labor force with an ever-larger stock of capital per worker, and that was another source of the growth in output per worker. In Denison's estimates, however, the contribution is modest; increases in the stock of capital per worker accounted for less than one-quarter of the productivity advances of the postwar years. But as we shall see, the implication of this result is *not* that government policies affecting saving and investment are unimportant.

After 1973 productivity growth slowed sharply. Why? We do not know the main reasons. The amount of capital per worker did not grow as fast in the 1970s as it had in earlier postwar decades, but that only explains a small part of the post-1973 fall in productivity growth. Denison pinpoints several other contributors to the decline. But, even after having done so, the developments that Denison could identify were responsible for less than half the slowdown.

For a long time, one popular contender for the role of villain in explaining the slowdown in productivity growth was the sharp rise in energy prices that occurred in the 1970s and 1980s. Obviously the higher price paid for foreign oil reduced the purchasing power and well-being of American consumers. But in addition, some analysts saw it as a major contributor to the fall in productivity growth. The downturn in productivity growth was not confined to the United States. It was worldwide, and it began everywhere after 1973, coincident with the first big surge in world oil prices. As explained in memo 10, a sharp run-up in oil prices sets in motion recessionary forces that reduce aggregate demand while also generating inflationary pressures that make it difficult for monetary policy to be eased as a means of combating the recession. These are temporary problems; after a while, the economy absorbs these short-run effects, and employment and inflation return to normal. But even in the long run, the path of productivity growth can be affected.

Energy can be considered, with labor and capital, as an input into the production process. When energy prices rose sharply between 1973 and 1981, business firms shifted toward less energy-intensive methods of means of production, using more capital and labor to produce goods and services. But that shift, while an appropriate response given the higher costs of energy, had side effects in reducing productivity. Some investments that would have been devoted to improving output per worker went toward energy conservation, some of the new energy-saving production techniques required more capital or more labor than the old ones, and some high-energy-using capital was made prematurely obsolete. The overall productivity of the economy is now lower than it would have been had energy prices and the intensity of energy use stayed where they were in 1973. Thus, say some, the rise in energy prices was a major factor in explaining the fall in productivity growth after 1973.

There are two reasons, however, why these developments cannot explain any large part of the post-1973 fall in productivity growth. First, energy consumption by business firms in 1973 represented less than 5 percent of their production costs. The switch away from energy use toward other, less efficient means of production that took place, in the effort to avoid some of the 200 percent increase in real energy costs to business between 1973 and 1981, was not big enough to explain much of the productivity slowdown. Second, real energy prices plunged sharply after 1985, and adjusted for general inflation, are now only 50 percent higher than in 1973. And yet productivity growth has not rebounded since 1985, as it would have begun to do if energy prices were the main culprit. In sum, rising energy prices played some role in the productivity slowdown but cannot explain most of the phenomenon.

Conceivably, the slowdown in productivity growth reflected a diminution in the pace of technological progress, after a generation of unusual growth around the world. The pace of the postwar advance in technology may indeed have been unsustainable, reflecting a catch-up after twenty years of depression and war, but no one has been able to verify that hypothesis. One of the serious shortcomings of the Solow-Denison techniques for studying growth is its treatment of the role of technology, which shows up as a residual after the role of everything else has been imperfectly estimated. It is still difficult to understand why, in the aggregate, the pace at which technological improvements were being introduced into the workplace slowed so suddenly and so dramatically.

In the end, economic studies to date have not convincingly identified the reasons for a good bit of the productivity slowdown. And so people have been straining to find explanations: unsatisfactory performance by American management, a loss of the work ethic among American workers, and so on. But it is not necessary to pin down the principal causes of the productivity slowdown in order to design policies to do something about it. Even if a football team can't figure out exactly why its running game has deteriorated, more aggressive line play and better blocking should improve it. And even if a fall in investment was not responsible for much of the productivity slowdown to date, the government can nevertheless help stimulate higher productivity growth by taking steps to expand national saving and investment through a reduction in the federal budget or, as some people would urge, through tax incentives for private saving and investment. The government can also promote reform and put more resources into education or try to speed up the advance of technology by increasing support for research and development. And so the memos that follow examine in some detail three major factors that affect economic growth: the volume of national saving and investment; the quantity and quality of education; and the advance of technology, especially as it is influenced by research and development.

Most of the things that the federal government can do to improve the long-term rate of economic growth require citizens to sacrifice some current consumption—private and public—to achieve results in the future. And the beneficial payoffs take effect only gradually. Even then, growth-promoting policies yield results that seem, at least on the surface, quite small, perhaps several tenths of a percentage point in sustained economic growth.[3] There are simply no dramatic supply-side miracles waiting to be discovered. Given the inherent difficulties of moving the long-term growth rate through government policies, however, modest positive results are important. In addition, the effects of very small changes in the economic growth rate, sustained over many years, cumulate into respectable results, unfortunately long after the next election.

Good or bad demand-side policies typically generate good or bad economic results relatively quickly. But good or bad supply-side policies have long-delayed payoffs.

APPENDIX: CALCULATING THE SOURCES OF ECONOMIC GROWTH

Solow, and those who in the past three decades have expanded on his work in calculating the sources of growth, make one key assumption on which economists rely heavily for many kinds of studies: on average, and in the long run, worker skills, educational investments, physical capital, and other productive factors get rewarded roughly according to how much each adds at the margin to the total value of production. If college graduates, on average, are paid $7,500 a year more in wages than high school graduates, that implies that the employed person with four years of college education contributes, on average, $7,500 more to the value of production than a high school graduate, partly because of intellectual and other abilities and partly because of the college education. If business capital investments earn a 10 percent return on capital employed (before taxes), this is because the addition of $1 million more in plant and equipment to the production process—while holding the size of the work force, the educational qualities of workers, and other elements of the production process constant—can add, on average, $100,000 a year worth of extra output.[4]

In calculating the sources of the growth in GNP during any period, each additional unit of labor is assigned a contribution equal to its wages and each dollar's addition to productive capital a contribution measured by its profit rate (including interest). Suppose, for example, that during some five-year period, GNP grew by 9 percent, that labor received 70 percent of total income while payments to capital (profits, depreciation, and interest) accounted for the remaining 30 percent. If employment rose by 5 percent during the period, we would say that labor contributed 3.5 percentage points of the 9 percent GNP growth (5 percent growth in employment times labor's weight of 70 percent). And if the stock of capital grew by 10 percent, we could conclude that capital contributed 3 percentage points of the GNP growth (10 percent growth in capital times capital's weight of 30 percent). In this example, labor and capital together would have contributed 6.5 percentage points (3.5 for labor and 3 for capital) and the remaining 2.5 percentage points would be the Solow residual, the growth explained by the advance of technology and other unmeasurable factors.

By similarly noting the difference in average wages connected with differences in educational attainment (years of high school or college attended, and so on), some part of the 3.5 percentage point contribution of labor to the GNP growth can be broken down into that part attributable to an increase in the average educational attainment of the labor force and that part owing to the sheer increase in numbers of workers.

NOTES

1. Robert M. Solow, "Technical Change and the Aggregate Production Function," *Review of Economics and Statistics*, vol. 39 (August 1957), pp. 312–20.

2. Edward F. Denison, *Trends in American Economic Growth, 1929–82* (Brookings, 1985). Denison assumes that the historical reduction in average working hours increased worker productivity so that some of the resultant decline in labor input did not have an effect in reducing output. In table 21–1, I recalculated Denison's results to remove that assumption. The effect is to in-

crease the negative influence of declining working hours and raise the residual but by small amounts.

3. I am referring to the rate in advanced industrial societies, where an appropriate economic structure is already in place. I am not considering societies, such as the ones in Eastern Europe and Latin America, which are fundamentally restructuring themselves.

4. The assumption is not as naive as it first sounds. For example, we typically observe racial discrimination not so much in minorities being underpaid in high-paying, highly productive occupations but much more in their being restricted to low-productivity, low-paid occupations. The marginal productivity theory of how factors of production are paid is not a theory about what is or is not ethical in the distribution of income. Rather it is a theory about how business managers behave when confronted with the costs of hiring or of using different factors of production.

MEMORANDUM **22**

TO: The President

FROM: CEA Chairman

SUBJECT: **Saving, Investment, and Capital Formation**

Capital formation, education, and research and development are the sources of economic growth examined in the remainder of these memos. I start with capital formation. What is it, how much of the nation's growth can be explained by it, and to what extent did the slowdown in capital formation contribute to the recent decline in national productivity growth?

A nation's stock of capital encompasses the resources invested in past years that contribute to the current production of output and the generation of income. The capital available to contribute to today's production is an inheritance of saving and investment decisions made in the past.

Many things are appropriately included in the term "capital," not only tangible capital in the form of machines, factories, and houses, but also the vast intangible capital assets the nation has built up from the resources devoted over the years to the education and training of today's work force. (The sixty-year-old worker possesses educational capital toward which resources were devoted more than fifty years earlier.) And in a similar vein, the government and business firms pour funds into research and development to create an intangible stock of technological knowledge. But I will confine this memo to a discussion of tangible capital, in the form of machinery and equipment, nonresidential structures, housing, and business inventories. By the end of 1989, the total gross stock of public and private tangible capital (excluding military weapons but including residential housing) that had been built up by investment over the past years amounted to $21 trillion, almost four times the value of that year's GNP. On average, it takes $4.00 in tangible capital to produce $1.00 of output.

SAVING AND INVESTMENT

Apart from the possibility of overseas borrowing, a nation can increase capital stock only by saving. As an earlier memo explained, national saving is that part of national output or income not devoted to private or government consumption. Thus saving is the annual flow of national resources made available for investment by the nation's refraining from consuming all of its income. Investment is the use of those resources to build productive assets in the form of plant, equipment, and houses, while capital is the total stock of such tangible productive assets that have been accumulated as the nation has saved and invested over the years. Each year some of the capital is retired as it reaches the end of its useful life, and some of it gradually loses efficiency even before it is retired. And so part of investment each year has to go to replacing the capital that is "lost" to the productive system that year. What's left over represents net additions to the capital stock.

It does a country no good to refrain from consumption (that is, to save) without devoting equivalent resources to producing goods for domestic investment or for an export surplus (that is, foreign investment). An attempt to increase national saving without an equivalent increase in investment will simply lead to a decline in aggregate demand, a recession, and a buildup of unemployed labor and capital resources. But in this memo, dealing with the supply side of the economy, I will assume that government monetary and fiscal policies are successful in matching demand to supply and keeping the economy on a high-employment track— any increases in national saving are matched by increases in investment and do result in higher capital formation. There are three forms of tangible capital: business investment in plant, equipment, and inventories; residential construction; and public investment in roads, dams, and other infrastructure. The magnitude of such investment is shown in table 22-1.[1]

Unfortunately, the standard studies of the role of capital in economic growth do not estimate the contribution of capital investment by government. Clearly public investment in highways, airports, and other infrastructure has contributed importantly to American economic growth. While growth studies measure the contribution to national output of private capital by observing the income it earns, the output of most

TABLE 22-1. Capital Stock and Investment in the United States, 1989
Billions of dollars

Item	Gross capital stock at year end	Investment in 1989
Business	10,019	607
Residential housing	7,010	231
Government (excluding military)	3,699	121
Total	20,728	959
Addendum: 1989 GNP	5,248	...

government capital—for example, roads, schools, dams—is not sold on the market and earns no profits. Consequently, it is far more difficult to estimate the contribution of such investment, and people are widely at odds on how productive various types of government investment are.[2] Because they ignore public investment, the growth studies and the discussion here underestimate, by a modest amount, the contribution of capital investment to U.S. economic growth.

THE ROLE OF CAPITAL FORMATION IN PRODUCTIVITY GROWTH

Over the past three hundred years in most of the Western world, production has become more capital intensive. Each successive generation of workers has had more capital to work with, not only directly in the form of more complex and expensive machinery on the factory floor, but indirectly in the form of increasing capital tied up in the trucking fleets, communications networks, and power plants that back up the production line and distribute its products. Increasing capital intensity is not merely the story of a historical process, it is an option available at any moment to today's business firms. If it is relatively inexpensive to get the funds to acquire new capital (with stock prices high and interest rates low), while labor is relatively dear, it will pay business firms to increase capital intensity—that is, to choose production techniques that use an increased amount of capital per worker.

Expanding the amount of capital per worker does not mean that each worker has more of the same kind of machines to work with. Rather, at any moment of time, a firm can choose from an array of technologically feasible production techniques. By choosing one with more complex and automated machinery, additional materials-handling capability, greater reliance on large inputs of electric power, or perhaps by centralizing production in one location and employing more transportation capital, firms can substitute capital for labor. Output per worker rises. Of course, this increase does not typically happen quickly. Firms do not junk the production facilities they just installed a few years ago. But if economic conditions—the cost of capital, the cost of labor, and the technological possibilities—call for it, firms make changes in capital intensity as they gradually replace old machinery and expand into new facilities.

There is an important connection between the continuing discovery of new technology and an increase in capital intensity. Between 1929 and 1989, the nation's stock of business fixed capital increased by 290 percent while the business work force rose by only 125 percent, representing a big (74 percent) increase in the ratio of capital to labor. But if the array of technological alternatives open to business firms had remained where it was in 1929, such a large increase in the capital-labor ratio would never have occurred. Businesses would eventually have exhausted the possibilities of improving profits through the adoption of more capital-intensive techniques, and with no new technologies entering the array, further increases in capital intensity would not have been profitable even at very low interest rates. On the one hand, steady increases in the capital-labor ratio push down the return from further investment in capital-intensive processes. On the other hand, the advent of more advanced new technology opens up new ways to use capital more intensively and restores the profitability of making further capital investments. It has been said that the history of business enterprise is "a race between capital accumulation and technological progress," the former pushing down the return from new investments, the latter raising it again.

In any event, at a given moment, individual business firms have available many technologically feasible ways of making investments that substitute capital for labor in the production process and raise average output per worker. If the price is right, they will make additional investments of that kind.

FIGURE 22-1. The Effect of a Rise in the Investment-GNP Ratio

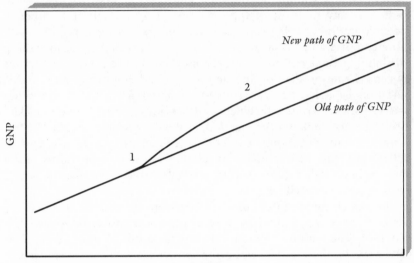

PAYOFF FROM ADDITIONAL CAPITAL INVESTMENT

A rise in the share of national income devoted to saving makes it possible to expand investment, increase capital stock per worker, and raise the level of output per worker. For a while, the growth of GNP will speed up. Eventually GNP will resume its old growth rate, but along a permanently higher path (figure 22-1). It will take some time to reach the new higher path, and it will be convenient to measure the effect of higher saving and investment as the speedup in the growth rate that occurs as national output is moving from the lower to the higher path (from point 1 to point 2 in figure 22-1).

By employing the basic Solow-Denison assumption—that is, that the rate of return to capital, averaged over good and bad years, tells us how much an extra unit of capital services will add to output—we can crudely estimate the payoff from additional investment. Potential net national product (NNP) in the United States is now growing at a little under 2 percent a year, with the labor force rising at a 1.2 percent rate and output per worker advancing at a little less than 1 percent annually.

If net national saving were raised by 1 percent of GNP and maintained in-definitely at the new higher level, and all of the additional saving were devoted to increasing domestic investment, the annual growth rate of potential GNP would be speeded up over the next decade by about 0.1 percent, in the form of a faster rate of productivity growth.

This seems like a disappointingly small payoff from additional saving and investment. Increasing the net national saving rate from its current 3 percent to, say, 5 percent would be no small matter, representing a 60 percent increase in saving. Yet it would, according to Denison-Solow type calculations, add only about 0.2 percent to the current growth rate of potential GNP.

Arguments have been advanced that the Denison-Solow techniques understate the historical contribution of investment to economic growth and are correspondingly too pessimistic about the future payoff from additional investment. Some part of technological advance is incorporated into new capital goods. Higher investment thus generates faster technological progress; consequently, an increase in investment would do more to speed up growth than emerges from "static" calculations of the Denison-Solow type. But if the underlying pace of technological advance doesn't speed up, an increase in the new technology embodied in capital through additional investment in one year simply leaves less to be incorporated by investment in subsequent years. Although the payoff from capital investment would indeed be raised temporarily, it would be followed by a period of lower payoff. Thus it has long been agreed among economists studying the growth process that even though some new technology is embodied in new investment, that fact does not invalidate the basic Denison-Solow results.

Arguments have been made that as firms invest in technologically up-to-date capital goods, they engage in a learning process that leads them to make further technological advances. A related view centers around the proposition that a large fraction of industrial research and development is done by firms producing capital goods. Hence an expansion in the market for capital goods would induce an increase in R&D and therefore an acceleration of technological progress. But even if correct, this argument would suggest that the appropriate government policy is to promote and subsidize more R&D directly rather than get to the same end indirectly, and probably more expensively, by inducing an increase in investment.

The chief case for assigning a greater role to investment in the growth process, however, rests not on these conceptual arguments but on the striking empirical observation, shown in figure 22-2, that across industrial

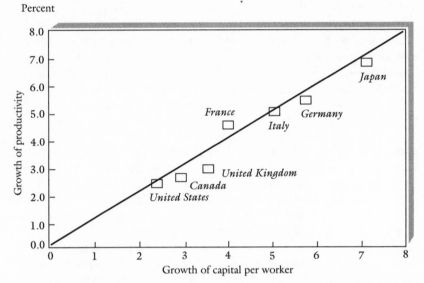

FIGURE 22-2. Capital Accumulation and Productivity Growth among OECD Countries, 1950–79

Percent

countries, a higher rate of accumulation of capital per worker produces a much greater improvement in the growth of productivity than is consistent with the Denison-Solow estimates. As shown in figure 22-2, each 1 percentage point extra growth of capital per worker seems to have added 1 percentage point more growth in labor productivity—more than three times as much as would be expected from the standard growth models.

A more careful look at the data and consideration of the circumstances in which Europe and Japan found themselves after the war blunt the arguments against the Denison-Solow findings. In the 1950s, 1960s, and early 1970s, the United States was the clear technological leader; it had in place much more advanced technology than did Europe or, especially, Japan. The bigger the technological gap between a particular country and the United States, the bigger the backlog of immensely profitable investment opportunities to be exploited by investing large sums in new equipment that embodied the advanced technology. Large capital investments and their associated technology borrowed from the United States could be put into place without significantly exhausting the huge stock of still-unexploited investment opportunities. Thus the greater the annual rate of investment, the larger the leap forward in new technology and productivity. But for the United States, already at the frontier—and for other countries once they catch up—the backlog of as-yet-to-be-exploited technology is not so large, and the payoff from investment, while still significant, is less than appears from the relationship shown in figure 22-2. The balance of the evidence suggests that the growth from additional saving and investment is not likely to be larger by a substantial margin than what is estimated from the Denison-Solow type studies.[3] But these matters are not yet settled in the economics profession.

CAPITAL FORMATION AND THE POST-1973 PRODUCTIVITY SLOWDOWN

A decline in the rate of capital formation played only a modest role in the slowdown of productivity growth after 1973. After 1973, the rate of growth of the American labor force picked up substantially owing to a growing inflow of women and young people into the labor force. A larger fraction of domestic investment had to go simply to equip the new labor force entrants with an average amount of capital per worker, leaving a reduced fraction available to raise the amount of capital available per worker. And so capital's contribution to the growth of labor productivity fell. But this reduced contribution of capital accounts for only one-tenth, or at most one-fifth, of the fall in productivity growth after 1973. And even after 1980, when the national saving rate in the United States fell sharply, resort to large-scale borrowing from abroad attenuated the accompanying reduction in domestic investment. Consensus among those who study productivity is fairly wide that whatever the disagreements about the relative importance of capital investment in explaining economic growth, the fall in productivity growth since 1973 cannot be blamed primarily on a low rate of capital formation.

In sum, capital's contribution to the growth process has been positive and important, but not huge, and the decline in productivity growth since 1973 cannot be traced in any large way to a falloff in capital formation.

WARNING: FRACTIONS OF A PERCENT ON THE GROWTH RATE ARE IMPORTANT

The payoff from additional saving and investment is measured only in tenths of a percent on the potential growth rate. That does not mean that government policy need not concern itself too much with the national saving and investment rate. It is devilishly hard for government to increase the growth rate dramatically by any set of measures. Indeed, if governments could do so and count on large, observable, and prompt results, most countries in the world would be growing much faster than they are now. If the payoffs were large and quick, it would be politically easy to undertake difficult measures to improve growth.

One of the few things that a government can do to promote growth with some confidence of success is to raise the national rate of saving and investment, principally but not solely, through eliminating budget deficits and even running surpluses, together with a policy of easier money and lower interest rates. A 2 percentage point increase in the net national saving rate, devoted to raising domestic investment, would, by the end of three decades, increase net national product some 4 percent. A small number indeed. But even after allowing for the higher saving rate, that would provide over $900 a year in extra consumption (private and public) for the average family in the next generation.

MAINTAINING THE STATUS QUO TAKES INVESTMENT

In a modern capital-intensive economy, like those of the United States, Europe, and Japan, it takes a great deal of investment each year simply to keep things going, as is evident from table 22-2. From 1987 through 1990 business firms invested an average of $530 billion a year, or 11 percent of GNP, in new plant and equipment. About three-fifths of that investment was needed simply to replace machinery, equipment, and structures that had ended their useful lives and were being retired from service. Another one-fifth was required to equip the additional people who came into the work force each year with an average amount of capital per worker; without that investment, capital per worker would have declined, exerting a downward force on productivity. In the end, less than one-fifth of business investment, amounting to about 2 percent of GNP, was available to increase capital per worker and make a contribution to the growth of productivity.

One of the implications of the data in table 22-2 is that what seem to be small changes in the share of GNP devoted to investment translate into large proportionate changes in the growth of capital per worker. Suppose we could increase gross business investment from just under 10 percent to 12 percent of GNP. That would be an increase of one-fifth in

TABLE 22-2. Uses of U.S. Business Investment, 1987–90

Uses of investment	Billions of 1987 dollars	Percent of GNP
Total business investment in plant and equipment	530	11.0
Replacing retired capital	319	6.7
Additional capital needed to equip new workers with the existing average amount of capital per worker	108	2.3
Amount available to increase the stock of capital per worker	103	2.2

the business investment share. But the investment required to replace worn-out plant and equipment retired each year would not immediately change, nor would the amount of capital needed to equip additions to the work force. The increased investment would go toward increasing the stock of capital per worker; the annual addition to the stock would approximately double, from $100 billion to $200 billion. And so, even though each additional 1 percent the nation saves and invests contributes only a small fraction of 1 percent to the growth of national output, that small fraction can easily be wiped out, or doubled, by relatively modest changes in the share of income that is saved and invested.

NOTES

1. All of the capital stocks are measured in terms of what it would have cost to reproduce them in 1989. They are gross stocks—that is, before the deduction of accumulated depreciation allowances. Government capital excludes military goods.

2. A recent widely cited study by David Aschauer of the Federal Reserve Bank of Chicago concludes that in the postwar period $1 of public investment has been three to four times as productive as $1 of private investment. But in my judgment, with some support from a recent study of the Congressional Budget Office, the Aschauer study provides excessively optimistic estimates of

the productivity-enhancing effect of government infrastructure investment. I will return to this issue in memo 25. See David Ashchauer, "Is Public Expenditure Productive?" *Journal of Monetary Economics*, vol. 23 (March 1989), pp. 177–200; and Congressional Budget Office, *How Federal Spending for Infrastructure and Other Public Investments Affects the Economy* (Washington: Congressional Budget Office, 1991).

3. A major recent study of U.S. economic growth by Harvard economist Dale Jorgenson and several associates also assigns a much greater role in economic growth to investment than does Denison. But a large part of the difference arises from how the terms are defined. The Denison estimates in table 21-1 refer to the nonresidential business sector of the economy. Jorgenson also includes, in his measures of output and capital input, the shelter services produced by residential housing and the services that consumers receive from the stock of durable goods they own. But these outputs are almost 100 percent generated by capital, with no contribution from labor. And when they are added to the business sector, they substantially raise the contribution of an "average" input of capital to the growth process. In addition, the Jorgenson study is based on the use of gross output, and for technical reasons, the contribution of capital formation to the growth of gross output, everything else being equal, will always be higher than its contribution to the growth of net output (or national income), which Denison examines. See Dale W. Jorgenson, Frank M. Gollop, and Barbara M. Fraumeni, *Productivity and U.S. Economic Growth* (Harvard University Press, 1987).

To: The President

From: CEA Chairman

Subject: **Raising National Saving and Investment:
A Target for the 1990s**

Memo 4 documented the drop in national saving during the 1980s, from an average of about 8.2 percent of national income in the previous three decades to about 3 percent at the beginning of the 1990s. The fall in private saving and a rise in the federal budget deficit contributed equally to this decline.[1]

THE CONSEQUENCES OF THE 1980S DECLINE IN NATIONAL SAVING

Consuming more than one's income is, for a time, a pleasant experience. But it has future costs. As mentioned in memos 4 and 10, the fall in national saving led about equally to a decline in domestic investment and an increase in overseas borrowing. In the years ahead the United States will be paying for its 1980s consumer binge in two ways: the lower domestic investment will lead to lower productivity growth, which reduces the advance of national living standards. And the overseas borrowing created debts to foreigners on which interest has to be paid, which reduces the national income available for use here at home. If the United States had been borrowing abroad to support a very large volume of investment in productive assets, as it did during large parts of the nineteenth century, it would be paying the overseas interest costs out of an augmented national income, generated by the high level of investment, and it could break even or come out ahead in the process. But the overseas borrowing of the 1980s financed consumption rather than productive investment and thus will worsen rather than improve future living standards.

The fall in national saving during the 1980s was the principal cause of the high real interest rates that characterized that decade. For both borrowers and lenders the relevant measure of interest rates is the "real" interest rate—the nominal rate of interest less the rate of inflation.[2] The high interest rates were the mechanism by which the nation adjusted to the fall in national saving. The high interest rates not only discouraged total investment but, perhaps equally important, biased the investment that did take place away from long-term and toward short-term projects. Increases in interest rates particularly penalize investments with a long-term payoff. Imagine borrowing $1,000 to make a one-year investment, while paying a 4 percent real interest rate on the borrowed funds. At the end of a year the investment project must have a net return of at least $40 to break even. If the interest rate were to rise to 6 percent, that one-year investment would have to return $60, a 50 percent increase. But now consider an investment that doesn't pay out until the fifteenth year. To break even at a 4 percent interest rate, the investment must earn $800. If the interest rate now rises to 6 percent, that same investment must return $1,400 to break even, an increase of 75 percent in the required yield. To look at it another way, all of the potential fifteen-year investment projects yielding between $800 and $1,400 dollars, which would have been worthwhile to undertake when the interest rate was 4 percent, are suddenly no longer profitable when the interest rate rises to 6 percent. And of course it is not just investment in physical assets that is affected. Clearly, the willingness to undertake research or market development projects with long-horizon payoffs is similarly discouraged.

Many of those who worry about the deterioration of American competitiveness in world markets argue that American business executives are too concerned with short-term results and much less willing than their Japanese or European counterparts to play the role of patient investors. In fact, however, American executives may be no less farsighted than their foreign competitors. They may simply have been responding rationally to the necessities imposed by a decade of unprecedentedly high interest rates.

HOW MUCH SHOULD THE COUNTRY SAVE?

Would returning to the saving rate of the pre-1980 years be appropriate? If so, what target would be appropriate? Raising national saving means forgoing national consumption, through higher taxes that will reduce private consumption or through a cut in public consumption. Increasing saving is not painless, and the country should have some rationale for the choice it makes.

One possible approach would be to say that the government should remain in a position of neutrality by balancing its own budget—neither augmenting nor reducing private saving—thereby accepting the aggregate saving outcome that emerges from the individual decisions of the nation's households and business firms. Based on the situation in 1989 and 1990, such a neutrality rule, requiring that the government move to balance its budget but no more, would raise the national saving rate from 3 percent to 6.5 percent, restoring about two-thirds of the decline that took place in the 1980s.

The neutrality rule, however, is flawed for several reasons. In the first place, there is nothing sacrosanct about the aggregate national saving rate that emerges from the decisions of individual savers. Millions of lower-income families, for example, would prefer to set aside at least modest amounts for the future but are so pressed by the exigencies of their limited incomes that they cannot. Moreover, the returns that savers, especially lower-income savers, can get for their money, after inflation and after taxes, may not be reflective of the much larger payoffs that could be obtained nationally by investing in productive assets.

Second, and perhaps more important, the federal government at this point cannot afford to be neutral about national saving. As explained in memo 1, the early years of the next century will witness a large increase in the number of retirees drawing social security benefits relative to the size of the work force who will be paying taxes into the social security system. The country is now accumulating large surpluses in its social security and other retirement trust funds to help pay for those future benefits.[3] Currently, accumulating these annual surpluses is the right thing to do, given the prospective growth in the number of retirees who will be receiving payments.

These financial accumulations, however, will not prevent the increased numbers of retirees from becoming a burden to the next generation of workers. The retirees of the future will be using their social security benefits to purchase goods and services. An increased share of national output and income will have to provide those goods and services, and a corresponding amount of output and income, therefore, will not be available for the workers of the future to use for themselves. The only way the United States can use today's financial surpluses to provide for

TABLE 23-1. Federal Budget Overall Deficits, 1992, 1997
Billions of dollars

Budget	1992	1997
Retirement funds	103	151
Operating budget	− 393	− 405
Total deficit[a]	− 290	− 254

a. Deficits exclude deposit insurance and Desert Storm contributions.

tomorrow's retirees and prevent their enlarged numbers from becoming a burden to the next generation is to adopt appropriate federal budget policies. Under such policies, the surpluses in the retirement trust funds would be employed to increase national saving and investment over and above what they otherwise would have been. The additional investment would expand the stock of productive assets and raise future national output and income.

By the middle of the current decade the magnitude of the annual trust fund surpluses, which should be used to augment national saving, will amount to about 2.5 percent of national income.[4] Under current policies, however, the nation is not using the retirement surpluses to add to national saving. Rather the surpluses are partially financing large deficits in the rest of the federal budget. For example, the overall budget deficit of some $250 billion projected for 1997 is composed of a $400 billion deficit in the operating budget, partly offset by large surpluses in the retirement funds (table 23-1).

Granted that the surpluses in the retirement funds should be used to increase national saving, what is the level of national saving to which they should be added? That is, apart from the extra saving needed to meet the demographic bulge of retirees several decades from now, how much should the nation be saving? I have explained why this matter can not simply be left to the decisions of the marketplace, but that caveat doesn't provide an answer.

Theorists studying the process of economic growth have developed some fairly esoteric rules defining an "optimal" national saving rate. But those rules depend on so many special circumstances as to be of little help. One rough and ready but basically sensible approach to the problem is to ascertain how much of its national income the nation would have to save and invest at home simply to preserve the current rate of growth in productivity (output per worker), assuming that other factors affecting productivity growth continue on their current path. The national saving needed to undertake that investment, without relying on importing any saving from abroad through foreign borrowing, would constitute a conservative "business-as-usual" baseline. To that amount can then be added the annual accumulation of trust fund surpluses, and the total would be the overall national saving target.

This approach to choosing a national saving target is indeed conservative. As already discussed, the current rate of productivity growth is low by postwar standards. Moreover, the proposed target does not allow for any net American investment abroad, something that did occur in most years before 1980. Nevertheless, even if the target is chosen conservatively, the United States is currently still well below it.

Calculating the Saving Target

Maintaining the current modest rate of productivity growth would require a national saving rate out of national income smaller than the saving rate of earlier postwar decades. That is so for three reasons. One, the growth of the labor force has slowed, so it now takes less aggregate investment to equip each new cohort of entrants to the labor force with an average amount of plant and equipment. Two, the amount of capital per worker is now growing more slowly than it did earlier. As noted in memo 21, this is one reason, though not a dominant one, for the post-1973 slowdown in productivity growth. And three, the prices of computers and related equipment (per unit of computing services delivered), which now account for a large part of business investment, have fallen and continue to fall sharply. Consequently, each dollar of saving now delivers a "bigger investment bang for the buck" than was true in earlier years. But given the depressed rate of American productivity growth, the country ought to take advantage of the reduction in capital goods prices not to lower its saving rate but to buy more investment goods. And so in calculating the business-as-usual saving target, I have not reduced it to reflect potential future declines in investment goods prices.

In light of all these considerations, the nation would have to save about 4.5 percent of its national income in the decade of the 1990s. That would provide a little more than the private investment needed to keep output

TABLE 23-2. A National Saving Target for the 1990s
Percent of national income

Components of saving target[a]	Percent
Business as usual	4.5
Saving needed to keep productivity growing at 1979–87 rate (steady state profit rate)	
Retirement surpluses	2.5
Additional saving needed to invest trust fund surpluses in productive assets	
Total	7.0

a. Private saving includes and government saving excludes the annual surplus in state and local governments' pension funds for their own employees; and national income = net national product.

per worker growing at its current rate (table 23-2). To that business-as-usual saving one must add the annual accumulation of the social security and other retirement trust funds, which for the decade as a whole will average about 2.5 percent of GNP. In total, therefore, the nation ought to be saving some 7 percent of national income in the decade of the 1990s, a little less than it did on average during the three decades preceding 1980. The 7 percent saving target for the 1990s is not much lower than the earlier postwar average of 8.2 percent. The decrease in national saving requirements, because of a slower growth in the labor force and the other factors just outlined, is largely but not fully offset by the increase in saving needed for demographic reasons to avoid the extra burden on the future working generation occasioned by having to pay social security benefits to a sharply expanded population of retired people.

CAN WE COUNT ON AN INCREASE IN PRIVATE SAVING IN THE 1990s?

Some observers have argued that the fall in the personal saving rate that began in the late 1970s can be traced to the decline in the proportion of the population in the high-saving age groups—people thirty-five to sixty years old. They also predict, optimistically, that as the baby boomers born in the 1950s mature into the high-saving age range, as is now occurring, the personal saving rate will recover. Unfortunately, this application of the life cycle theory doesn't fit the facts very well. In the first place the proportion of the population aged thirty-five to sixty began to decline in the 1960s, well before the drop in personal saving took place. And the decline in that age group leveled out and began to edge up in the 1980s, while the saving rate continued to plummet.

An even more telling set of facts against the demographic explanation has recently been provided by Brookings scholars Barry Bosworth, Gary Burtless, and John Sabelhaus.[5] They analyzed newly available data that provide estimates of saving by different age, income, and other demographic groups at different times over the past several decades. They found that a fall in the saving rate has occurred in virtually all demographic groups. Using the data on saving by various age groups, they were able to estimate what the overall saving rate would have been if there had been no changes in the demographic composition of the population over the past several decades, and they found that saving would still have fallen almost as much as it actually did. In other words, little of the fall occurred because of the shifting age composition of the population. Correspondingly, there is no reason to believe that the current growth of the middle-income age group can be counted on to bring back the higher saving rates of earlier decades.

Some people have cited the 1980s boom in the stock market as the cause of the fall in private saving during that decade. The argument posits a restoration of saving in the 1990s on the assumption that the stock market rise will not continue at the abnormal pace of the 1980s. As explained in memo 6, consumers do respond to increases in the value of their wealth by decreasing their saving. But according to empirical studies of the relationship between stock market prices and consumer spending, the drop in private saving during the decade was far too large to be explained by the behavior of stock prices.

CONCLUSION

No one can confidently predict what will happen to the private saving rate in the coming years. Nevertheless, given the absence of any good evidence to the contrary, there is little choice but to base national economic policy on the assumption that the private saving rate will not rise spontaneously. Only deliberate public policy will move the United States toward the targeted national saving rate of 7 percent.

NOTES

1. As explained in memo 3, for simplicity, the term "national income" is used in these memos to denote the income generated in the production of net national product. This use is slightly different from the terminology of the Department of Commerce, which defines national income in that way except that it excludes the value of sales and property taxes.

2. Memo 8 discusses why the real interest rate is the one that matters for most economic decisions.

3. In fiscal 1992, the federal government's retirement trust funds for military and civilian employees were scheduled to have an annual surplus of some $36 billion.

4. The hospital trust fund of medicare is grossly underfinanced. The 2.5 percent of national income includes a 0.3 percent pro forma allowance to reflect an increase, not yet legislated, that will be needed in the medicare trust funds.

5. Barry Bosworth, Gary Burtless, and John Sabelhaus, "The Decline in Saving: Some Microeconomic Evidence," *Brookings Papers on Economic Activity 1: 1991, pp. 183–241.*

Memorandum 24

To: The President

From: CEA Chairman

Subject: **Increasing National Saving and Investment: Some Guiding Principles**

Designing and promoting policies to increase private saving and investment is a favorite indoor sport on Capitol Hill, with many presidential candidates and a vast number of business lobbyists participating in the game. Most of the policies include tax concessions, principally benefiting the middle class and the rich, to induce them or the firms they manage to save or invest more. Small wonder that the game is popular among many lobbyists. This is not to say that such schemes should be discarded on sight—self-interested parentage should not deprive a proposal of careful examination, but it should warn us to examine it with beady eyes. Numerous studies exist about the potential effects of changes in taxes on saving and investment. I have no intention of loading anyone down with a long set of evaluations of particular schemes or studies. Rather, I want to outline a set of generally applicable principles that apply to the relationships between national saving and investment on the one hand and federal tax and fiscal policies on the other, which should help you make judgments about policy issues as they arise. I will then provide some middle-of-the-road perspectives—that is, estimates that are in between the views of the optimists and the pessimists—of what might be achieved by way of higher national output and income through a policy that converted the large federal budget deficits of the 1980s into modest budget surpluses by the middle of the 1990s.

A FEW PRINCIPLES

Let's start by assuming the economy is operating at high employment levels, with aggregate spending sufficient to take off the market all the goods that the economy can produce when it is operating at potential; there is no problem of deficient demand. For the economy to increase its investment in new capital goods, resources somehow have to be freed to produce the additional machines and structures. Under these circumstances, several basic economic principles come into play that must be observed in government policies dealing with saving and investment. If these rules are ignored, the results of the policies are likely to be quite different from what the policymakers intended and will usually be counterproductive.

> Principle 1: With one exception, it is impossible to increase national investment without taking steps to increase national saving; the resources for additional capital formation must be provided from additional saving.

As long as the economy is already producing at its potential, it cannot devote more of that production to investment goods without first reducing the production of goods devoted to consumption by consumers or government. It must, in other words, consume less and save more. The one exception is that if a nation's credit is good abroad, it can borrow the additional resources from overseas, importing more than it exports and running a trade deficit. But the United States has just gone through a decade of very large trade deficits and is still borrowing abroad. Even if it were possible to attract a greater inflow of foreign lending on a sustained basis, such a policy would be much less effective than an increase in national saving as a means of promoting a faster growth of American living standards. The reason is that part of any increase in national income made possible by investing sums borrowed abroad would have to be used to pay the interest on the higher overseas borrowing and would not be available to raise living standards. And so, at least for the immediately foreseeable future, economic policy ought to be made on the assumption that "Rule 1" holds absolutely—if we want more investment we have to save more.

> Principle 2: The adoption of special tax or other incentives to reward investment, unless offset by tax increases or spending cuts elsewhere in the bud-

get, is likely to increase the favored form of investment at the expense of other forms of investment or at the cost of a higher trade deficit.

This principle arises from a critical characteristic of investment spending: if unaccompanied by an increase in national saving, it increases aggregate demand by much more than it increases aggregate supply. As earlier memos pointed out, the initial effect of the higher investment outlays in creating an additional *supply* of GNP will be relatively modest and will take a long time to come to fruition; in its first year, an increase of $1.00 in annual investment outlays will add only about $0.10 to the annual *supply* of gross national output. But it will add more than $1.00 to aggregate *demand*. Assuming that the economy is already operating at or near its potential, the introduction into the federal budget of tax incentives or other measures that successfully stimulate business investment spending will, therefore, lead to excess aggregate spending in the economy as a whole. And to avoid inflation, spending will have to be cut back somewhere else in the economy.

There are two policy options available. First, budget policy can be made more restrictive. Other taxes can be raised to restrict consumer spending, or government expenditures can be cut. But if these budgetary actions to reduce national consumption and raise national saving are not taken, then to nip the excess spending in the bud, the Federal Reserve will have to raise interest rates in order to squeeze out demand somewhere in the economy. As mentioned in earlier memos, higher interest rates will dampen consumer spending on autos and perhaps on other expensive durable goods. But the rate will mainly affect various forms of investment spending. Housing construction will clearly suffer. The higher interest rates will also diminish the net profitability of business investment and thus undo some or all of the stimulating effect of the tax incentives. And if, as is usually the case, the tax incentives are concentrated on tangible investments in plant and equipment, there will be a negative impact on intangible business investments with long-term payouts, such as research or market development.

The other major effect of the higher interest rates is likely to be an increase in the trade deficit; the higher interest rates make the dollar more attractive and drive up its overseas value, penalize American exports, and promote higher imports. Thus, without accompanying measures to increase national saving, tax incentives or subsidies undertaken to stimulate investment at home, are likely to result in higher overseas borrowing.

Principles one and two are derived from a more general one that is critical for policymaking.

Principle 3: Once the economy is at high employment, any government measures that lead to additional spending, including measures designed to induce greater supply, must be accompanied by measures to reduce spending elsewhere, since the supply response will virtually always be smaller and occur more gradually than the demand response.

If taxes are reduced to stimulate investment or research and development or work effort, then taxes must be raised elsewhere to restrain some other kind of spending, *or* government spending must be cut, *or* monetary policy must be tightened to do the necessary job of spending restraint through higher interest rates. Similarly, even though it may well be true that an increase in government spending on infrastructure investment adds as much to the growth of supply as an equal investment by the private sector, spending somewhere else in the economy must be cut to make room for the added investment outlays by government. And if we insist on adopting supply-side tax concessions, without also adopting offsetting budgetary policies to neutralize the aggregate spending consequences, then we will have the job done for us by higher interest rates, which may well undo a good part of the supply-side gain.

To state the matter baldly, the demand management arm of fiscal policy concerns itself with the changing overall level of spending in the economy, while fiscal policy aimed at supply management policy has to be carried out by changing the composition of spending. To get more output and income in the future, we have to change the pattern of national spending in the present, toward more saving and more investment.

The economic history of the 1980s starkly illustrates the consequences of ignoring the two principles outlined. Those who designed the budgetary policies of the 1980s pointed to the success of the Kennedy-Johnson tax cuts of 1962 and 1964 as evidence of the success of supply-side policies. But the rapid and sustained economic expansion under way in those years arose not from an acceleration of the growth of supply but from the successful stimulation of demand, which had fallen below supply at the beginning of the decade. In a similar vein, whatever the tax reductions of 1981 did to expand potential GNP they, with large increases in defense spending, did far more to expand aggregate demand. At first, with the economy in the depths of recession, greater demand posed no problem, since there were plenty of unused resources that could be put back to work by an expansion of demand. But once the recovery was well under way, the Federal Reserve—to avoid excess demand and inflation—had little option but to pursue a policy of monetary stringency, yielding a decade of unprecedentedly high interest rates. (See figure 17-1 to see how high real interest rates were compared with the ones in earlier decades.) And so, despite the lower tax rates and improved incentives, investment spending as a share of GNP fell and overseas borrowing rose.

INCREASING NATIONAL SAVING

Once we recognize the need to increase national saving as a prerequisite for higher capital formation, how do we go about it? Let's start with simple arithmetic. Saving means "not consuming." To save more, the nation must spend less on private or public consumption. Policymakers can choose from two approaches. One, the nation can adopt policies designed to raise private saving. Two, the government can increase public saving, that is, it can reduce its budget deficit or go further and move into surplus. It can do so by raising taxes to reduce private income and private consumption. Or it can reduce spending (on items other than productive public investment). Either way, the government will have lowered the share of national income devoted to public or private consumption and thereby raised the national saving rate.

PRIVATE SAVING

During wartime it has been possible to raise the private saving rate by appeals to patriotism accompanied by well-publicized campaigns to buy "war bonds." But in normal times the major practical way the government influences private saving is through tax incentives that raise the return people can get from their saving. The tax rate on income from capital can be cut, or the current deductions for interest payments on consumer borrowings (that is, home-equity loans) can be reduced. In either case, the after-tax return from saving rises.

On the surface, at least, what happened to personal saving in the 1980s is hard to reconcile with the view that raising the return to saving produces great increases in saving. During that period, real interest rates—that is, nominal interest rates less the inflation rate—reached unprecedentedly high levels for the modern American economy. The real interest rate on long-term corporate bonds, for example, averaged about 6.5 percent, versus the 1.5 to 2 percent averaged in the three decades preceding 1980. Marginal income tax rates, especially on the upper income groups who do most of the saving, were slashed, so that the after-tax return rose even more than the before-tax return. And during most of the 1980s, individual retirement accounts, with their tax-free savings feature, were available. Despite this concatenation of circumstances driving up the reward to saving, the saving rate fell sharply.

Proponents of enlarged saving incentives respond to these facts by suggesting that other economic developments would have pushed down the saving rate even more had it not been for the favorable interest rate and tax climate. But as explained in memo 23, the two most often cited reasons for the saving decline in the 1980s—the stock market boom and the decline in the high-saving age group as a fraction of the population— cannot explain any significant part of the drop in saving. Nevertheless, the experience of the 1980s, when saving fell despite an increase in the return to saving, though a powerful piece of evidence, is not by itself conclusive proof that saving will fail to respond significantly to changes in the rate of return. What does economic theory suggest, and what do those research studies show that cover longer periods and make allowance for other factors affecting saving?

Economic theory by itself cannot tell us whether an increase in the after-tax reward for saving will raise or lower saving. That is because a rise in the return to saving has two effects, which go in the opposite direction. On the one hand, an increase in the interest rate or other return to saving reduces the amount a person has to save in order to achieve any given wealth objective for the future (for example, for retirement income). On this account a rise in interest rates would tend to lower saving. Thus, when interest rates rise, employers whose pension plans provide a fixed level of benefits to future retirees can get by with making smaller annual contributions to their pension funds. But a rise in interest rates also increases the future reward for each additional dollar of saving set aside today, and that should tend to raise the amount people save. There is no a priori reason why the latter of these two forces should outweigh the former. And so we have to turn to empirical studies of the relationship between saving and interest rates to determine how people respond to higher rates of return.

One prominent study of the effect of rates of return on saving, completed in 1978, concludes that a 1 percentage point rise in the real after-tax return will reduce consumption spending by as much as 2 percent.[1] But other studies tend to show much smaller responses. Most of the empirical evidence is not favorable to the proposition that household saving reacts in any big way to changes in the return to saving. As one of the leading macroeconomic textbooks sums up the state of the evidence, "Typically, research suggests the effects [of a rise in interest rates on saving] are small and certainly hard to find." [2]

A tax incentive to private saving, which takes the form of some kind of tax reduction, raises the budget deficit, and to that extent *lowers* national saving. It must therefore stimulate private saving by more than the tax loss if it is to have a positive effect on the overall national saving rate. Obviously, an across-the-board reduction in personal income tax rates is not an effective approach if the only objective is to increase national saving. Since taxes on all income—not just income from capital—are reduced, the revenue losses are much greater than the induced increase in private saving, by any of the saving response estimates.

Suppose part of the income tax was replaced with a value-added tax. The tax would affect only that part of income spent for consumption; income devoted to saving would not be subject to tax. The loss in income tax revenues could be neutralized by the revenue from the value-added tax and any stimulus to private saving would be fully reflected in a rise in national saving. But the addition to national saving would be modest. One recent study by the Congressional Research Service estimates that the introduction of a 6 percent value-added tax (generating $150 billion of revenues in 1991) and use of the proceeds to reduce the personal and corporate income tax by one-quarter would increase private saving by about 0.5 percent of national income.[3] While some might judge a large-scale substitution of a value-added tax for the income tax a worthwhile exercise, in practical terms, this is not the route by which a major increase in national saving is likely to come —certainly not an increase that would raise the U.S. national saving rate from the depressed level of the late 1980s (3 percent of national income) to or near the 8 percent of national income that characterized the first three decades after the Second World War.

Because of these drawbacks to generalized saving incentives, practical attention has been concentrated on specialized incentives such as individual retirement accounts, under which taxpayers may shelter from taxes a limited amount of their savings—typically $2,000 for an individual and $4,000 for a family. Unfortunately, however, the individuals and families who do most of the saving already have wealth much larger than these limited amounts, and will simply convert some of their wealth into IRAs to earn the tax advantage without doing any more saving. Some families who might not have saved $4,000 in a year may indeed increase their saving, but, net, the amount of additional saving per dollar of tax loss is not likely to be favorable. There have been several attempts to use consumer survey data to determine the overall effect on household saving of the IRAs that were introduced in the 1980s. Several studies do suggest that they were effective. But other studies have come to the opposite conclusion. At this stage, the most favorable judgment that can be rendered on the effectiveness of such devices is the Scotch verdict "not proven." And, in any event, whether the net outcome is a small plus or a small minus, such tax devices are not likely to generate a large increase in national saving. The only realistic way of reaching that goal is to increase public saving.

PUBLIC SAVING

Increasing public saving as a share of national income is fairly straightforward economically, even though it is difficult politically. We have to cut the budget deficit (or raise the surplus) by raising taxes or reducing expenditures. There are several qualifications to this simple statement. First, we are not interested in cutting the deficit for its own sake, but as a means to increase national investment in productive assets. And so expenditures on productive public investments ought not to be cut (and perhaps should even be increased). That principle, however, is easier to state in general terms than to apply in specific cases.

Government investment doesn't normally have to meet the test of the marketplace, and many projects undertaken don't provide enough future benefits to cover their costs. For years, billions of dollars were spent on federal water resource projects for navigation and irrigation that were notorious boondoggles, providing pork for regional political interests but offering precious little to national output. Indeed, the federal government heavily subsidized the construction of irrigation projects to increase agricultural output, while simultaneously paying farmers elsewhere to cut back production. Now, when people in arid areas like southern California face severe water shortages, they find that the highly subsidized public water projects of earlier years have committed huge amounts of the available water to low-value agricultural irrigation.

Many people have questioned whether or not federal subsidies for the construction of subways provided benefits greater than costs, and much of the investment in the late 1970s and 1980s in alternative energy sources seems to have been poorly directed. A recent detailed study of the highway system has concluded that if the United States reformed the way it invests in and charges for highways, the country could improve the services of the highway system and reduce congestion with the expenditure of only a modest increase in what is now being spent.[4]

The public sector ought to be investing in precisely those projects that offer a decent return to the nation but for one reason or another cannot succeed as private sector investments. But that fact usually makes it exceedingly difficult to decide which public investment programs are or are not likely to have a national payoff. Although sound economic principles can indeed proclaim that one ought not to cut the budget deficit at the expense of productive investment in infrastructure, the real trick is in deciding and convincing Congress and the voting public what is productive. Some types of public investment need to be expanded—later on, for example, I will suggest the need for far more public investment in civilian research and development. In short, my aim is not to denigrate the potential worth of many forms of public infrastructure investment, but to warn against the view that anything that qualifies as public infrastructure is automatically deserving of budget support.

A second qualification to the bald proposition that a decrease in the federal budget deficit adds an equivalent amount to national saving concerns the possible effect on private saving of any tax increases that were undertaken as part of the budget-cutting exercise. To the extent that higher taxes discourage private saving, the lower budget deficit will not add dollar for dollar to national saving. Suppose, for example, that taxes are raised by $10 billion and the budget deficit is reduced by the same amount. If, in response to the $10 billion reduction in its after-tax income, the private sector cuts saving by $1 billion and consumption by $9 billion, *national* saving will rise by $9 billion—$10 billion through the lower budget deficit, offset by $1 billion of lower private saving. In other words, only that part of the tax increase that results in lower consumption spending will add to national saving; any effect of the tax increase in discouraging private saving will reduce the effectiveness of the deficit cut as a device for increasing national saving. Most of any general tax increase on individuals—through income, sales, or value-added taxes—will end up as a reduction in private consumption, but there will also probably be a small reduction in private saving. Thus, most, if not all, of any deficit reduction will show up as an increase in national saving even if the deficit reduction is brought about by a tax hike.

A MINORITY VIEW

A small but influential group of economists argues that the conventional wisdom about the effect of budget deficits on national saving is wrong. According to this group, changes in the budget deficit are offset dollar for dollar by changes in the opposite direction in private saving. The argument rests on two key assumptions about household behavior. One, individuals are very foresighted and plan for the very long term; in particular they foresee that a tax cut today, paid for with a budget deficit and federal borrowing, will lead to a tax increase in the future because the government cannot keep running deficits forever. Two, people do not plan only for their own welfare, they give equal weight to the welfare of their descendants and save to make bequests to them. Thus a tax increase that comes along after they are dead is seen nevertheless as affecting them; it is the equivalent of a reduction in their bequests.

Given these assumptions, when the government cuts taxes and runs a deficit, these infinitely foresighted, highly benign families save all the proceeds of the tax cut to provide the financial resources for themselves or their descendants to pay the inevitably increased taxes in the future. (And the interest they earn on their saving matches the extra tax increase that will have to be made to pay the interest on the debts the government is piling up.) According to this view, the government cannot force the community, through changes in taxes financed by borrowing, to alter the way they have already decided to allocate their resources over the time spans of their own lives and those of their descendants.

It is hard for most noneconomists to feel much sympathy for this point of view and the assumptions about human behavior that underlie it. I sympathize with the skepticism. But viewing human beings as highly rational, efficient, and extremely foresighted calculators is to many economists what the apple was to Eve—a temptation they cannot resist. It's an immense aid to the formulation of precise and mathematically elegant propositions about economic affairs. In fact, the evidence for the United States is against the proposition. The experience of the 1980s flies in the face of the theory; the federal budget deficit ballooned to unprecedented levels, but instead of private saving rising, as the theory would require, it collapsed. Moreover, the weight of evidence from several empirical studies of saving behavior lies against the theory.[5] Most, though not all, of any cut in the budget deficit will end up as an addition to national saving; it will not be negated by an offsetting decrease in private saving.

THE IMPLICATIONS FOR FEDERAL BUDGET POLICY IN THE REMAINDER OF THE 1990S

In memo 23 I estimated that a national saving rate of about 7 percent of national income might be a reasonable target for government policy to aim at for the middle of the 1990s. Memo 23 also explained why it would be rash to count on a spontaneous rise in household saving to produce the necessary saving increase. And, as discussed in this memo, the private saving rate is not likely to respond significantly to changes in taxes or special tax incentives. Let's assume, therefore, that the private saving rate remains unchanged at its recent (1987-90 average) level, some 7 percent of NNP. It would appear that the government sector of the economy as a whole would have to achieve a budget balance if the overall national saving target of 7 percent of NNP is to be attained (table 24-1).

There are a number of reasons, however, why we should set a goal for a modest *surplus* in the federal budget rather than a balance. When the federal deficit is reduced, there may be some offsetting reductions in private saving. Lowering the deficit will require measures, such as tax increases or entitlement reductions, that will initially lower household income and therefore household saving. (Memo 26 examines the view that higher taxes on investment income might also reduce the incentive to save.) The deficit reductions will reduce interest rates, and some would argue that will reduce private saving. On balance the reductions in private saving are likely to be small, but not zero. To reach the national saving target, we will have to do somewhat more than balance the budget, we will have to run a surplus. Moreover, to the extent that the remainder of the decade witnesses continuing state and local deficits, even though of small size, the federal budget will have to run an offsetting surplus.[6] Further, even under the most optimistic assumptions, the target of budget balance for the government as a whole would not be achieved before the late 1990s. We cannot and should not try to make up fully for lost ground, but we might edge our goal up a bit in recognition of the earlier shortfalls. Finally, even with the best economic management, occasional years of

Table 24-1. Meeting the National Saving Target
Percent of national income

Saving	Percent of national income[a]
Saving target	7.0
Saving availability	7.0
Private saving, at current (1987–90) rate	7.0
Required government deficit versus	0.0
projected government deficit	−3.6

a. National income = net national product.

slower than normal economic growth are likely, perhaps even recession. The budget in normal years should therefore have a modest surplus to take that likelihood into account. For all of these reasons, it would make sense to aim for a surplus in the federal budget of about 1 percent of NNP in order to have a reasonable chance to achieve the overall national saving goal of 7 percent of NNP. If the goal were reached by 1997, the federal budget target would require a budget surplus of some $70 billion for that year. In early 1992, after the negotiated budget compromise of 1990, the Congressional Budget Office projected that the baseline budget deficit in 1997—that is, the deficit that would result by then if federal defense and civilian programs and tax laws were continued under current policy with no changes—would equal $250 billion, or 3.6 percent of NNP.[7] Thus, as of early 1992, budget policy was $320 billion or 4.6 percent of NNP short of the 1997 target. And so, to meet the national saving target, some combination of tax increases and expenditure cuts sufficient to produce a $320 billion improvement in the budget balance would be needed.

Notes

1. Michael J. Boskin, "Taxation, Saving, and the Rate of Interest," *Journal of Political Economy*, vol. 86 (April 1978), pt. 2, pp. S3–S27. For a critique of the Boskin study, see E. Philip Howrey and Saul H. Hymans, "The Measurement and Determination of Loanable-Funds Saving," *Brookings Papers on Economic Activity 3:1978*, pp. 655–85, and Boskin's response on pp. 694–700.
2. Rudiger Dornbusch and Stanley Fischer, *Macroeconomics*, 5th ed. (McGraw-Hill, 1990), p. 289.

3. See the study of Jane Gravelle of the Congressional Research Service reported in Congressional Budget Office, *Effects of Adopting a Value-Added Tax* (Washington, February 1992), p. 53, n3.

4. Kenneth A. Small, Clifford Winston, and Carol A. Evans, *Road Work* (Brookings, 1989).

5. See, for example, Martin Feldstein and Douglas W. Elmendorf, "Government Debt, Goverment Spending, and Private Sector Behavior Revisited: Comment," *American Economic Review*, vol. 80 (June 1990), pp. 589–99; and Douglas B. Bernheim, "Ricardian Equivalence: An Evaluation of Theory and Evidence," *NBER Macroeconomics Annual 1987* (MIT Press, 1987), pp. 263–304.

6. State and local governments are running large annual surpluses in the pension funds for their employees. But we have classified these funds as private saving, which is how the pension funds of other employers are classified. Changing the classification of the state and local pension funds by including their surpluses in the overall government surplus would not change the end result as far as the calculation of the needed federal budget surplus is concerned. Private saving would be lower than shown in table 24–1, and the needed government surplus would be correspondingly higher.

7. Congressional Budget Office, *The Economic and Budget Outlook: Fiscal Years 1993–1997* (Washington, 1992).

M EMORANDUM **25**

To: The President

FROM: CEA Chairman

SUBJECT: **Raising National Saving and Investment I: The Economic Consequences**

In one context or another we have already discussed what occurred in the American economy because of the large drop in the national saving rate during the 1980s coupled with the anti-inflationary monetary policy of the Federal Reserve: unprecedentedly high interest rates, a drop in domestic net investment, and a large trade deficit matched by an inflow of funds from abroad (see memos 4 and 10). Now let's assume that steps were taken, as outlined in memo 24, to convert the projected $250 billion federal budget deficit into a $70 billion budget surplus in stages over the next five years. The national saving rate, which would otherwise be about 3.5 percent of national income, would rise to, and indeed exceed, the target of 7 percent. And let's also assume, what is in any event quite probable, that the Federal Reserve will accompany the restrictive budget measures with an easing of monetary policy sufficient to keep aggregate demand growing and unemployment close to the high-employment level. In that case, the developments of the 1980s would be reversed.

Real interest rates would fall, the availability of credit would increase, and the higher national saving would be used in some combination of two ways: the United States would run a lower balance-of-payments deficit and import less saving from abroad; and domestic investment would increase. In turn, these developments would gradually improve U.S. living standards. The higher domestic investment would increase the growth of U.S. productivity and the smaller overseas debt would reduce overseas debt service payments, so that more of the national income could be retained and enjoyed at home. While it would be foolish to try to predict the precise magnitude or form of the increase in living standards, I can provide some ballpark estimates.

The major steps needed to convert a $250 billion budget deficit into a $70 billion surplus ought to be enacted into law at the beginning of the budget reduction program—for example, gradually phased-in tax increases and expenditure cuts—and the Federal Reserve should announce its intention to help maintain the growth of GNP during the transition period. Although these actions would not eliminate the skepticism of financial markets about the sustainability of budget reduction programs, they should go a long way in that direction. Long-term borrowers and lenders would expect short-term interest rates to fall in future years and that expectation should lead to prompt and sizable reductions in long-term rates. The fall in interest rates following an increase of 4 percentage points in the nation's saving rate could be substantial, perhaps on the order of 2 percentage points. In the middle of 1990, before the 1990–91 recession began, real interest rates on high-quality corporate bonds were about 5 percent (a 9.5 percent nominal rate less 4 percent inflation). If we can assume that those real interest rates would remain roughly unchanged in the absence of any budget action, then converting the $250 billion deficit into a $50 billion surplus by 1997 could produce real interest rates in the neighborhood of 3 percent or even less.

There is one reason to believe that this conclusion is too conservative and one reason to suggest it might be too optimistic. A comparison of the national saving-investment balance that would result from the suggested budget program with earlier postwar history suggests the possibility of even lower real interest rates. During the period between 1959 and 1980 the national saving rate averaged 8.2 percent of national income, of which 7.8 percent was invested domestically and 0.5 percent was invested abroad through a trade surplus. Real interest rates on long-term corporate bonds averaged a little less than 2 percent during the period. But as just outlined, it will only take domestic investment of something like 4.5 percent of national income during the 1990s to equip a more slowly growing labor force and keep the capital-labor ratio growing at its recent pace. Thus, national saving at the 7 percent target would be a good bit more abundant relative to investment demand than it apparently was in the earlier postwar decades, and real interest rates should be lower than they were then. Because of the buildup in the public retirement trust funds and the desirability of raising the growth of national wealth and income, memo 23 set a national saving target for the 1990s to provide a relative abundance of saving, more than required simply to meet current investment demand out of domestic saving. Everything else being equal, this abundance of saving should push interest rates below their earlier postwar levels.

Everything else is not equal, however. Capital moves much more freely among countries in response to favorable overseas interest rates and other returns than it did in earlier decades. As U.S. interest rates fall relative to rates abroad, less capital will flow into the country and more out of it. This pattern will tend to limit somewhat the potential decline in interest rates. Moreover, we have to consider the possibility that the reconstruction of the Eastern European economies may raise the demand for international capital and limit the potential drop in rates. On balance, the drop of some 2 percentage points in real long-term interest rates seems a reasonable estimate of what might happen, but with a good bit of uncertainty attached to it.

CHANGES IN THE STRUCTURE OF THE U.S. ECONOMY

The rise in national saving and the fall in interest rates will generate two principal changes in the structure of the economy: an increase in domestic investment and an improvement in the trade balance—more exports and fewer imports. But how much of each are we likely to get? Memos 9 and 10 outlined how the growing mobility of international capital has affected the internal behavior of all of the large industrial countries. Whereas, in the earlier days of the postwar period, changes in national saving principally resulted in changes in domestic investment, in more recent years an important fraction of any changes in saving showed up as changes in a country's trade balance. Now, when national saving rises in one country, and interest rates in that country fall, foreign investors become less interested in buying bonds or making loans in that country, the currency declines, and the trade balance improves, with exports rising and imports falling. And so, some of the reduction in consumption (the mirror image of the rise in saving) is matched by a rise in exports and a substitution of domestic production for imported goods rather than by an increase in domestic investment.[1]

Though many circumstances can affect how the change in national saving will be split between alternative uses, several recent studies suggest that a little more than half might go to domestic investment and a little less than that to a better trade balance.

THE LONG-TERM GAIN IN OUTPUT AND INCOME

Raising the supply capability of the economy by increased saving and investment is a gradual process that takes place over several years as the capital stock and national productivity are boosted from the old path of growth to a newer one. Policies that aim at an increased growth of potential GNP have to be viewed in relation to several decades, not several years. What might be accomplished in that framework by a budget policy that converted the 3.6 percent of NNP budget deficit now projected for the mid- and late 1990s into a surplus of about 1 percent and sustained that policy for several decades?

First, as noted in memo 24, p. 265, a small part of the improvement in the federal budget position may be offset by a decline in private saving. I assume that the change from a budget deficit of 3.6 percent of national income to a 1 percent surplus would lead to a gain in the national saving rate of a little less than 4 percent.

If we assume that some three-fifths of the increase in national saving is channeled into higher domestic investment and two-fifths into a better trade balance, what would be the long-term gains to the economy? First, domestic investment. On a Denison–Solow-type calculation, an increase of approximately 2.3 percentage points in the share of NNP devoted to domestic investment, gradually achieved over the next five years and then maintained for the subsequent two decades, would lead to an NNP at the end of the period 3.5 to 4 percent above what it would otherwise have been. And for some time thereafter, if national saving is maintained at the higher level, the gain in income will increase further.

The second improvement to American living standards would come from the reduction in the balance-of-payments deficit and the consequent reduction in the amount of national income that has to be paid abroad in interest payments on the debt that is incurred to finance those deficits. If, as assumed above, two-fifths of the rise in national saving goes toward reducing the balance-of-payments deficit, then once the improved budget position and higher national saving rate were fully in place, the balance-of-payments deficit should be lower each year by 1.6 percent of NNP. Since the 1990 current account deficit was about 2 percent of NNP and falling, reaching the national saving target would wipe that deficit out.

After five years of phase-in and two decades of full effectiveness, the cumulative effect of the lower balance-of-payments deficit and the reductions in foreign capital inflows would result in an improved balance of payments overseas for interest and dividends and other investment income, amounting to about 2 percent of NNP.[2]

As a result of the rise in domestic investment, the productivity and real wages of American workers should rise more or less in line with the investment-induced growth in NNP—some 3.5 to 4 percent by the time the program had been fully in effect for two decades. An additional 2 percent gain in NNP would arise from an increased inflow (decreased outflow) of overseas earnings. Moreover, I have made no allowances for any growth-promoting side-effects attributed to investment by the new growth theories, such as a larger volume of R&D (see memo 22).[3]

WILL INVESTMENT DEMAND BE SUFFICIENT?

Recall that the national saving target was explicitly chosen to make saving more abundant relative to investment demands. I calculated that investment of 4.5 percent of national income would be required to maintain, or slightly surpass, the current growth of productivity but proposed a saving target of 7 percent of national income. However, an increase in saving not accompanied by an equally large increase in investment, either at home or abroad (in the form of an improved trade balance), would lead to a decline in aggregate demand, a fall in GNP, and an increase in unemployment. So far, the assumption has been that, with the cooperation of the Federal Reserve, investment demand and the trade balance would rise to match the higher national saving. Is that a reasonable assumption? Could the country safely pursue a much more restrictive budget policy and still achieve reasonably full employment?

As noted earlier, several of the forces that create domestic investment opportunities are less powerful than they were in earlier postwar decades, when investment demand did indeed match the 8.2 percent national saving rate that characterized the period. In particular, the growth of the labor force and the overall pace of technological advance have apparently slowed down. A big increase in investment under these conditions would lead to a significant acceleration in the growth of the business capital stock relative to the growth of the labor force and the growth of technological knowledge. In turn, as discussed in memo 22, this development implies that business firms would have to be satisfied with a lower rate of return on their investment projects. However, falling real interest rates would lower the cost of capital and make it possible for business firms to accept a lower return on new investment. The lower interest rates would also, through the process described in memo 4, lower the value of the dollar and improve the trade balance. The role of the Federal Reserve, through an easier monetary policy, is to supplement the fall in interest rates (which would occur in any event) sufficiently to produce the increase in investment and the trade balance needed to keep aggregate demand growing in line with potential GNP.

Is there a possibility that real interest rates cannot be forced low enough to do the job? Lower interest rates are effective in stimulating housing construction. Empirical studies of the factors determining changes in business investment in plant and equipment assign a positive role to falling interest but not a very powerful one. However, the fall in the rate of return to capital that would occur if domestic investment increased as much as projected is not likely to be very large, so the fall in interest rates might not have to be very great. Some rough calculations suggest that if increases in domestic investment matched three-fifths of the increase in national saving, as suggested above (the remainder going toward an improvement in the trade balance), and if business and housing investment shared that increase in their historic proportions, the average rate of return on new business investment projects might be driven down by perhaps 1.2 percentage points from its current level over the next several decades. That does not seem like an impossibly large drop to be overcome by reduced real interest rates. Even if domestic investment did not rise as much as assumed above, the growing international mobility of capital would almost surely provide an outlet for America's increased saving. In that case the improvement in productivity would be somewhat less and the improvement in the trade balance (and its associated reduction in overseas interest payments) somewhat more than just projected.

All in all, given the very high level of real interest rates that now prevail in the United States and, lately, around the world, and the apparent rising demand for capital abroad, it seems highly probable that the higher saving and actions of the Federal Reserve could push rates down far enough to maintain high employment—that is, to insure that the combination of higher domestic investment and an improved trade balance was large enough to absorb the resources freed by the reduction in national consumption. Although this conclusion is not 100 percent certain, that uncertainty should not stand in the way of aiming for a federal budgetary surplus of the magnitude suggested. In the best of circumstances, the target will only be approached gradually, and if it should turn out, contrary to expectations, that the easier monetary policy and the lower interest rates are not bringing forth enough domestic investment or trade balance improvement, some of the tax increases or entitlement spending cuts can be eliminated or postponed. The politics of doing so, should it prove necessary, are hardly likely to prove difficult.

PUBLIC INVESTMENT

So far we have assumed that all of the resources freed by the increase in national saving would be used to raise private investment and improve the trade balance. But shouldn't some of those resources be used to increase investment in public capital, both tangible capital and human capital? Recent studies by economist David Aschauer (cited in memo 22) conclude that in the postwar U.S. economy an extra dollar of public investment in tangible capital (infrastructure), especially for transportation purposes, has had a payoff in higher GNP equal to three or four dollars of private capital. If that were true, public investment should clearly take preference over deficit reduction for a large share of any funds made available from tax increases, defense spending cuts, and other budgetary economies.

These claims for the highly superior efficacy of public infrastructure investment, however, are much greater than warranted by reality. Just at the time that national productivity growth was beginning to taper off, in the late 1960s and more so in the early 1970s, the public investments associated with the building of the massive interstate highway system were winding down, as were the public school building programs necessitated by the postwar baby boom. By statistically relating productivity growth to the level of public investment over the period, this coincidence of events will suggest a causal relationship far stronger than in fact exists. In a recent study of the relationship of public investment to national productivity growth, the Congressional Budget Office casts substantial doubts on the estimates that assert vastly larger payoffs to public than to private investment (see memo 22). Thus, for example, the results obtained from studies like those of Aschauer change massively when relatively modest changes are made in the years covered by the study or in the specifications of the data.

Since there is a wide range of types of public investment, it serves no purpose to argue about the relative merits of public investment in general. Some traditional public investments, such as the building of dams for the supply of irrigation water, are widely known as losers—their benefits are much lower than their costs. But there are also some types of public investment for which the payoff to added expenditures is likely to be quite large. For example, memo 28 will argue that federal investment in civilian research and development would have a very high payoff, larger than is likely to be achieved by the average private investment. And as I will also argue in memo 27, impressive evidence indicates that American economic growth would be significantly speeded up by improvements in the quality of the nation's elementary and secondary education system. But the extent to which improvements require additional public investment, rather than major institutional reforms in the educational system, is a question that can be addressed only by evaluating specific proposals. In the end, there is no substitute for a case-by-case analysis of potential investment opportunities. And even the best studies will leave an irreducible amount of uncertainty for policymakers to resolve through informed judgment and intuition.

The growth projections made in the scenario above could almost certainly be improved by channeling some of the resources freed through budgetary actions into selected, high-priority public investments rather than using all such resources to lower the budget deficit and increase private investment. But it would be highly surprising if the best analysis and judgment dictated a policy mix radically different from long-term historical experience—by far the largest share of additional resources available for investment ought to go toward private investment at home and abroad, but with a healthy amount reserved for public investment. In current budget accounting, all government spending, whether for investment or consumption, is lumped together for purposes of calculating the budget deficit. A decision to devote some of the funds from tax increases or reductions in government consumption spending to high-priority public investments would reduce the degree to which the official budget deficit was reduced or a surplus achieved. But that is a matter of accounting convention. Such a policy would not diminish the real extent to which national saving and national investment were increased.

Policy Lessons

The policy choices and alternatives described in this memo illustrate the following essential principles discussed in earlier memos:

—The most effective way to increase national saving is through federal budgetary policy.

—When budgetary policy becomes more restrictive, a shift toward an easier monetary policy by the Federal Reserve can keep the GNP and employment moving up along their old path, provided the shift to budget restriction is not too large in any one year and that the Federal Reserve is given a little time to act before the budgetary restrictions come into effect. While there is undoubtedly a limit to the size of the federal budgetary surplus that could be supported by the Federal Reserve, a modest surplus could most likely be successfully handled.

—The mix of monetary and fiscal policy can thus be altered to change the structure of GNP, keeping the level unchanged. A shift in budget policy, from deficit toward surplus, will lead to some combination of increases in domestic investment—housing construction and business investment—and in net foreign investment. (Remember that net foreign investment can be positive—a trade surplus, or negative—a trade deficit). Given the increased mobility of capital across national borders, we might now expect a little more than half of the saving increase to be absorbed by increased domestic investment and the remainder by a reduced trade deficit.

—Some share of the resources freed by tax increases or spending cuts should be used selectively for public investments, based on case-by-case evaluations rather than on some general principle that investment in infrastructure ought to get the lion's share.

So far this discussion about the economic consequences of changing the budget deficit into a surplus has not considered the possibility that the tax increases that would undoubtedly be necessary to achieve the budget surplus might themselves impair private economic incentives and thereby offset some or all of the favorable growth consequences otherwise achievable with the new budget policy. Moreover, the discussion did not consider the possible role of providing some tax incentives for private investment as part of the overall growth strategy. Memo 26 will fill in both of these gaps.

Notes

1. This picture is the mirror image of what happened to the United States in the 1980s when national saving declined sharply.

2. This calculation, to be conservative, assumes that the real rate of return to be earned by reducing America's net debtor position is a little less than the rate earned on domestic investment.

3. All of the estimates in the preceding paragraphs assume that the federal budget is converted from a deficit of 3.6 percent of NNP to a surplus of 1 percent, and that this in turn leads to an increase in national saving of a little less than 4 percent. The target of a small federal budget surplus includes, as noted, a safety margin, so that if the surplus were achieved and maintained and the private saving rate stayed at 7 percent of NNP, the economy would slightly surpass the saving goal set out earlier in memo 23.

To: The President

From: CEA Chairman

Subject: **Raising National Saving and Investment II: Tax Changes and Their Effects**

Even though some combination of increases in domestic investment spending and in the trade balance would probably be sufficient to make up for any economic slack caused by the move to more restrictive budgetary policies, the combination may well be unsatisfactory. Conceivably, for example, the rise in domestic investment could turn out to be smaller and the shift in the trade balance larger than the 60–40 split that we have assumed. In that case the improvement in productivity and the real wages of American workers would be smaller while the savings in overseas debt service and the return to the owner of capital would be larger than implied by the estimates in memo 25. It might make sense not simply to let market forces make that decision about the split between domestic and foreign investment but to take steps to increase domestic business investment at the expense of improvements in the trade balance. Similarly, an additional dollar invested by business in plant and equipment would almost surely generate a larger gain in national output and income than the typical additional dollar invested in private housing construction.

ALTERING THE COMPOSITION OF INVESTMENT

The principal way for the government to influence the broad structure of investment is through tax policy. The investment tax credit could be reinstated, providing a tax credit against purchases of business equipment (and, in a modification to the old credit, also against new factory buildings). Alternatively, business firms could be allowed to accelerate their depreciation deductions for tax purposes, which would increase their cash flow early in the life of an investment and decrease it later. This allowance would be the equivalent of an interest-free loan on the investment. A more radical alternative has been to allow business firms to expense immediately the cost of plant and equipment purchases, while disallowing the deduction of interest payments on business borrowing. Besides stimulating investment, this approach removes the current bias in the tax code that favors debt over equity financing. Another possibility, which I will discuss in a later memo, is to improve and enrich the current tax credit for investment in research and development.[1]

Any tax concessions made to stimulate business investment would increase the demand for investment goods.[2] Since we are assuming that the economy is not in recession but at full employment, the additional aggregate demand would threaten higher inflation. And so the business tax incentives would have to be offset by additional tax increases elsewhere in the economy, or, failing that, the Federal Reserve would have to tighten money and raise interest rates to restrain demand. Either alternative poses difficult issues for decision.

Suppose it is decided to make up the revenue losses caused by the tax incentives by tax increases elsewhere. If the purpose of the tax incentives is not to be frustrated, the offsetting tax increases could not be levied principally against income from capital; they would have to be borne principally by workers and consumers. Since, to achieve the targeted budget surplus, taxes in any event would have to be raised, an additional tax burden on the average voter would surely increase the political difficulty of securing acceptance for the whole package. And a tightening of interest rates by the Federal Reserve would reduce housing construction as well as increase the trade deficit. Thus, a policy of increasing the domestic investment response to the saving increase requires trade-offs involving difficult political and economic considerations as well as questions of equity. Economists have no special advantage in making (as opposed to explaining) those kinds of trade-offs. That's what presidents, congressional representatives, and senators are elected to do.

A partial disallowance of interest deductions on home mortgages would also dampen the response of housing investment to the new budget policy and correspondingly favor additional business investment and improvements in the trade balance.[3] Here again, changes in the structure of taxes can be used to influence the response of the economy to the shift in budget policy. But, as in most such cases, the political difficulties in the way are formidable.

THE CAPITAL GAINS TAX CUT

The controversy over the effectiveness of using tax incentives to stimulate saving and investment has been most heated in the recent political debate about the extent to which a cut in the capital gains tax would increase economic growth. Advocates on each side of the argument—those who believe it would greatly increase investment and growth and those who argue that its effects would be small—have cited existing economic studies or commissioned new ones to support their side of the argument.

The Congressional Budget Office (CBO) in 1990 examined the six existing studies and conducted two of its own. Of these eight studies, five estimated that a major cut in the capital gains tax would contribute little if anything to economic growth, and three reached the opposite conclusion. The CBO concluded that these three studies (one by the Council of Economic Advisers under President Bush) were flawed and that "cutting taxes on capital gains could not be counted on to significantly boost output and increase economic growth."[4] The results of one representative study, cited by the CBO, imply that the effect on investment incentives of a cut in the capital gains rate from 28 to 20 percent would be the equivalent of less than a two-tenths of 1 percentage point increase in the after-tax return to savers.[5] Moreover, even if cutting capital gains raised GNP somewhat, it is highly unlikely that the increase in income and the higher realization of capital gains would generate enough additional tax revenue to offset the revenue losses caused by the lower tax rate, as is argued by some proponents of capital gains tax cuts.

It is impossible in this memo to do justice to the arguments and counterarguments. But several points are important. One of them illustrates a principle spelled out earlier: a tax incentive or other measure that increases the demand on the part of business for investment goods cannot increase aggregate investment in the economy unless national saving is also increased. Otherwise the increased demand for the type of investment good favored by a tax incentive will drive up interest rates and squeeze out less-favored types of investment (including foreign investment by U.S. citizens), leaving aggregate investment the same. The CBO points out that two of the three studies simply assumed that private saving would be perfectly responsive (in the economist's jargon, would be infinitely elastic) and would rise to match the increase in investment demand stimulated by the capital gains tax cut without any increase in interest rates. A capital gains tax cut would raise the return to certain investments and raise the reward to saving. But, as noted, even the most favorable reading of the evidence would not warrant the assumption of an infinitely responsive saving rate. Those studies that allowed for some, but not for infinitely elastic savings responses, produced much less optimistic results. Moreover, to the extent that the estimated stimulus to economic growth from the capital gains cut is scaled back, the likelihood that such a tax cut would pay for itself with higher revenues diminishes to the vanishing point. Over the longer run, a capital gains tax cut will almost surely lose revenue, add to the budget deficit, and offset some or all of the higher saving the tax cut might otherwise stimulate.

One particularly dubious argument is often made in support of a cut in the capital gains tax, namely, that a cut would generate a large increase in the flow of venture capital to innovative business firms. The picture is conjured up of sharply improved incentives and new sources of funds for capital-starved electronic wizards, genetic engineers, and other high-tech entrepreneurs. But this image is highly misleading. A 30 percent capital gains exclusion (the policy measure most often proposed) would mean that a successful entrepreneur in a high-risk venture could look forward to selling out his shares and realizing 80 percent instead of the current 72 percent of his gains.[6] Without suggesting that the increased return would have no effect, I believe it is unlikely that this kind of incentive would change the decision of an entrepreneur who was contemplating whether to undertake a highly risky business venture.

The case is even stronger that a cut in the capital gains tax would not make a big difference in the amount of outside capital available to venture capital entrepreneurs. According to the major venture capital trade association, the flow of net new private capital committed to venture capital firms in 1987 was only $4.9 billion—a pittance compared with the $139 billion raised in capital markets that year by nonfinancial corporations. A 1985 study by the Treasury Department and a more recent update by James Poterba of the Massachusetts Institute of Technology found that over 80 percent of the capital for venture capital comes from sources who do not pay personal income taxes and would not benefit from a change in the capital gains provisions of the personal income tax—institutional investors, foreigners, and corporations.[7]

In sum, while economic studies can be cited to support either side in the heated controversy about the growth-stimulating consequences of a cut in capital gains taxes, my reading of the evidence suggests that the skeptics are more likely to prove correct. Most important, opening up again the differential between the tax rate on ordinary income and the tax on capital gains would recreate incentives for taxpayers to convert ordinary income to capital gains, to invest in tax shelters, and otherwise to distort economic activity in the interest of tax savings, incentives that were greatly reduced or eliminated in the tax reform of 1986. Even apart from considerations of equity in the distribution of tax burdens among different income classes, a simple cut in the capital gains tax gets very low marks as a desirable way to promote higher economic efficiency and higher growth.

There are some good arguments for *indexing* capital gains for tax purposes. Twenty thousand dollars of common stocks bought ten years ago might be worth about $60,000 now, and a sale of those stocks bringing a $40,000 capital gain would require someone in the 28 percent tax bracket to pay a tax of $11,200. But $10,000 of the capital gain simply reflected inflation in the economy; the value of the stock would have to increase by that much just to stay even with the general rise in prices. The "real" capital gain was not $40,000 but $30,000. Allowing taxpayers to recalculate the purchase price of their assets to reflect inflation, before calculating the capital gain, would, reasonably, subject them to a tax only on the real gain.

One must bear in mind several considerations, however, before immediately concluding that indexing is an idea whose time has come. In the first place, earnings that take the form of capital gains can be sheltered indefinitely without any taxes until the asset is sold, and those tax-sheltered earnings can earn a return. Other forms of income are taxed when earned. This fact gives a tax advantage to capital gains, offsetting some or all of the excess inflation tax. Second, as long as capital gains are indexed against inflation while the inflation premium in interest rates continues to be eligible for deduction from income for tax purposes, it would be possible to "game" the tax system. Especially when inflation is high, it would pay to borrow and invest the proceeds in stocks or other assets whose prices tend to rise with inflation. But devising an administratively feasible way to calculate the inflation premium in interest payments is an exceedingly difficult task. On balance, allowing indexing of capital gains might be worthwhile, despite its problems, in return for another major reform—taxing the (indexed) value of capital gains at the death of the asset holder. Currently, a person can accumulate capital gains and pass the higher-priced assets on to heirs who can then use the appreciated value as the basis for calculating their own capital gains when the assets are later sold. Much income completely escapes taxes through this route.

SOME MORE GENERAL PRINCIPLES

An important principle about the relationship of tax policy to the task of increasing national saving and investment can be distilled:

> The total amount of investment, foreign and domestic, undertaken by a country cannot exceed its national saving. Except as they succeed in raising national saving, tax incentives favoring investment cannot change the aggregate amount of investment. But within the total determined by national saving, tax incentives can be used to a limited degree to change the mix of investment. Incentives favoring business investment, for example, can be used to increase domestic business investment at the expense of housing construction and the trade balance.

TAX INCREASES AND SUPPLY-SIDE EFFECTS

I have already argued that the gradual phase-in of a much more restrictive budgetary policy need not lead to a deficiency of aggregate demand and higher unemployment. With the cooperation of the Federal Reserve, the lower interest rates resulting from such a policy should stimulate enough investment spending and improvements in the trade balance to keep aggregate demand from declining and to prevent an economy at full employment from slipping significantly below that level. In other words, the country should be able to avoid any major demand-side problems encountered in the transition to a more austere budget policy. But even with large cuts in defense spending, shifting the federal budget from a $250 billion deficit to a $70 billion surplus (an improvement equal to 4.6 percent of national income) would clearly be impossible without a sizable tax increase. Could the supply-side consequences of the tax increases—that is, unfavorable incentive effects—be large enough to wipe out all or a large part of the long-term gains in potential GNP estimated in memo 25 to flow from the new budget policy? That is the question to which I now turn.

How big would the tax increases have to be to achieve the budget objectives set out above? Obviously the answer depends on how much spending could be cut, as issue that is as much political as economic. Nevertheless I can outline some possibilities. In the first place, reducing the budget deficit by tax increases or spending cuts brings a bonus in the form of lower interest payments on the debt. Thus, if approximately $235 billion of deficit reduction through tax increases or expenditure cuts were gradually put in place by say, 1997, an additional saving in interest payments on the debt would automatically be realized, amounting to perhaps $80 billion or $90 billion a year. Some $55 billion of these savings would occur because of a reduction in the national debt below projected levels, and $25 billion to $35 billion from the lower interest rates made possible by the large deficit reduction (although the full effect of lower rates on federal interest premiums might not be felt until after 1997). Thus some combination of spending reductions and tax cuts of $235 billion a year would, with the interest bonus, produce the targeted $320 billion of budget improvement.

It would hardly seem radical, with the cold war ended, to reduce the defense budget by 1997, in dollars of constant purchasing power, 35 to 40 percent below what it was in 1992, on the way to an even lower number in subsequent years. Some reduction is already included in the CBO budget projections that I have been using, but an additional $60 billion in expenditure saving would be realized by the cut suggested above. Civilian budget expenditures in many areas have already been seriously reduced by the budget stringency of the past decade. Domestic discretionary programs—those whose annual expenditures are determined year-by-year in appropriation bills and are not determined by legal entitlement legislation—have been reduced from 4.8 percent of GNP in 1980 to about 3.7 percent in 1992 and further large cuts seem unlikely. However, spending for entitlement programs, especially medicare and medicaid, have grown rapidly. Conceivably, a major restructuring of the nation's health care system might make it possible to realize substantial costs savings for the country as a whole. But those savings are not in hand, and insofar as the federal budget is concerned, any savings are likely, at least initially, to be equal or exceeded by the cost of providing for the 35 million to 40 million Americans who lack adequate health insurance. Nevertheless, out of the $1,180 billion civilian outlays (excluding interest) projected for 1997, it ought not to be unreasonable to find savings sufficient to finance some high-priority program increases and squeeze out something like $35 billion in net expenditure reductions.[8] That would leave $140 billion to be raised by a tax increase, equal to 2 percent of national income.

Would the negative incentive effects of a higher tax burden significantly offset the favorable supply-side consequences of the higher national saving rate that the proposed budget policy would produce and thus reduce these gains? Suppose, at one extreme, that all of the increase in taxes came from an across-the-board boost in personal income taxes. That would require a 21 percent increase in income tax revenues. The 15 percent rate might, for example, go to 18 percent and the 31 percent rate to 38 or 39. Would the lower after-tax return to saving, brought about by the tax increases, induce consumers to save a smaller percentage of their income?

As noted earlier, some studies suggest that consumption does not respond to changes in the after-tax return to saving. If we use an estimate of the response halfway between zero and the very high estimate cited in memo 23, an income tax increase of the size proposed above might lower private saving by some $35 billion. In my judgment even that is too high. In any event the vast bulk of the deficit improvement would flow into higher national saving. And any tax-induced reduction in private saving could be avoided by concentrating the tax increase on consumption-type taxes—a general sales (or value-added) tax or more narrowly concentrated excise taxes on specific goods such as energy or polluting emissions. Moreover, a successful program that produced a sustained improvement in the budget deficit amounting to 4.6 percent of national income would gradually lower the federal debt and federal interest payments sufficiently to allow the initial tax increase—and any adverse supply-side effects—to be reduced steadily as the years went on.

For a general sales or value-added tax, a two-way trade-off exists. Even the relatively modest effect of higher taxes in penalizing saving would no longer be present, but the sales or value-added tax would fall heaviest on people in the lowest part of the income distribution. Taxes on energy consumption or pollution present a somewhat more favorable trade-off. They have minimal effects on saving, and they penalize the consumption of social "evils." But energy taxes fall especially hard on people who have long commutes or otherwise depend on auto travel. Income taxes have the largest relative effect in discouraging private saving (although not an absolutely large effect) but tend to be fairer in their incidence.

Higher taxes, whether income or sales taxes, also lower the after-tax reward for work, and we must consider how much that effect will diminish the supply of labor in the economy. Again, as in the case of private saving, there is no unanimity in the economics profession about the extent to which the labor supply is affected by changes in the after-tax wage. A series of carefully controlled social experiments was carried out in the 1970s to determine the effect of various forms of welfare programs and negative income tax proposals on work effort. The results are applicable principally to workers at the lower end of the income distribution; they suggest that the labor supply of male family heads changes very little in response to changes in taxes, but that secondary earners, chiefly wives, do respond through changes in labor force participation and in hours of work to changes in taxes. The overall response, that is, the *elasticity*, of the labor supply to changes in tax rates, as observed in these experiments, is small— each 1 percent increase in after-tax wages, induced by a cut in taxes— would induce less than a 0.1 percent change in the amount of labor supplied. Other studies, based on statistical surveys, which included workers at all income levels, give different results, but they generally show a larger overall elasticity, with the major effect coming from secondary earners. One well-known and often-cited study finds a much more substantial response of work effort by husbands to changes in tax. Moreover, studies suggest that the greater the progressivity of the tax, the larger the effect in reducing labor supply. To the extent this is correct the labor supply effect of a tax increase would depend upon the nature of that increase; a progressive rise in income taxes would have a larger effect than the imposition of a broadly based sales or value-added tax.[9]

As part of a program to raise national saving, an increase in taxes would have two kinds of effects on the labor supply. On the one hand, the tax increase would depress after-tax wages and initially cause a reduction in the supply of labor, especially among secondary earners. As noted, an increase in income taxes is likely to curtail labor supply by more than a broad-based sales or value-added tax. On the other hand, the higher domestic investment made possible by the budget program would gradually raise real wages. After the program had been phased in and was fully in effect for several decades, the induced rise in real wages should offset part of the initial labor supply effect and probably much of it if the additional revenues came from a sales or value-added tax. And, in any event, as noted earlier, the growing reduction in interest payments on the federal debt would allow the initial tax increases to be relaxed in later years.

THE BALANCE

A budget policy, starting in 1993, that gradually converted the projected $250 billion budget deficit now likely for 1997 to a $70 billion surplus and then maintained that surplus (as a share of national income) for twenty years, would, by the end of that time, raise the annual level of national income by about 5.5 to 6 percent. If income taxes were raised to produce the revenues needed for the budget program, the rate of return earned by private savers would be modestly reduced. But, as pointed out earlier, the loss of private saving on that account is likely to be small, and so only a small portion of the potential gain would be lost through that route. And that result could be guaranteed by using a sales or value-added tax as the device to raise the revenues—incentives for private saving would not be affected. There would be some immediate reduction in the amount of labor supplied to the economy, especially from secondary and part-time earners, larger with income than with value-added taxes. But this initial effect would gradually be reduced as the faster advance in productivity raised real wages to compensate for the higher taxes and the growing reductions in interest payments allowed a reduction in the tax burden. All in all, adverse supply-side offsets, especially with a sales or value-added tax, should be small.

The gains in national income would not come free, of course. Initially, consumption spending would have to fall through the medium of higher taxes and lower federal transfer payments (principally reduced interest payments on federal debt). But even though consumption became a smaller share of national output, output itself would rise. By the end of the period we have examined (a five-year phase-in and then two decades of the higher national saving rate), consumption would have risen by some 1.5 to 2 percent above where it would have been in the absence of the budget program. And for some time thereafter the net gain would widen further.

CONCLUSION

We explored the gains in national income that could be realized from a large-scale budgetary program to convert the projected budget deficits to a small surplus over the next five years. The game is worth the candle. The initial reduction in consumption would pay off in higher consumption later, and American living standards would rise. However, the gains, while clearly worthwhile, are preceded by a period of reduced consumption, are not huge, and only gradually appear over many years.

The fundamental reason is that additional investment in physical capital, *by itself*, yields a modest return in higher national income. Moreover, I have used conservative estimates of the payoff to additional investment and have not followed the "new" school of growth theorists who suggest that expanded investment spending generates extra benefits to the economy not measured by its rate of return—for, example through inducing a higher volume of research and development spending by business (see memo 21).

Whether or not added investment automatically carries with it additional benefits, such as greater volumes of research and development, clearly a strategy to speed up the exceedingly sluggish pace of American productivity growth should not place sole reliance on expanding saving and investment. That is an important policy objective because it is one thing the federal government has the policy tools—even if not the political will—to achieve. But, historically, the amounts saved and invested over the years were not the most important elements underlying the nation's economic growth. Of most significance were those developments connected with the advance of human knowledge, specifically the quantity and quality of education and the advance of technological progress. According to Edward Denison's accounting (see memo 21), improvements in these two areas probably accounted for some 70 percent of the growth in productivity between 1929 and 1982. The government can influence the quantity of education available to young people and can have some effect, although much less, on its quality. It can also influence the pace of technological advance through policies that directly and indirectly expand the amount and kind of research and development carried on in the nation. And so memos 27 and 28 examine policies to increase the contribution to growth made by each of these two factors, *education* and *research and development*.

Notes

1. The national income statistics do not treat business expenditures on research and development as "investment"; they are treated as a current cost of doing business and, in effect, reduce profits and business-retained earnings. Statistically, therefore, an increase in business research and development would show up not as a rise in investment but, ironically, as a reduction in private (business) saving. Nevertheless, such a policy would tend to increase national productivity growth, and, as explained in memo 27, possibly by more than an equivalent amount of resources devoted to investment in tangible plant and equipment.

2. I am assuming that business firms would use all of the additional revenues from the tax incentives for investment and would not raise dividends (which would tend to increase consumption spending).

3. An economically more rational, but even more politically dangerous approach, would be to leave the interest deductibility of mortgage payments un-

touched but to tax the "implicit" net income accruing to homeowners in the form of the rental services they receive from their ownership of the house they live in.

4. Congressional Budget Office, "Effects of Lower Capital Gains Taxes on Economic Growth," *CBO Papers* (Washington, August 1990), pp. 2–3.

5. Alan Auerbach, testimony before the Senate Committee on Finance, March 28, 1990, cited in CBO, "Effects of Lower Capital Gains," pp. 14–15.

6. The top marginal tax rate on capital gains is 28 percent; 72 percent of the capital gain is kept by the seller. Excluding 30 percent of the gain from income would lower the effective rate to 20 percent, leaving the seller with 80 percent of the proceeds. And when we consider that the payment of the tax on the income from the investment can be deferred indefinitely, until it is realized as a capital gain, the difference between the two situations is even less pronounced. Thus, an investor plowing the income from his or her investment back into the business and selling out at the end of, say, seven years, and then paying a capital gains tax at the top marginal bracket rate would pay an effective rate of 20 percent under the current law and 14 percent under the 30 percent exclusion. (This illustration assumes a real discount rate of 5 percent.)

7. James M. Poterba, "Capital Gains Tax Policy toward Entrepreneurship," *National Tax Journal*, vol. 42 (September 1989), pp. 375–89, cited in CBO, "Effects of Lower Capital Gains," p. 29.

8. Over $25 billion in saving could could be realized by taxing social security benefits, which now receive highly favorable treatment, in the same way that private pension benefits are taxed. While this is a tax increase, not an expenditure cut, it is a relatively equitable way of reducing the net cost to the government of entitlement benefits. And because the tax is levied on the social security benefits of retirees, it should have few if any disincentive effects on either work effort or saving. The federal government's contribution to paying the cost of physicians' services under medicare (Part B) has risen from the 50 percent intended at the time medicare was originally enacted to something like 75 percent at the present time. The premiums charged to those covered by medicare could be raised toward the original 50 percent; a 5 percentage point increase in the cost share covered by premiums would yield about $7 billion a year.

9. Jerry A. Hausman, "Labor Supply," in Henry J. Aaron and Joseph A. Pechman, eds., *How Taxes Affect Economic Behavior* (Brookings, 1981), pp. 27–83; Jerry A. Hausman and James M. Poterba, "Household Behavior and the Tax Reform Act of 1986," *Journal of Economic Perspectives*, vol. 1 (Summer 1987), pp. 101–19; Don Fullerton, "On the Possibility of an Inverse Relationship between Tax Rates and Government Revenues," *Journal of Public Economics*, vol. 19 (October 1982), pp. 3–22; and Gary Burtless, "The Work Response to a Guaranteed Income," in Alicia H. Munnell, ed., *Lessons from the Income Maintenance Experiments* (Federal Reserve Bank of Boston, 1986), pp. 22–52.

To: The President

From: CEA Chairman

Subject: **Education**

Those who have studied the sources of economic growth agree that increases in the educational qualifications of the American labor force have contributed greatly to the growth in its productivity. The importance of education to productivity growth can also be observed in other countries—the education of a country's work force is an important determinant of its output and income per worker.

The Education and Skills of the Labor Force

Growth studies rely on the central assumption that economic payoff to education—the higher productivity associated with additional years of education—can be measured by examining the differences in earnings among people with different amounts of education. In the late 1970s, for example, average incomes of full-time (male) workers varied according to years of school completed, as shown in table 27-1. The number of years of school completed by American workers has been growing steadily since the country was founded. That growth has continued throughout the postwar period. Using data like that shown in table 27-1, Edward Denison found that between 1929 and 1982 the increase in schooling accounted for some 0.4 percent a year of the 1.6 percent annual growth rate in productivity.[1] Moreover, that 0.4 percent a year contribution of education was roughly the same in all the major subperiods, including

291EDUCATION

TABLE 27-1. Income Disparity by Years of Schooling

Education	Ratio
High school dropout	0.84
High school graduate	1.00
1–4 years of college	1.48
5 or more years of college	1.68

the years after 1973. The recent productivity slowdown cannot be attributed to a tailing off in the growth of years of schooling among American workers. Other researchers, using more detailed data and some refinements of technique, basically confirm these findings.

The traditional growth studies have relied on data about the quantity of education, as measured by years of school completed. But what about quality? It is widely believed that in recent years the quality of American education has deteriorated. Scores on the Scholastic Aptitude Test (SAT) started a long period of decline after the mid-1960s. Students born in 1945 and tested in 1963 achieved an average score (math plus verbal) of 980. Seventeen years later, in 1980, the cohort of students born in 1962 and tested in 1980 averaged a score of only 890, a 10 percent decline. Could that not be at least one cause of the productivity slowdown?

Most of those who have carefully investigated the question concluded that the decline in educational test scores was unlikely to have been significantly responsible for the slowdown in productivity growth *to date*. It has been estimated that about half of the decline in the SAT scores (and all of the decline before 1973) occurred because an increasing proportion of the high school population was taking them; the tests were reaching further and further down into the ability pool, and quite naturally the average declined. More important, the decline in test scores that began in the late 1960s affected only new entrants to the labor force, and those entrants weren't a large enough proportion of the whole labor force to have been associated with the decline in productivity growth that began occurring in the late 1960s and became worse in the 1970s. Finally, the slowdown in productivity growth was a worldwide phenomenon and occurred in countries whose educational performance is constantly being held up as examples of success.

Recently, a careful study by John Bishop of Cornell University has suggested that the drop in SAT scores may adversely affect productivity in the future.[2] In the first place, the evidence strongly suggests that prior to the late 1960s the general intellectual achievement of American students, as measured by various tests, had been rising steadily at least since the turn of the century. The evidence also shows that improved intellectual achievement is associated with higher wages and higher productivity. Thus some fraction of the growth in American productivity before 1970 depended on a continuing rise in the quality of education and the intellectual level of the American work force (aside from the improvement simply because of increased years of schooling). To the extent that average test scores measure intellectual achievement—and to a significant extent they do–simply maintaining the earlier (pre-1970s) growth rate of productivity would have required continued improvement in test scores. The decline in scores that occurred after the late 1960s was thus more serious than appears at first glance.

In the decade of the 1970s the downturn in test scores of new entrants to the labor force did not play a large role in the reduction of productivity growth, simply because—as noted above—those young workers formed such a small segment of the overall work force. But, as Bishop warns, the fraction of workers whose test scores fall below the earlier trend is steadily growing as more and more of the work force consists of cohorts of workers who graduated from school after the late 1960s. Even if the recent recovery in test scores continues and represents a real improvement in intellectual achievement, scores will remain for a very long time below the point they would have been had the trends of the 1950s and 1960s been sustained. Thus Bishop calculates that even on the optimistic assumption of continued recovery, the average quality and productivity of the work force in 1990 was 3.6 percent below where earlier trends would have put it, and by the year 2000 the quality shortfall will be 5.5 percent. That's a huge amount. It means a loss of about $250 billion in GNP below its earlier growth path. Although these estimates probably exaggerate the effect of the fall in test scores—it may be unreasonable to have expected the 1950s and 1960s improvements to continue forever—the evidence is strong enough to establish the distinct likelihood that test scores do measure intellectual achievement, even if imperfectly; that improved intellectual achievement of the labor force is associated with productivity growth; and that the post-1960s decline in test scores will be increasingly damping the growth of American productivity, even if some recovery in scores takes place.

Business Practices and the Quality of Elementary and Secondary Education

Not only has the apparent intellectual achievement of American high school students declined, but a volume of evidence has accumulated indicating that American elementary and secondary students are not nearly as well prepared as their counterparts in other advanced countries. The American educational system has some advantages over those of many other countries, especially in encouraging independent thinking and innovation. But in imparting knowledge and skills, especially in math and science, American education prepares students far less well than the school systems of many other countries. On standardized tests, American students score much lower than do students of similar age in foreign countries, and the discrepancy seems to grow as the students advance though the elementary and secondary school system. As the most egregious example, the test scores of American students at the end of high school were four grade equivalents behind those of Japanese students with the same number of years in school. But American students at the high school and elementary levels also score poorly compared with students in virtually all other advanced countries. In almost none of the comparisons can the poor U.S. results be explained by the phenomenon that a larger fraction of U.S. students finish high school than is the case in other countries. In a recent report, the National Science Foundation summed up the evidence this way: "Thus, U.S. 10-year-old students in science ranked in the middle of the countries, lost ground by age 14, and scored at or near the bottom by the 12th grade."[3]

There is some reason to believe that those American students who attend college—at least the better four-year colleges—begin to catch up to their foreign counterparts. Certainly competition is intense among foreign students to attend the top American institutions of higher learning. But approximately half of the young people graduating from high school do not go to college; the other half enter the labor force directly from high school.

Over the years, scores of studies have documented the relationship between what a worker scores on tests measuring competence and subsequent productivity in the workplace. Research conducted for the armed forces amply demonstrates the same point. There is clearly a cost to the nation, in forgone productivity and income, that can be associated with the low intellectual achievement of the average American worker who has recently entered the work force after high school.

The same John Bishop cited above has identified at least one potentially removable cause for the poor performance record of American high school students.[4] He assembled a large body of evidence that shows that despite the positive relationship between the productivity of young workers (who have not attended college) and prior educational achievement, there is little connection between the earnings of young male workers during the first five to ten years of work and their educational achievement, and only small gains for young women. For those students not going on to college, there are thus few economic incentives to do well in high school and to score well on performance tests. And, on average, American high school students, not surprisingly, spend a much smaller share of their time in school and are commonly believed to do less homework than their foreign counterparts.

James Rosenbaum of Northwestern University points out that college-bound students have substantial incentives to perform well in high school, and their teachers and administrators have incentives to promote that objective.[5] These incentives are effectively enforced by the colleges who penalize poor work and reward good performance. But for students not aspiring to college, the performance incentives are lacking for student and teacher, because future job and income prospects are not related to school performance. As Rosenbaum notes, a tacit conspiracy exists among students and teachers—if you don't hassle me, I won't hassle you.

Why do employers ignore the positive relationship between prior student achievement and high productivity? Why don't the better students get the better jobs and earn the higher wages? The answers are not entirely clear, but Bishop suggests some probable ones. Although tests are available for measuring performance, though imperfectly, in basic language, math, and other skills, concern over potential racial bias led the Equal Employment Opportunity Commission to issue guidelines in 1971 that led to a sharp decline in the tests' subsequent use by employers. Moreover, unlike the high schools in many other countries, most U.S. high schools do not provide transcripts and teachers' referrals to potential employers. And finally, as Harvard's Richard Murnane suggests, many of the widely used tests do not measure problem solving ability at all well, and problem solving ability is the most important skill in the workplace.[6] Since there is a tendency to teach to tests, students are not well prepared or tested for precisely those traits that will be most useful to them in the workplace.

THE ECONOMIC CONSEQUENCES
OF THE EDUCATIONAL SHORTFALL

A sharp increase in the inequality of income has accompanied the slow growth of the American economy since the early 1970s. As we have already seen (figure 20-2), after 1973 average family income grew very slowly. Furthermore, the income of the bottom 40 percent of families fell, while income for the top 20 percent, and even more striking, for the top 5 percent, grew handsomely. Perhaps the most important aspect of that rising income inequality is the widening gap between the wages of the college educated and the wages of workers, especially young ones, with a high school or less than high school education. Thus, a recent study by Frank Levy found that in 1986 the average annual earnings of a male, aged twenty-five to thirty-four, with four years of high school were 16 percent lower than they were in 1973 (after adjustment for inflation), while the earnings of the average college graduate were approximately unchanged.[7] Even more dramatically, another study that examined changes in wages for high- and low-paid employees found that by 1990 the wages of the bottom 20 percent of American workers (the lowest paid and presumably the least educated and the least skilled) had fallen some 25 to 30 percent below the point they had been in 1973.[8] Harvard's Richard Freeman and some of his colleagues have estimated that only a modest fraction (20 to 30 percent) of the fall in the relative wages of the less educated took place because of loss of high-paying semiskilled jobs in manufacturing industries such as steel and autos.[9] Rather, it principally reflected an across-the-board decline in wages of the less educated and less skilled in all industries. Moreover, the lower earnings did not reflect a shift in job creation in American industry toward low-skill and away from high-skill jobs. If that had been true, there would have been a surplus of the college educated and a shortage of less well-educated workers, and the relative wages of the college educated population would have been bid down relative to the wages of the high school educated, rather than up as was the case. The problem, in short, is not a scarcity of skilled jobs but a shortage of skilled workers.

It may well be true that no absolute decline has occurred in the educational accomplishments and skills of those entering the labor force out of high school. But as technology advances, American industry and other business firms are increasing the technological sophistication and the skill requirements in the workplace. Unless the average level of skills and problem solving capabilities among the high-school educated work force continually improves, employers are increasingly forced to downgrade the skill content, the productivity, and the wages of many jobs at the lower end of the skill distribution.

The problem of educational quality is made more acute by the increasing globalization of modern production. As transportation costs have fallen around the world, and multinational firms have invested heavily in the rapidly developing countries of the Pacific rim and elsewhere, American workers compete far more often with a worldwide industrial labor force. The old sources of comparative advantage, abundant raw materials and cheap capital, have become much less important, while the human skills of management and workers in mastering high-quality, technologically advanced methods of production, transportation, distribution, and finance have become much more important. Markets for American goods and services produced by skilled, competent, and well-educated workers are expanding rapidly, and international trade is a force boosting the wages of such workers. But correspondingly, American workers with low skills and poor education are increasingly competing with the work force of lower-income but rapidly industrializing countries.

A country whose educational and training institutions continued to improve the skills of one-half of its new labor force entrants (college and post-college graduates) while holding constant the skills of the remainder would experience a growing maldistribution of income in the absence of any world trade. But that result will be even more striking as economic and technological developments internationalize world markets. This wave of developments will not recede. Improved education and skill training, not protection, is the answer.

POLICY RESPONSES

The evidence is overwhelming that the quality of American elementary and secondary education leaves much to be desired and that the level of American productivity and living standards has been and will continue to be lowered by that deterioration in quality. The discipline of economics does not offer specific proposals to deal with this problem. But it can provide a few tips. In particular, economics stresses the importance of incentives.

Incentives for Students

John Bishop, correctly I think, has put his finger on one serious problem and pointed in the general direction of what might be done to improve the situation. Employers should be able to reward previous achievement at the high school level by assigning jobs and wage levels on the basis of that performance as indicated by grades and achievement test results, in turn creating some incentives, which apparently do not now exist, for young people to do better in high school even when they are not going on to college. The federal government could sponsor the research and validation needed to improve existing tests, or design and validate new ones, that better measure future performance for white and minority youth. Emphasis should be on testing for problem solving skills. In a related vein, those states that do not have standardized statewide tests should adopt the requirement that all schools administer them. With the states, the federal government could help develop the institutional framework and the privacy protection that would make it feasible for employers, even small- and medium-sized ones, to request and receive in timely fashion high school grades and standardized test scores from high schools, for job applicants (with, of course, the consent of the applicant).

Incentives for Schools

Better incentives in the form of a future wage payoff from good perfor-mance should motivate students to put forth more effort. Schools and teachers also need better incentives. It is not the province of economics to design incentives for educational institutions. Nevertheless, the logic of economics would generally favor suggestions, which have been put forward recently, urging the decentralization of local systems, eliminating large slices of central educational bureaucracies, giving more power to principals and teachers in individual schools, and in particular providing parents with the right of choice among individual schools.[10] While the analogy with the marketplace is far from perfect and should not be pushed to the limit, economic history and analysis strongly confirm the benefits for consumers of having vigorous competition among the providers of consumer services and can attest to the spur to performance imparted by the threat of loss of markets.

Finally, in considering these matters, one must bear in mind the simple arithmetic of schools and labor markets. Realistically, better incentives for students and schools and other improvements in educational quality would only begin to affect the performance of high school graduates some years down the pike. In turn, each year's cohort of new workers represents only about 2 to 3 percent of the total labor force. Thus, even educational improvements set in motion immediately would not reach half of the labor force until after the year 2020. And so we should consider means to upgrade the skills of today's adult workers. In the end, hard-headed analysis may indicate little promise for a large-scale effort to educate adult workers. But it would be a mistake to neglect this possibility in the absence of such a negative finding.

NOTES

1. Edward F. Dension, *Trends in American Economic Growth, 1929–82* (Brookings, 1985), p. 114.

2. John Bishop, "Is the Test Score Decline Responsible for the Productivity Growth Decline?" *American Economic Review*, vol. 79 (March 1989), pp. 178–97.

3. National Science Board, *Science and Engineering Indicators—1989* (Washington: Government Printing Office, 1989), p. 28.

4. John Bishop, "Incentives for Learning: Why American High School Students Compare So Poorly to Their Counterparts Overseas," in Commission on Workforce Quality and Labor Market Efficiency, *Investing in People: A Strategy to Address America's Workforce Crisis*, Background Papers, vol. 1 (Department of Labor, 1989).

5. James E. Rosenbaum, "What If Good Jobs Depended on Good Grades?" *American Educator*, vol. 13 (Winter 1989), pp. 10–15, 40–42.

6. Richard J. Murnane, "Education and the Productivity of the Work Force: Looking Ahead," in Robert E. Litan, Robert Z. Lawrence, and Charles L. Schultze, eds., *American Living Standards: Threats and Challenges* (Brookings, 1988), pp. 215–45.

7. Frank Levy, "Incomes," in Lawrence and Schultze, *American Living Standards*, pp. 108–53.

8. Chinhui Juhn, Kevin Murphy, and Robert Topel, "Why Has the Natural Rate of Unemployment Increased over Time?" *Brookings Papers on Economic Activity 2: 1991*, pp. 75–133.

9. McKinley L. Blackburn, David E. Bloom, and Richard B. Freeman, "The Declining Economic Position of Less Skilled American Men," in Gary Burtless, ed., *A Future of Lousy Jobs? The Changing Structure of U.S. Wages* (Brookings, 1990), pp. 31–67.

10. See John E. Chubb and Terry M. Moe, *Politics, Markets, and America's Schools* (Brookings, 1990).

To: The President

From: CEA Chairman

Subject: **Technological Advance**

In the long run, the advance of scientific knowledge, and its translation into new and improved products and methods of production, is the most important force contributing to economic growth. If, to use a fanciful example, the major industrial countries of the world had saved and invested as much as they actually did over the past two centuries and given their citizens the years of education that they have provided, but such countries still had access only to the science and technology of the late eighteenth century, today's output, income, and living standards would be a tiny fraction of what they are. We would have transportation by horse, barge, or sailboat. We would have a little power from waterdriven mills, but we would rely mostly on power from human or animal muscle. We would have no refrigerated foods or electric lighting, no synthetic materials, oil refineries, or aluminum smelters, no antibiotics, X-rays, or sterile procedures, no hybrid high-yield grains, or powered farm machinery. Indeed, without the progress of science and technology the amount of investment that could profitably have been undertaken would long ago have shriveled to the level needed simply to replace the existing capital stock that then existed. And people would not have sought, nor would governments have provided, the education we have become used to. A world of primitive technology would have far less need for, and offer far fewer rewards for, education.

Progress in science and technology occurs along a spectrum, ranging from fundamental advances in scientific knowledge to commercially feasible improvements in consumer goods and production processes. In some

TABLE 28-1. Sources of Support for U.S. Nondefense Research and Development by Type
Percent of total

Source	Basic	Applied	Development
Federal government	61	34	8
Industry	20	59	91
Other (university and so on)	19	7	1
Total	100	100	100
Share of total research and development in each sector	18	27	55

ultimate sense, most advances in commercial and industrial technology are traceable to earlier advances in scientific knowledge. If scientific progress stopped, advances in economically useful technology would also eventually grind to a halt. But at any point in history, most of the improvements in product design and production techniques that generate economic growth are more humble in origin and come from some combination of applied research, planned development efforts, trial and error, and plain old tinkering. In seeking to advance science and technology, the government has two tasks: to promote basic scientific research and accomplishment and to do what it can, though its capacity is limited, to foster the translation of scientific advances into industrially and commercially useful technology.

The basement tinkerer still exists, but organized research and development efforts produce most scientific advances and technological improvements in modern economies. Research and development (R&D) activities fall into three major categories: basic research, applied research, and development. In the United States, the federal government finances a very large share of the nation's basic research, is a much smaller (though still substantial) supporter of applied research, but outside the defense industries, the U.S. government contributes only a tiny fraction of the total cost of development work, almost all of which is commercial or industrial (see table 28-1).[1]

By its nature, basic research produces results that are not proprietary. Since the results very quickly become common knowledge and cannot usually be patented, those who carry out the research often cannot capture the benefits. The benefits to the whole country from basic research are much higher than the benefits that can be captured privately by those who undertake the research. As a consequence, the return to private industry from investing in basic research projects is likely to be small, even though the return to society as a whole is high. The private incentives are insufficient to underwrite the costs and the risks of basic research. Without public financing, the private sector would undertake far too little basic research.

At the other end of the spectrum is the process of converting basic and applied research results into commercially usable improvements in products or processes. Here, private firms can, at least to some extent, reap the rewards of successful efforts. Although knowledge gradually leaks out to competitors, a combination of patents, secrecy, and the advantage of learning by doing can, for some time at least, allow firms that carry on applied research and development projects to earn a satisfactory return for undertaking the investment and bearing the risk of unsuccessful projects. Outside of defense, therefore, the federal government has tended to concentrate support for R&D on basic research.

Under the Reagan administration the government became especially reluctant to support civilian research beyond the category of basic. But three exceptions to this broad policy have long been in effect: first, the government has traditionally been the principal funding source for R&D in the space industry, most of which does not involve basic research. (Only one-quarter of NASA's R&D is classified as basic.) Although commercial uses of space have grown, commercial payoffs alone would never have come close to supporting the necessary R&D. But for reasons (real or perceived) of national prestige, entertainment value, and national defense the government itself has created and supported this highly R&D-intensive industry.

Second, the federal government has sporadically supported several large-scale projects aimed at commercially feasible new technologies: the Clinch River breeder reactor, the supersonic transport (SST), and several large projects undertaken to learn how to gasify coal and extract oil from shale are among the most prominent. The federal government's rationale has varied from case to case. When foreign governments support the development of a highly risky commercial venture that is competitive with an American industry, but too risky for private firms in that industry to undertake on their own, the federal government is sometimes successfully pressured to launch its own development project, for example, the

SST. The U.S. government also responded to the energy crises of 1974 and 1979 by supporting large-scale development of alternative energy sources (coal gasification and shale oil).

Most often these federal government ventures into commercial R&D projects have yielded highly disappointing results. Few became commercial successes, but, as might be expected, most were kept going even after it became obvious they would not be successful. Not surprisingly, the political system often chose them and then, because they created local and regional jobs, preserved them as long as possible despite the signs of commercial failure.[2]

Indeed, in a governmental system of divided powers, in which 535 locally elected congressional representatives and senators help to call the shots and executive branch managers make risky decisions without having any of their own money at risk, it is very difficult for the federal government to use hard-headed economic and business criteria to select, and when appropriate to close down, applied research and development projects of a commercial nature.

Third, recently the federal government has supported several research and development ventures jointly undertaken by consortia of individual firms in high-technology industries. Joint ventures have been started or are seriously under consideration in the fields of semiconductor manufacturing techniques (Sematech), supercomputers, superconductivity, and high-definition television. Some of these projects are supported by the Defense Department. But America's fear of losing its competitive edge to other countries, especially Japan, who are pursuing large and potentially successful research and development ventures in these areas, has motivated the federal government's participation. It is too early to issue a report card on these joint federal-industry ventures, but none of them yet seems a great success, perhaps because the companies participating in the venture do not have the incentive to assign their best people to a project whose results they have to share equally with their competitors. It is indeed striking that Japanese industry finances 98 percent of industrial research activities and the Japanese government only 2 percent.

Despite the political and managerial advantages of having the federal government concentrate most of its R&D support on basic research, a large body of evidence suggests that the nation now needs to develop some improved political and administrative mechanisms that would allow it to manage, rationally and with nonpolitical criteria, greatly increased research funding for research and development projects beyond those in the purely basic research category.

First, several careful economic studies have documented that the *private* rate of return to industrial and commercial R&D averages about 25 percent, roughly double the return on investments in plant and equipment.[3] Private firms apparently underinvest in what seem to be highly profitable R&D projects. (If firms were as willing to invest in R&D as in other assets, they would gradually exhaust the superior opportunities available and push down the average rate of return on R&D investments toward that of other projects.) Perhaps private firms are reluctant to invest appropriately large sums in R&D because large-scale R&D projects are very risky: on average the return is good, but the chance for any one or several large projects to turn into a lemon is very high. Management will not "bet the firm" on one throw of the dice. In this situation the government has a legitimate role to play—it is large enough to pool risks and play the averages; it will not go down the tubes because some large ventures fail.

The same studies that documented the very high private return to R&D demonstrate that the total social return is larger yet, averaging perhaps 50 percent. Despite patent laws, industrial secrecy, and the advantages of learning by doing, the results of successful research leak out to industry generally, so that society as a whole gains more than is captured in the returns to the originator of the research. The case for governmental action to stimulate more R&D is thus strengthened even more.

Despite the excellent case that can be made for more extensive government support for civilian R&D, the U.S. federal government's support is low. In 1989 federal civilian R&D expenditures were $23 billion. But of this amount, $12 billion were for the space program and the National Institutes of Health. These areas of research, especially the health research of NIH, produce important social benefits. But the spillover effects on national productivity growth are probably modest. And the $11 billion remaining for all other civilian purposes was a tiny share in relation to the nation's 1989 GNP of $5 trillion. In allocating support for civilian research and development, the U.S. government's priorities are markedly different from those of other industrial governments (table 28-2).

A nation can be in the front rank in the quality of its science and still do poorly in translating scientific advances into economically successful innovations that improve national productivity. Great Britain seems to be such a case. In contrast, Japan's achievements in science have not been outstanding, but it has been preeminently successful in translating scientific advances into commercially profitable innovations and improving on technological discoveries made elsewhere.

TABLE 28-2. Government Support for Civilian Research and Development, 1987

Percent of total support

Type of research	United States	Germany	Japan	United Kingdom	France
Health, environ- ment, space	59	13	9	16	15
All other	41	87	91	84	85
Total	100	100	100	100	100

Japan's concentration on the commercial development of the R&D shows up in several ways. For example, in Japan the number of science and engineering degrees awarded (relative to the size of the twenty-two-year-old population) is about the same as in the United States—5.2 percent for Japan versus 4.8 percent for the United States. But in Japan 85 percent of those degrees are in engineering and only 15 percent are in science. In the United States 60 percent are in science and only 40 percent are in engineering. Surveys of citations in scientific articles around the world show that relative to its population Japanese authors receive the greatest number of citations in engineering journals but the lowest in mathematics.

None of this means that the United States must imitate the Japanese. But the evidence strongly suggests that the United States needs to devote more energy and resources toward moving scientific and technological discoveries out of the laboratory and onto the production line. In turn, the federal government should develop the institutional capacity to provide efficient, politically sanitized, and greatly expanded support for generic and precompetitive research and development—the kind of research that is a necessary prelude to the development of an economically useful technology but that does not directly produce a commercially salable product or process.

Currently, the federal government provides a limited tax break for private R&D—a 25 percent tax credit for R&D expenditures in excess of a base period amount. The current tax credit has some problems.[4] For example, when a firm is deciding whether to undertake a large R&D project, it has to consider that a large jump in one year's R&D expenditure raises its base and reduces the R&D credits available in subsequent years. With some improvements to reduce the flaws in the system, this is one of the very few areas of the tax code where it would be worthwhile to enlarge on special tax credits and deductions. But there is a limit to how much this form of support can be expanded. The availability of a tax credit for R&D gives firms a strong incentive to undertake "creative" and hard-to-police accounting, which assigns the largest possible share of firm costs to the category of R&D. The more generous the tax credit, the larger the incentive.

The task of designing the proper institutions to select and manage such support efficiently is a daunting one. But economic logic, common sense, and some experience with the way the political and bureaucratic system operates offer useful guidelines. First, and perhaps most important, any R&D grant program for commercial and industrial research must require a substantial commitment of private equity funds. Those who apply for the grants must put their own money at risk. Second, in contrast to some past federally supported commercial R&D projects, the support should not take the form of guaranteed loans. Such loans have two faults: they remove the risk of failure from the private operators of the project and they do not count as budget outlays, thus escaping the discipline of the budget process. Third, the government should, as much as possible, limit financial support to "precompetitive" research, that is, to research designed to establish underlying technological parameters and possibilities rather than R&D that directly results in a marketable product or process. The financing of the latter should be left to private firms who alone can exercise the kind of market judgments needed to judge this type of research. Finally, an ideal goal would be to set up a procedure similar to the peer review process that NIH uses to make decisions about the allocation of its funds. Certain funds are targeted for each area that is to be supported, and panels of outside experts, not directly subject to the supervision of Congress or the executive branch, decide which proposals among the ones competing for R&D grants are worthy of support. For precompetitive industrial and commercial R&D, the government could allow consortia of firms in certain industries to apply for support. More analysis is needed to determine whether such a procedure would enable the federal government to support research on a large scale. Nonetheless, developing an efficient, politically neutral procedure is a worthwhile goal.

CONCLUSION

Although technological progress is in the end the most important ingredient of economic growth, governments have only a limited ability to speed up the pace of advance. Nevertheless the government's role is important.

Right now the federal government faces two challenges. First, it must greatly increase budgetary support for civilian research and development in areas other than health and space and finance it in a way that does not add to the budget deficit. Second, policymakers must design institutional arrangements that allow the government to financially support, in a politically neutral way, those R&D activities that help convert basic scientific advances into economically viable products and processes. In this task, institutional innovation should go hand in hand with the expansion of the federal R&D budget. Without new institutions to insulate the program from politics, we would almost surely get more political pork than technological advance.

NOTES

1. The data in the table include a modest amount of defense-related R&D funded by industry.

2. A recent book by Linda R. Cohen and Roger G. Noll, *The Technology Pork Barrel* (Brookings, 1991), provides detailed case studies of six federal commercialization ventures in the R&D field and documents the severe political and managerial problems facing the government when it tries to select and operate such projects on criteria related to commercial and economic success.

3. Edwin Mansfield and others, "Social and Private Rates of Return from Industrial Innovations," *Quarterly Journal of Economics*, vol. 91 (May 1977), pp. 221–40; and William J. Baumol, Sue Anne Batey-Blackman, and Edward N. Wolff, *Productivity and American Leadership: The Long View* (MIT Press, 1989).

4. See Martin Neil Baily's testimony in *Permanent Extension of Certain Expiring Tax Provisions*, Hearings before the House Ways and Means Committee, 103 Cong. 2 sess. (Government Printing Office, forthcoming).

P A R T **4**

Summary

To: The President

From: CEA Chairman

Subject: **A Summary of These Memos and How They Differ from What Others Might Have Told You**

In barebones form, without the qualifications and nuances, the major policy conclusions and implications from these memos can be summarized in a few pages:

There are two major goals of macroeconomic policy: *economic stability*—keeping unemployment and inflation low; and long-run *economic growth*—encouraging advances in productivity, incomes, and living standards.

—Economic instability arises principally from fluctuations in total demand (spending) relative to the economy's supply capabilities (potential GNP). Recessions and high unemployment come about when total demand falls short of potential. When demand exceeds potential, inflation rises. Economic stabilization policy is thus mainly concerned with managing total demand to keep it roughly in line with potential GNP.

—One problem that often plagues economic stabilization policies is that inflation responds only slowly and stubbornly to changes in aggregate demand. Wage and price increases do not moderate very quickly in the face of modest increases in unemployment and weakening markets. Inflation in the United States is not on a hair trigger, waiting to explode on the occurrence of small amounts of economic overheating. But, once a rise in inflation does occur, for whatever reason, a big dose of economic slack and unemployment must take place to bring it down again.

—Over the short and medium run, say one to four years, governmental policies can have large effects on the overall level of demand and spending in the economy, but it is not easy to choose the proper policy instrument, in the right magnitude, at the correct time. Through fiscal policy—changes in tax rates or expenditure programs—the federal government can stimulate or restrain total demand. But for economic and political reasons, fiscal policy is a blunt instrument that cannot easily and quickly be turned in one direction or another. It is not normally a useful tool for smoothing moderate fluctuations in demand. Countercyclical changes in tax or expenditure policy are best saved for dealing with large and protracted recessions or booms.

—Through monetary policy, the Federal Reserve can restrain or stimulate total demand by injecting or removing reserves from the banking system, thereby changing the money supply and influencing interest rates and the availability of credit. Monetary policy should be the first line of defense in economic stabilization policy.

—Monetary policy also has its limitations. A significant and variable delay occurs between the time the Federal Reserve acts to change bank reserves and the ultimate effects on economic activity. Highly aggressive and ambitious efforts to prevent all fluctuations in economic activity, which rely on uncertain and sometimes erroneous forecasts of the future—and there are no other kind—could exacerbate economic instability. Because the relationship between the money supply and the level of economic activity is not a stable one, especially in recent years, following the monetarist prescription of fixed growth of bank reserves and money supply would be unwise. The Federal Reserve should generally "lean against the wind." It should ignore minor fluctuations in demand. It should stimulate total demand when demand is significantly below potential GNP. But it should modify policy gradually, not try to do all at once what may eventually be necessary to achieve targets for demand and spending. It should deal similarly with rises in demand whose magnitude or speed threaten an increase in inflation.

—A major "supply shock"—typically, a large and sustained jump in world oil prices—raises the costs Americans pay for a major raw material, simultaneously boosting inflation and curtailing demand. The rise in the price of gasoline and other energy products, much of it paid to overseas oil producers, reduces the purchasing power of Americans and their spending on other goods and services falls. Additional wage increases, to recover some part of the loss, then produce higher inflation and threaten the onset of a new wage-price spiral. And keeping the one-time rise in costs from setting off a period of rising inflation requires stiff demand restraints, not small cuts in demand.

—These characteristics of our price and wage system have several consequences for stabilization policy. First, because inflation is costly to eliminate, the Federal Reserve should lean just a bit to the anti-inflationary side when it has to resolve uncertainties about how to act. Second, when a large and sudden rise in world oil prices or some other sizable supply shock occurs, stabilization policy faces a real dilemma. If demand is stimulated to offset the recessionary consequences, inflation is aggravated. If demand is reduced to minimize inflation, the recession is worsened. For oil supply shocks, prevention rather than cure is the best policy. This aim suggests the strong desirability of building a large strategic stockpile of oil, of long-run measures to reduce dependence on oil imports, and of a foreign policy that gives high priority to avoiding the political disruption of Middle Eastern oil supplies.

—After the deep 1981–82 recession, the U.S. economy experienced eight years of uninterrupted recovery despite massive budget deficits, unprecedented fluctuations in the exchange rate for the U.S. dollar, a stock market crash second only to the Great Depression, and a $200 billion savings and loan fiasco. The recession that finally came in 1990–91, while unusually long, was shallow by historical standards. Barring a new major oil shock, the likelihood is high that monetary policy can continue to do a reasonably good, even if imperfect, job of stabilizing demand and preventing large recessions or inflation in the years ahead. That forecast assumes, however, that American voters and their elected representatives continue to give the Federal Reserve the political freedom to do what is necessary for stabilization, including at times large and painful doses of tight money and high interest rates.

—In sum, on matters of economic stabilization policy, these memos argue that monetary policy can fight inflation and recession, even though imperfectly. They therefore urge principal reliance on an activist, albeit slightly cautious, monetary policy. Fiscal policy is an effective, but blunt, tool for stabilization. Fiscal stimulus should, therefore, be used only during deep and protracted recessions.

—Growth policy is supply-side policy; it is concerned with the growth of supply, or potential GNP—the amount that the economy can produce when operating at reasonably full employment. In the long run the overwhelmingly most important source of rising per capita incomes and living standards is the growth of supply. Increasing demand can speed recoveries from recession, but it cannot safely increase output and income beyond the economy's capacity to produce goods and services. Supply-side measures typically have only modest effects in any given year, but if sustained, these policies can produce large cumulative gains.

—Growth of per capita and per family income depends in the long run largely on the growth in output per worker. The growth of output per worker and family income slowed sharply after the early 1970s. From 1948 to 1973 real (inflation-adjusted) income per family rose by 3.1 percent a year; from 1973 to 1990 it rose by only 0.5 percent a year. Although some decline from the high growth of productivity and income during the early postwar decades may have been inevitable, the current rate of growth is low by any historical standard.

—A host of microeconomic policy measures can affect the level and growth of output supply: trade policy, environmental and other regulations, minimum wages, agricultural policy, and so forth. This book has concentrated on three important macroeconomic contributors to the growth of supply and the policies that affect them: national saving and investment in new plant, equipment, and infrastructure; the amount and quality of education embodied in the labor force; and technological advance as it can be influenced by governmental support for research and development.

—National saving in the United States has collapsed in recent years, from more than 8 percent to 3 percent of national income. Private saving fell and government *dis*saving increased. Domestic investment also fell, but less than saving did. The difference was made up by an inflow of foreign saving, as we ran a substantial trade deficit and financed it by borrowing saving from abroad. The growth of American living standards is being reduced directly by the fall in national investment and indirectly by the rise in overseas borrowing (because we have to pay debt service to foreigners for the debts we have incurred).

—In order simply to maintain the current relatively low rate of growth in national productivity and living standards, and to raise national income by an additional amount, so that the large prospective increase in the ratio of retirees to the working population will not place a huge burden on future generations of workers, the United States needs to restore its national saving and investment rates to a point close to the 8 percent rate of earlier decades.

—While even centrist economists disagree somewhat, few believe tax incentives can boost private saving enough to restore America's national saving. And so the rise in national saving will have to be achieved principally by eliminating the projected federal budget deficits, and if possible, converting them into modest budget surpluses. Reaching that goal will require a large tax increase, deeper cuts in defense spending than are now budgeted, and control of rapidly escalating budget outlays on entitlement programs, especially for health care. Memo 26 supported the proposition that the disincentive effects of the tax increases necessary to close the deficit would offset little of the resulting gain in national output and income.

—Improving the quality of education, especially at the elementary and secondary level, is the second principal route by which to raise the rate of economic growth. According to virtually all studies, increases in the amount of education per worker have been a major factor underlying economic growth in the United States over the past half century or more. But various international test comparisons suggest that the quality of American elementary and secondary education is well below that of other countries; that it has not kept up with rising demand for skilled workers on the part of industry; and that this educational shortfall is contributing to the slowdown in economic growth and to the growing maldistribution of income in the United States. But in this case a correct diagnosis of the problem does not immediately tell us how to respond. Spending more money alone will probably do little good.

—Two proposals were sympathetically reviewed in this book. First, half of the new entrants to the labor force each year do not go beyond high school. Performance in high school, as measured by grades and various test scores, seems to be positively associated with worker productivity. But students with better grades do not earn higher wages, at least for the first five or ten years after entering the labor force. Those not going on to college have little economic incentive to do well in school. Employers have little access to high school grades or test performance. Under appropriate safeguards, that situation should be remedied. With the choice of jobs and initial pay more closely related to high school performance, some improvement in the motivation to learn should occur. Second, there should be widespread experimentation with recent proposals to allow parents more freedom to select which public schools their children can attend. The introduction of more competition into the public school system is likely to create incentives for improved performance. Because these two approaches, even if highly effective, will have only a very gradual payoff in terms of a more productive work force, expansion and improvement of worker training programs deserve high priority.

—The national payoff to additional research and development expenditures is very high, perhaps on the order of 50 percent annually, a rate that is far above the typical return to conventional investment. But because private firms cannot capture all the rewards from many types of R&D— the results tend to spread quickly to competitors—too little R&D gets done with purely private funds. Yet the U.S. federal government provides surprisingly little support for civilian research and development other than for health and space. A great expansion of support for civilian research outside of health and space is clearly warranted. But the provision of additional funds in the budget is not sufficient to remedy the situation. Under current budgeting practices in Congress the R&D funds would probably be distributed heavily along pork-barrel lines, with a much smaller payoff than is potentially available. Substantial additional funding should go hand in hand with the development of a more politically insulated way of allocating the funds among private industries and firms, perhaps along the lines of the peer review process used by the National Institutes of Health.

The most important single policy message from these memos can be summed up as follows:

In the short run, changes in the nation's economic fortunes are dominated by changes in aggregate demand. Policies to stabilize demand can make a large contribution to improving the country's well-being by minimizing periods of high unemployment and inflation.

In the long run, however, demand management is far less important than policies to promote the growth of supply. Unlike stabilization measures, such policies typically produce gradual and initially imperceptible changes in the nation's ability to produce goods and services. But these changes can cumulate over the decades and generations to generate substantial improvements in living standards. Continuing progress in the nation's living standards depends heavily on growth of capital, improvement in the skills and knowledge of workers, and scientific and technical advances.

WHAT OTHER ADVISERS MIGHT HAVE TOLD YOU

At the beginning of these memos I said that they would represent a mainstream and centrist point of view. But it would be strange indeed if other economists, even those who are more or less in the broad middle of the spectrum of opinion, would not disagree on one or more of the issues I have addressed. In this concluding memo, I want to make clear on what issues other economists would have given you different advice from mine on the nature or size of the effects of particular policies.

THE MODERATE CONSERVATIVES

In the 1950s, 60s, and 70s, one way moderate conservatives (for example, Arthur Burns, Herbert Stein, Allan Greenspan) differed from moderate liberals (Walter Heller, James Tobin) was in their assessment of the relative dangers of inflation and unemployment. Moderate conservatives were usually rather slow to recommend expansionary policies to fight a recession but quick to urge restrictive policies to prevent inflation. Moderate liberals were more expansionist minded, urging the use of voluntary "incomes policies" as a means of pushing the economy to higher levels of demand and employment without increasing inflation. The moderate liberals also tended, on the whole, to have less faith than the conservatives in the stimulative capabilities of monetary policy and were more likely to urge fiscal stimulus in recessions.

More recently however these differences have narrowed substantially. With interest rates at historically very high levels—giving monetary policy much room to operate in a stimulative direction—and with fiscal policy hamstrung by huge structural budget deficits, most centrist economists would rely on monetary policy as the principal stabilization tool. And after the inflation of the 1970s, and the pain of the massive 1981–82 recession necessary to wring it out, moderate liberals are somewhat less ambitious in their expansionist views. Since Republicans have held the presidency since 1981 and "incumbency doth make expansionists of us all," conservative economic advisers have become more willing to urge the Federal Reserve to pursue expansionist policies during periods of economic weakness. And so on issues of stabilization policy, it is probably fair to say that the divergence of views among moderate conservatives and liberals has been reduced in recent years. With some difference in emphasis and detail, the two groups would accept the approach to stabilization policy I have urged.

There is one aspect of these memos, however, with which today's moderate conservatives, such as recent CEA Chairmen Martin Feldstein and Michael Boskin, and likeminded members of Congress (for example, Lloyd Bentsen and Robert Dole) would take issue. They would not subscribe to the pessimistic evaluation given in these memos to the effectiveness of such tax incentives as individual retirement accounts and capital gains tax cuts to increase private saving and investment. Indeed several prominent economists of a more liberal persuasion, such as Lawrence Summers (economic adviser to Governor Michael Dukakis in the 1988 presidential campaign) share some, although not all, of their views on the effectiveness of investment tax incentives (Summers is not a proponent of capital gains tax cuts but does favor restoration of the investment tax credit). While few subscribe to the extreme views of supply-siders of the early Reagan years, who promised miracles from tax cuts, they do postulate larger results from such measures than I do.

MONETARISM, OLD AND NEW

Memo 17 explained the views of the traditional monetarists, as exemplified by Nobel prize winner Milton Friedman. He would have the government, through the Federal Reserve, provide a fixed and stable growth of the money supply and reject efforts to pursue countercyclical monetary and fiscal policies. But, as that memo pointed out, financial deregulation and financial innovations in recent decades have blurred the distinction between the many forms of money (for example, checking accounts) and other financial assets (for example, mutual bond funds). As a consequence, households and business firms vary the proportion of their financial assets they want to hold in the form of money depending on interest rates and other economic developments. Correspondingly, the relationship between the quantity of money and aggregate demand and GNP is far more variable than it was in earlier periods—and even then the stability of the money-GNP relationship was not all that assured. Given a highly variable money-to-GNP relationship, maintaining a constant growth of the money supply could *de*stabilize the economy. In recent years among some economists a new monetarism has emerged, which reaches roughly the same policy conclusions as the traditional monetarist held but for different reasons. The new monetarism emerges in somewhat varied ways from several different but related strands of economic analysis, each of which rests on pessimism about the ability of the government to carry out a successful countercyclical policy. It argues that attempts to do so are likely to carry an inflationary bias and to reduce the long-term rate of economic growth.

Supply-Side Business Cycles

In this view, short-term fluctuations in GNP arise principally from sporadic changes in aggregate supply, not from swings in aggregate demand or spending, as these memos have portrayed. The effects of these "supply shocks" on total output are magnified and stretched out over time by various characteristics of the economic system. This view of the way that economic fluctuations occur implies that efforts to overcome recessions by stimulating aggregate demand through fiscal or monetary policy will not increase output—which is low because the supply potential has fallen not because demand is inadequate—but such efforts are likely to raise prices. I explained in memo 1 why I reject this analysis as the basis for policy formulation.

Rational Expectations—Flexible Prices

According to this view of the world, significant and lasting shortfalls of aggregate demand below supply would not occur in a modern free market economy, free of distortions from misconceived government stabilization policy. In such a world prices and wages would respond quickly to adjust demand and supply to each other. Moreover, these theorists argue, households, workers, and business firms base today's decisions on a rational forecast of what the future holds, taking into account a reasoned judgment about what is likely to be the course of government policies. If government monetary and fiscal policies were kept on an even keel, the appearance of a shortfall of aggregate demand below supply potential would lead to cuts in wage and price inflation, which would in turn eliminate the shortfall of demand. But firms and workers won't moderate their wage and price decisions when demand starts to fall if they expect that every downturn in GNP will produce an expansionary monetary policy. Thus, systematic countercyclical monetary policy won't lead to more stable output but, over time, to higher wage and price inflation.

If monetary policy were kept stable—a fixed growth in the money supply—then deficient aggregate demand would cure itself and a long-term bias toward inflation would be eliminated. Fluctuations in supply potential might still occur (that is, "real" business cycles), but trying to manipulate demand through monetary or fiscal policy cannot cure them. And, finally, long-term stability of government tax, spending, and monetary policy would reduce uncertainty about the future and encourage investment, risk taking, and economic growth. Even if the public did alter its desire to hold money relative to other kinds of financial assets, so that the money-GNP relationship tended to vary over time, the flexibility of wages and prices in an environment of stable government policy would adjust wages and prices in the "right" direction so that real GNP would not fluctuate sharply on this account. Memos 13 and 17 provided the main reasons for rejecting much of this line of reasoning and its policy prescriptions.

THE DEMOCRATIC LEFT

Several ideas about economic policy have been coming from the political left in recent years.

The Budget Deficit Isn't Such a Big Problem

Professor Robert Eisner of Northwestern University has been the major proponent of this view.[1] First, he believes that the deficit is overstated; it should be adjusted downward to reflect the effect of inflation in reducing the real value of the government's debt. Second, sharp reductions in the deficit would depress aggregate demand and employment beyond the capability of an easier monetary policy to restore it; we may need at least a good part of the deficit we have. And third, unemployment (even before the onset of the recession of 1990–91) is too high. That fact strengthens the reasons for not raising taxes or cutting expenditures.

In memo 18 I pointed out that while Eisner is correct in saying that the size of the federal budget deficit may be overstated, making his downward adjustment to the estimate of the budget deficit would require a similar reduction to the currently estimated value of private saving. The government deficit would be lower but so would private saving, leaving the abysmally low *national* saving rate unchanged by Eisner's correction. And several memos have given reasons why, under current conditions, an easing of monetary policy and the subsequent lowering of interest rates would be successful in maintaining a satisfactorily high level of aggregate demand as the federal budget was gradually reduced.

Give Top Priority to Infrastructure Investment

Many liberal economists and commentators believe that a large increase in public investment should be undertaken (in highways and bridges, airports, schools, and so on), even if this has to be done at the expense of the budget deficit. A policy that gave over-riding priority to public investment would be unwise for two reasons. One, in memo 25 I evaluated the claims, made in several recent studies, that a dollar of additional spending for public infrastructure of the traditional type would yield much higher payoffs than a dollar spent for private investment, and I concluded that, as a general proposition about public investment, these claims were unwarranted. And unless public investment has a much larger payoff than private investment, financing a large increase in public investment by running a larger budget deficit would not improve national productivity growth since it would, roughly dollar for dollar, displace private domestic and foreign investment.[2]

Two, the main areas usually cited as candidates for large infusions of public investment spending are highways, bridges, airports, and the educational system. But an innovative new study has recently concluded that by making a number of reforms in the way we design and pay for the nation's highway and airport systems, we could achieve the desired modernization and improvements at small added cost.[3] These reforms are likely to be politically difficult, and they may never be enacted. Thus it may ultimately be necessary to overwhelm the problem with more money. But priority should initially be given to educating Congress and the voters about the gains to be had from fundamental reform. Only if that effort fails should a large expansion of the infrastructure budget be undertaken and then only if taxes are increased to pay for it.

Memo 27 argued that big increases in spending for education may not help much unless the system is changed. Admittedly, the social and economic payoffs to big improvements in the quality of American elementary and secondary education are so high that additional public spending which seriously promised to achieve that end would be worth making even at the expense of some diversion from private investment. But no agreement has yet emerged on how to make school systems more effective. Some challenging proposals have been circulating. Some additional public funds may be needed to smooth the way for educational reform. Until we reform the system, however, a large increase in federal spending on education at the expense of the budget deficit—and a subsequent reduction of private investment—is not a promising way to increase national productivity and living standards. Additional public investment in civilian research and development could yield large benefits (see memo 27). In sum, although additional public investment is not likely to do as much as its ardent advocates claim, any major national program to raise taxes and cut defense spending, while devoting the bulk of the proceeds to deficit reduction, should also make provision for some increase in public investment. The appropriate public investment share is significantly greater than zero but surely less than that proposed by the ardent devotees of such investment.

INDUSTRIAL POLICY

Periodically over the past seven or eight years, liberal commentators and a few economists have urged the federal government to adopt some form of an "industrial policy." Exactly what the term industrial policy means has varied from time to time and proponent to proponent. The common thread is that the federal government should identify "strategic" industries (often, but not always, taken to mean high-technology manufacturing industries) and foster their growth through such measures as tariffs and quotas to keep out foreign competition, subsidies to assist exports, and support for large R&D ventures.

Industrial policy can be distinguished from the kinds of growth-promoting activities that have been urged in these memos—such as higher rates of saving and investment, improved education, and broad increases in R&D funds—by its insistence on the need for the federal government to identify and support specific strategic industries. Industries are considered strategic for various reasons, but chiefly because they are high-technology industries whose success spawns growth in other industries or because they are industries paying particularly high wages to large numbers of American workers. The high costs and large risks of research and development, and the support given by other nations to their own strategic industries, it is argued, make it impossible for competing American industries to grow and prosper without assistance or protection. Because most of the industries identified as strategic engage in international trade or are threatened by competition from abroad, greater governmental management of international trade flows is an important component of most proposals for industrial policy.

For the government to undertake an industrial policy along these lines would be misguided for three reasons. One, if the overall framework of economic growth policy is favorable, American manufacturing industries are perfectly capable of achieving reasonable growth and international competitiveness. Indeed, productivity in manufacturing has been rising a good bit faster than it has in the economy as a whole.[4] Two, there is absolutely no reason to believe that the federal government, or any single decisionmaking unit, could acquire the information or the knowledge needed to improve on the judgments the market makes about what is a winning industrial structure and where private investment and R&D resources ought to be allocated.

Three, even if a federal agency could somehow make the right choices, the American political system wouldn't let them occur. It is impossible in our political system for the government to pick and choose among firms, regions, and industries in the nonpolitical efficiency-driven way envisaged by advocates of industrial policy. Can anyone imagine some federal agency, subject as it would be to congressional oversight and appropriations, deciding that the future for the wool textile industry is hopeless, but that with public support, high fashion apparel is a good bet? And would anyone really want to trust decisions about selecting industries for assistance to the same political system that poured heavy subsidies into agriculture, the merchant marine, irrigation of desert farmland, the breeder reactor, and the supersonic transport, and that, furthermore, rarely if ever closes down a failed project?

WHAT TO RETAIN FROM THE DISSENTING VIEWS

I reject the central policy prescriptions from a number of dissenting groups. Nevertheless, each group message offers some valid points.

Tax Incentives for Saving

On my reading, most of the evidence demonstrates that tax incentives are not likely to be very efficacious in raising private saving. But the evidence is not all of a piece, and one should keep an open mind. Perhaps future research will suggest a more optimistic prospect for the use of one form or another of a certain incentive.

Supply-Side Business Cycles

These memos have stressed that, apart from occasional shocks to the system from disruptions in oil supplies, economic instability typically arises from fluctuations in aggregate demand around a slowly changing supply potential. But several times in the nation's modern history, the level or rate of growth in supply potential has fallen rather abruptly—most recently, the severe slowdown that occurred in the rate of growth of potential that began in the recession of 1974–75 but wasn't fully recognized for some time. Some reasonable caution is therefore warranted in designing antirecession monetary and fiscal policy, especially when recovery is under way, to avoid the danger of stimulating aggregate demand beyond the country's supply potential (which may have slipped below earlier estimates).

Rational Expectations

These memos stressed the limitations of the "rational expectations—flexible prices" school of analysis and their essentially hands-off approach to government stabilization policy. Nevertheless, in some markets, especially most financial markets, the prices of assets (stocks, bonds, options, and so on) do move very flexibly, and the expectations of market participants about the future are a major driving force. Government policymakers have to steer a difficult line between two opposing considerations. They must always be aware that some markets—especially, again, financial markets—may quickly react to what they foresee as the future implications of current government actions. Thus, an easing of current monetary policy, if it is widely believed to herald a period of excessively easy money, may cause long-term interest rates to rise, not fall as policymakers may wish. At the same time, policymakers must have the sophistication to understand that the pronouncements of financial executives about government policy may sometimes be tinged with a hue of self-interest.

The Critique from the Left

One does not have to believe that a huge dose of infrastructure investment is the principal answer to slow economic growth in order to acknowledge that national output could be raised by carefully selected increases in public investment programs. The key is a careful analysis and selectivity in determining what public investment programs do yield substantial benefits relative to costs, and a recognition that such investment is not free: we must pay for it, either with higher taxes or reduced spending on other programs. Deficit finance is an option but a bad one because it displaces private investment (domestic or foreign).

And the advocates of industrial policy do have a point in their argument that the federal government's support of civilian research with potential industrial and commercial payoffs is woefully inadequate. But as argued in memo 28, larger outlays are not the only response. Indeed federal funds could be diverted to fill many barrels of pork. Rather a newly devised selection process is needed to enable the federal government to allocate funds for such research on the basis of economic rather than political and parochial criteria. If that were done, a substantial increase in federal R&D supports would indeed be warranted.

Notes

1. Robert Eisner, *How Real Is the Federal Deficit?* (Free Press, 1986).

2. The additional deficit will reduce national saving. There will be some combination of decreases in domestic private investment and increases in the trade deficit. The increase in national income made possible by the additions to the stock of public capital will approximately match the combined effects of a lower stock of private capital and higher overseas debt service.

3. Kenneth A. Small, Clifford Winston, and Carol A. Evans, *Road Work* (Brookings, 1989).

4. The official estimates of manufacturing productivity may have overstated its growth in the past decade. But even after allowing for that fact, productivity growth in manufacturing in the 1980s returned close to what it was in the earlier postwar decades. See Edward Denison, *Estimates of Productivity Change by Industry* (Brookings, 1989), p. 20, table 2-1.

INDEX

Abraham, Katherine, 165
Aggregate demand
 Defined, 16
 Fiscal policies influencing, 16–17, 27–
  28; discretionary changes in budgets,
  207, 209–11; government expenditures, 196–99; taxes, 200–03, 211–
  12
 Fluctuations in: economic instability, 8,
  57–58; measure of volatility, 60–61;
  multiplier and acceleration effects,
  61–63; sources, 19–21
 GNP and changes, 28–29, 219–20
 Inflationary response to changes, 129,
  132–34, 142
 Interaction between supply and, 15–16;
  determination of output and employment levels, 18–21
 Monetary policy influence on: to
  achieve economic stabilization, 93–
  94, 210–11, 214–15, 272–73; creation of money, 173–76, 184–86;
  credit system, 176–79; interest rate
  changes, 87–93, 179–80, 183–84,
  190–92; long lags between economic
  results and, 186–87; to prevent excessive, 190–91
 Prices and, 129, 132–34, 144–45
 Role in cyclical fluctuations, 19, 22

Role in short-run economic performance, 19, 24–25
Saving-investment balance and, 58–60
Wages and, 133, 143–49
Aggregate supply
 Interaction between demand and, 15–
  16; determination of output and employment levels, 18–21
 Policy to change composition of GNP,
  29
 As potential GNP, 17–18; growth, 25
 Role in cyclical fluctuations, 19, 21–23
 Sources of change, 19–21, 28–29,
  220–21, 228, 230; capital formation,
  236–39; education, 290–98; government investment-type spending, 28,
  33, 196–97; tax policy 32–33, 201,
  203, 220, 283–86; technological advance, 228, 230, 299–305
Aschauer, David, 245n, 274

Balance of payments, U.S., 35–36
 Capital account, 100
 Components, 98–99
 Current account deficits, 100–01
 National saving target for reducing
  deficit, 271–72
 See also Trade balance